THE SELF-HELP REVOLUTION

THE SELF-HELP REVOLUTION

Edited by
Alan Gartner
*Co-Director, National Self-Help
Clearinghouse,
Graduate Center, City University of New York*

Frank Riessman
*Co-Director, National Self-Help
Clearinghouse,
Graduate Center, City University of New York*

Volume X, Community Psychology Series

Series Editor: Bernard Bloom, Ph.D.

 **HUMAN SCIENCES PRESS, INC.**
72 FIFTH AVENUE
NEW YORK, N.Y. 10011

Printed in the United States of America
123456789

Library of Congress Cataloging in Publication Data
Main entry under title:

The Self-help revolution.

(The Community psychology series; v. 10)
Bibliography: p.
Includes index.
1. Mental health services—Social aspects.
2. Self-help groups.   I. Gartner, Alan.   II.Riessman,
Frank, 1924—.   III. Series. [DNLM: 1.   Self-help
groups. WM   426S465 RA790.5.S36   1984   ]   362.2   82-21229
ISBN 0-89885-070-3

CONTENTS

5

THE COMMUNITY PSYCHOLOGY SERIES
SPONSORED BY

THE DIVISION OF COMMUNITY PSYCHOLOGY
OF THE AMERICAN PSYCHOLOGICAL ASSOCIATION

The Community Psychology Series has as its central purpose the building of philosophic, theoretical, scientific, and empirical foundations for action research in the community and in its subsystems, and for education and training for such action research.

As a publication of the Division of Community Psychology, the series is particularly concerned with the development of community psychology as a sub-area of psychology. In general, it emphasizes the application and integration of theories and findings from other areas of psychology, and in particular the development of community psychology methods, theories, and principles, as these stem from actual community research and practice.

TITLES IN THE COMMUNITY PSYCHOLOGY SERIES UNDER THE EDITORSHIP OF DANIEL ADELSON, FOUNDING SERIES EDITOR
(1973–1979)

Volume 1: Man as the Measure: The Crossroads, edited by Daniel Adelson

Volume 2: The University of the Urban Crisis, edited by Howard E. Mitchell.

Volume 3: Psychological Stress in the Campus Community: Theory, Research and Action, edited by Bernard L. Bloom.

Volume 4. Psychology of the Planned Community: The New Town Experience, edited by Donald C. Klein.

Volume 5: Challenges to the Criminal Justice System: The Perspectives of Community Psychology, edited by Theodore R. Sarbin.

UNDER THE EDITORSHIP OF BERNARD L. BLOOM
(1980–1984)

CONTRIBUTORS

BEDELL, JEFFREY R., Director, Adult Psychiatry, Florida Mental Health Institute, Tampa, Florida

BLIWISE, NANCY GOURASH, Post-doctoral Fellow, Human Development and Aging Program, University of California, San Francisco, California.

BORKMAN, THOMASINA, Associate Professor, Sociology, George Mason University

CLAFLIN, BILL, formerly Coordinator, Alcohol Education, Rockland County Community Mental Health Center, Division of Consultation and Education; Addictions Educator and Consultant, Ericksen Associates, Endicott, New York

EDMUNSON, EILEEN D., Director, Behavioral Medicine, Intervention Systems, Clearwater, Florida

GOLDNER, VIRGINIA, Assistant Clinical Professor of Psychiatry, Albert Einstein College of Medicine

GORDON, RICHARD, Associate Professor of Psychiatry, University of Florida, Gainesville, Florida

HUDIS, IRS, formerly staff member, Community Service Society's Natural Supports Program; Exxon Corporation

HUMM, ANDY, Project Director, the Center for the Advanced Study in Education, Graduate Center, City University of New York; Spokesperson, Coalition for Lesbian and Gay Rights

KATZ, ALFRED, Professor, Public Health and Social Welfare, University of California, Los Angeles, California

KNIGHT, BOB, Clinical Psychologist, private practice

LAVOIE, FRANCIE, Department of Psychology, Laval University, Quebec, Canada

LEVY, LEON H., Professor and Chair, Department of Psychology, University of Maryland, Baltimore County, Maryland

LIEBER, LEONARD L., Co-Founder and Executive Director, Parents Anonymous

LIEBERMAN, MORTON, Professor, Department of Psychiatry and the Human Development and Aging Program, University of California, San Francisco, California

MARIESKIND, HELEN I., Executive Director, Vision Services, An Agency for the Visually Impaired, Seattle, Washington

MELLOR, M. JOANNA, Fordham, University School of Social Services/Network Associates; formerly staff member, the Community Service Society's Natural Supports Program

MOWRER, O. HOBART, formerly Professor of Psychology, University of Illinois

RAIFF, NORMA FADOL, Director, Division of Research and Evaluation, Mon Valley (PA) Community Mental Health Center

RZETELNY, HARRIET, Hunter Brookdale Center on Aging; formerly staff member, the Community Service Society's Natural Supports Program

SILBERT, MIMI H., President, Delancey Street Foundation, Inc.

SILVERMAN, PHYLLIS, Associate Professor, Institute of Health Professions, Massachusetts General Hospital; Lecturer, Social Welfare, Department of Psychiatry, Harvard Medical School

SMITH, DIANA, nurse, mental health practitioner, Divorce Resource and Mediation Center, Cambridge, Massachusetts

WILLEN, MILDRED L., Psychotherapist, Pedersen-Krag Center, and the North Shore Psychotherapy and Counseling Service, Huntington, New York; Sponsor, Parents Anonymous

WOLLERT, RICHARD, Associate Professor, Department of Psychology, Portland State University

PREFACE

A collection of essays owes most to its contributors, to whom we are grateful for their willingness to share their work with us, in so spontaneous and generous manner.

Our work in the self-help mutual-aid field is one of the activities of the National Self-Help Clearinghouse and the New York City Self-Help Clearinghouse. We are grateful to our colleagues in those activities, Fran Dory, Carol Eisman, Audrey Gartner, William Lynch, Jr., and Rosemary Washington, as well as to Ethel Mingo and Susan Podbielski, who helped to produce the manuscript. While this book is not an activity of any direct source of support, we are grateful to several sources of support which have helped our work in the area— Sam Silverstein, the Experimental and Special Training Unit, NIMH: Tom McEnry, New York City Department of Employment; Vernon James, the Paraprofessional Branch, NIMH; and Richard Schloss, the Administration on the Aging, DHEW. Also, for ongoing support, we would like to express our appreciation to the leadership of the Graduate School and University Center, City University of New York, President Harold Proshansky, and Dean Solomon Goldstein, as well as to Mr. and Mrs. Mendek Rubin for their generous support of the New York City Self-help Clearinghouse.

INTRODUCTION

Few developments of recent years have as far-reaching potential for mental-health services as does the self-help mutual-aid phenomenon. On the one hand, there are a set of factors which strain the mental health system: growing and more diverse demands for services at a time of resource constraints; while at the same time there is increased questioning of the efficacy and nature of traditional professionally provided services. This comes at a time when the value of large institutions is being challenged. We are seeing, in effect, a convergence of factors in the society at large and in human-service practice. On the other hand, partially in response to those factors, there has been the growth of self-help mutual-aid activities. And the growth is but the tip of a very large iceberg: viz., an extensive study by the Office of Prevention, California Department of Mental Health (Roppel, 1979), reports that while 75 percent of those queried felt getting together with persons with similar health and mental health problems was good idea, only 9 percent had done so. There is, it seems, a considerable "market" for further growth of self-help mutual-aid activities.

This growth is shown both in the number of groups and of participants, and in the variety of problems addressed by such groups. And, as Alfred Katz points out in the last essay in this volume, these are developments of a worldwide nature.

The older, more established groups, such as Alcoholics Anonymous, and Recovery, Inc., founded 1935 and 1937, respectively, are continuing to grow: AA has nearly a million members, while Recovery, Inc. now enrolls over 7,000 members. At the same time, the range of problems being addressed by self-help mutual-aid groups continues to expand.

There are groups addressed to particular mental health conditions, namely Depressives Annonymous, Manic-Depressives Anonymous, Neurotics Anonymous, and Schizophrenics Anonymous (Evans, 1979, and Gartner Riessman, 1979, give extensive listings of self-help mutual-aid groups, with the latter including an extensive index both by type of "problem" addressed and geographic location of the group's headquarters). And there are groups concerned with the mental-health needs of various population groups. For example, the first section of this book includes descriptions of self-help mutual-aid groups of women (Marieskind), gays (Humm), drug abusers (Silbert), abusing parents (Lieber), the overweight (Goldner), the physically disabled (Silverman and Smith), and those who care for the aged (Mellor, Rzetelny, and Hudis).

This last group, a self-help mutual-aid among care givers, suggests a whole new area of development. It may well be that such groups among care givers, lay and professional, may be an answer to the "burnout" problem! One can look at two particular problem areas to which mental health programs direct services: among alcoholics (A.A., of course, but also more specialized groups such as the Calix Society, the National Association of Recovered Alcoholics in the Professions, and Women for Sobriety) and the drug dependent (Delancey Street Foundation, Narcotics Anonymous, Pills Anonymous). Or, to shift from population groups to a service aspect, prevention, we see that self-help mutual-aid groups provide two unique features. They offer social support to their members through the creation of a caring community, and they increase members' coping skills through the provision of information and sharing of experiences and problem solutions. Thus, it is no surprise that the Council on Prevention of the National Council of Community Mental Health Centers has identified self-help groups as an effective, efficient model of a program that is within the resources of community mental-health centers across the country. *(Self-Help Fostered by Community Mental Health Center*, 1979, pp. 1-2).

Another way to view the range of self-help mutual-aid groups is to note those which relate to parents and children. There are groups for pregnant women (Self-Help Education Initiative in Childbirth); for parents of "normal" newborns (Postpartum Educational Project); of those born prematurely (Premature and High Risk Infants); and for parents whose children die at birth (Aiding a Mother Experiencing Neo-Natal Death), or in the first year (National Foundation for Sudden Infant Death Syndrome); for adopted children seeking their natural parents (Adoptees' Liberty Movement Association), and for parents who have surrendered children for adoption (Concerned United Birthparents); for single parents (Parents Without Partners), mothers (Association of Professional Women Who Are Mothers) or fathers (Fathers' Rights); for those with "normal" children (Parent Care), those who are handicapped (groups for every disability), or

---

[1]As one of the characteristics of self-help mutual-aid groups is their lack of formality, record keeping is limited. There seems to be no doubt, however, that there has been a rapid proliferation of self-help mutual-aid groups. One study (Katz and Bender 1976), estimates that there are more than 500,000 such groups. And even casual review of either the popular or professional literature makes clear the growing attention to this growth. Indeed, in its review of the 1970's, the *New York Times* (January/1/80) reported that self-help mutual aid was the most significant development of the decade in the behavioral sciences.

[2]Each of the groups listed in the previous paragraphs is described in Gartner and Riessman, 1979. Killilea (1976) presents the most extensive schema of self-help groups.

who are dying (the Candlelighters); for parents who abuse their children (Parents Anonymous) and for the children who have been abused (Daughters and Sons United); and to shift to the other end of the spectrum, for those whose parents (or other relatives) are institutionalized (Friends and Relatives of the Institutionalized Aged).[2]

We need not belabor the point any further to assure the reader that whatever the concerns of a mental-health program, there are self-help mutual-aid groups addressed to the topic. But, of course, the mere existence of such groups does not connote the appropriateness of the mental-health community becoming involved in such activities. It is to this topic to which we now turn our attention.

As a review of the dates in the citations in the previous paragraph indicates, there is a recent rush of attention to issues of evaluation. As yet, there have been no large-scale longitudinal studies, and few with control groups. What has been found is suggestive, reinforcing of participants' reports of satisfaction, and a clear signal for further more systematic attention. With these caveats, among the findings particularly worth noting are those of Raiff concerning Recovery, Inc., and of Edmunson, Bedell, Archer, and Gordon on a program for deinstutionalized patients in Florida.

In both Recovery, Inc., and the Florida Community Newwork Development Program, persons with the problem play special leadership roles. These findings suggest that in the helping function there may be something especially therapeutic. Of course, this phenomenon is exactly what Riessman (1965) sought to capture with his "helper-therapy" concept. In its simplest form, this principle states that those who help are helped most.

Thus, an alcoholic in AA who is providing support to another AA member may be the one who is chiefly benefiting by playing this *giving* role. Furthermore, since all members of the group play this role at one time or another, they are all benefited by this helping process. In a sense, this is true of all helpers, whether they be professionals or volunteers but it is more sharply true for helpers who have the same problem as the helped, as is characteristic of mutual-aid groups. While all help givers may themselves be helped in a nonspecific way by playing the helping role (and this is an important matter), help givers who have a particular problem may be helped in that specific problem, whether they be alcoholics, drug addicts, smokers, underachievers, heart patients, hypertensives, diabetics, or so on. Dewar (1976, p. 81) points out that "It feels good to be the helper. It increases our sense of control, of being valued, of being capable. When children play by acting out helping relationships, they are more apt to seek to play the role of the helper than of the helped. It feels better. As a person organizes more of their identity around their activities and value as a helper, it gets harder to keep them from helping. It always seems more predictable that the helpers will benefit from helping, rather than the helped."

Numerous postulated mechanisms explain the potential power of the helper-therapy idea. Skovholt (1974, p. 62), seeking to describe and explain the helper-therapy principle, summarizes the benefits received from helping: "(1) the effective helper often feels an increased level of interpersonal competence as a result of making an impact on another's life; (2) the effective helper often feels a sense of equality in giving and taking between himself or herself and others; (3) the effective helper is often the recipient of valuable personalized learning acquired while working with a helpee; and (4) the effective helper often receives social approval from the people he or she helps." Skovholt hypothesizes that all four factors, rather than any one, make the helper-therapy principle potent.

There are at least three additional mechanisms to account for the fact that the person playing the helping role achieves special benefits: (1) the helper is less dependent; (2) in struggling with the problem of another person who has a like problem, the helper has a chance to observe his or her problem at a distance; and (3) the helper obtains a feeling of social usefulness by playing the helping role. The entire helper-therapy concept is derived from role theory, whereby a person playing a role tends to carry out the expectation and requirements of that role. In effect, as a helper the individual displays mastery over the afflicting condition—plays the role of a nonaddict, for example—and thereby acquires the appropriate skills, attitudes, behaviors, and mental set. Having modeled this for others, the individual may see himself or herself as behaving in a new way and may, in effect, take on that role of his or her own.

While key to understanding the activities of self-help mutual-aid groups, the "helper-therapy" principle does not stand alone in gaining an understanding of the processes of self-help mutual aid.[3] The group itself is a key factor.

The group provides support, reinforcement, sanctions, and norms; extends the power of the individual; provides feedback; and occupies time. While this last might normally be thought of as a negative, for a person seeking to overcome addictive behavior that had come to control and occupy one's entire life, involvement in the group helps to fill time and to replace the activities associated with the addiction. It is not uncommon, for example, for alcoholics to attend AA meetings many nights a week, both to give help and get help.

---

[3]For a fuller discussion of the "helper-therapy" principle, see Gartner and Riessman (1977).

Katz (1970) provides a useful overview of some of the processes of self-help that are related to the group:

1. Peer or primary group reference identification.
2. Facilitation of communication because members are peers.
3. Enhances opportunities for socialization.
4. Breaking down of individual psychological defenses through group action, open discussion, and confrontation.
5. Provision of an acceptable status system within which the member can achieve his place. Status is defined according to group goals and needs, and the individual's status within the social system of the group can be relatively clearly defined.
6. Simulation of or proximity to conditions of the outside world in the groups, as compared with the institutional setting or professional client-practitioner relationship.

These factors are particularly significant for people who have been excluded, for whatever reason, from society's mainstream. In the self-help setting, they can experience normal social contacts, as well as communication that is unhampered by irrelevant barriers. Most important, they can experience the opportunity for leadership. Although a self-help group or network may include professional or volunteer participation, or may even be the result of a human service worker's initial prodding, its potential for success is based on the active participation and commitment of its members. Those members must know that there is "room at the top."

While we have emphasized the similarities among the members of the group, there of course, are key differences in the membership, between old-timers and newcomers. In discussing the helper-therapy concept, we have noted that the old-timers benefit in the process of helping others. But there is benefit, too, for the newcomers. Festinger (1954) has argued that individuals are most influenced by persons whom they perceive as like themselves. Antze (1976, p. 326) supports this view: "The strongest influencers are those whom the the subject sees as like himself." For example, in the statement of the old-timer at the AA meeting that he is an alcoholic, but obviously under control, the new member sees what he or she can become. And, of course, the conviction as to the rightness of the group's way is most ingrained in that successful old-timer, and the newcomer is affected by the members with the strongest convictions.

A further aspect of many of the self-help groups is their ideological character. Ideology goes beyond the activity of the individual to involvement in something beyond oneself, to a broader commitment, and to social change. This is perhaps most obvious in women's and men's conscious-ness-raising groups and in parent groups that have worked for better condi-tions for their handicapped children. But it is also operative in the various stigmatized groups, such as gays, former offenders, stutterers, midgets, and other social outcasts, where the ideology of the group involves criticism of society and the demand for social change. This criticism is frequently directed at professionals and social agencies, as well as the larger society. The ideological perspective of the self-help group gives it force and convic-tion in dealing with these agencies and in feeling much more positively about itself and its condition.

While part of the force powering many self-help mutual-aid groups is antipathy, and in some instances antagonism, toward professionals and professional organization, in fact, with the large exception of AA and its off-shoots, the great bulk of self-help mutual-aid groups involves various forms of professional participation. Recovery, Inc. was founded by a psy-chiatrist, Abraham A. Low. Parents Anonymous was co-founded by a psy-chiatric social worker, Leonard Lieber, and has a professional sponsor (Willen, in this volume) for each group. Many of the large national health organizations—the American Cancer Society (Laryngectomy, Inc., Reach to Recovery), the American Heart Association (Stroke Clubs), the TB and Lung Association (Easy Breathers), the National Multiple Sclerosis Society (The Hopefuls), and the Epilepsy Foundation—sponsor self-help mutual-aid groups. And the fastest growing group, Make Today Count, for those with cancer and other life-threatening illnesses, includes a unique combina-tion of those with the illness, their spouses, their friends, and their care givers (Wollert, Knight, and Levy, in press). Caplan and Silverman at the Laboratory for Community Psychiatry at Harvard established the Widow-to-Widow helping program. Numerous community mental health centers sponsor self-help mutual aid groups (Claflin, in this volume), and the National Council of Community Mental Health Centers, at its 1979 annual meeting, made support and development of self-help mutual-aid activities a major national priority. Mowrer's essay in this volume properly addresses the issue of whether these developments are examples of coopera-tion or cooptation.

Great impetus is offered in the direction of cooperation by the Report of the President's Commission on Mental Health (1978). The Report gives both broad support to the need for the formal mental health care-giving sys-tem to relate to community support networks, as well as making specific recommendations, including the development by community mental-health centers of directories of self-help groups, encouraging referrals to such groups, training or retraining agency personnel to work with such groups, sponsoring of conferences between professionals and self-help group organizers.[4] The Experimental Training Division, NIMH, funds a unique program, "The Urban Training and Brokerage," at the Graduate School and University Center, City University of New York. It brings together leaders of self-help mutual-aid groups and professionals interested in self-help mutual-aid activities as trainers and trainees of one another.

Needless to say, there are dangers to such relationships, not only of co-optation, addressed by Mowrer, but of diversion and segmentation of the self-help mutual-aid movement, as well as the risk of its being viewed as the current fad, to be supplanted by some new panacea. We think that, while real, these and other dangers are avoidable, in part because of some of the pressures on the present professional care-giving systems noted earlier: this is a topic to which in the afterword we return.

Alan Gartner
Frank Riessman

---

[4]For further discussion of the implications of the Presidents' Commission Report for self-help mutual aid activities, see Riessman (1978).

Part I

THE GROUPS

Chapter 1

WOMEN'S SELF-HELP GROUPS

Helen I. Marieskind

Down through the ages, women have sought to teach themselves by meeting in groups and pooling information and experiences. They have done this for self-protection and in response to being denied advanced educational opportunities, as was the case with the groups organized by Christine de Pisan in 14th-century Venice, (Hurd-Mead, 1938) for "spiritual comfort," and to share "childbirth travails," as did the women meeting with Anne Hutchinson in 16th-century Puritan New England (Findley, 1939); or to learn elementary anatomy, basic sex education, nutrition, general hygiene, and common sense approaches to dress (no corsets) through attendance at the Ladies' Physiological Reform Societies in the 1830s and 1840s in the eastern United States (Blake, 1965).

Today, women who meet in self-help groups do so for many of the same reasons that their earlier counterparts gathered together. They have experienced frustration over the control which the medical profession maintains over their lives, at not understanding medical treatments, and receiving condescension when they sought information. With growing consciousness of the social forces which shape people's lives, women have begun to question their traditionally designated roles and have become angry at their sense of helplessness in the "scheme of things." By meeting in groups and sharing these feelings and questions, women have sought information, feeling confident that knowledge is power.

The self-help group which is specifically oriented to give women health knowledge, and particularly knowledge of their bodies, was initially begun in 1971 by Carol Downer of the Feminist Women's Health Center in Los Angeles. These first groups were organized around gynecology. They were intended to challenge medical stereotypes about women, to demystify the medical profession's therapies, and to dispel the ignorance among women about their anatomy and bodily processes, which leave them susceptible to stereotypes and mystifications. The concept of self-help rapidly expanded as a logical progression for women already meeting in consciousness-raising groups fostered by the women's liberation movement, and for those concerned about women's health and active in the movement to reform abortion laws.

Although self-help clinics or groups did, and do, take many forms, usually they are comprised of six to ten women, ideally from varied socioeconomic backgrounds, who meet together for about 10 weeks to exchange health information, to learn breast and vaginal self-examination, and to share gynecological and obstetrical experiences. More advanced self-help groups are strictly an educational process; they are not a health-services unit for the direct provision of care, although frequently they are sponsored by women's clinics which do provide services (Marieskind, 1976; Ruzek, 1979).

Goals of individual self-help groups vary according to the "theme" of the group, some examples of which are discussed here. Regardless of the theme, two goals are common to all women's self-help groups: to provide education on the topic which brought the group together and to aid women in realizing their own potential (Hornstein, 1976; Kleiber, 1978). Groups are careful to head off the takeover by a leader who will formulate direction. The establishment of goals by the whole group at the beginning of their meetings is one means of ensuring equitable participation by all members.

To achieve the first goal of education, women speak from their own experience. When information presented does not conform with other members' experience, the group supportively questions and thereby minimizes the risk of adding further misinformation to their knowledge. In the same vein, medical practices and stereotypes are discussed and evaluated. Members are also encouraged to seek clarification from other sources and to share this with the group. As happens in a gynecological self-help group, performing vaginal and breast examinations enables women to familiarize themselves with their bodies, and learn helpful preventive techniques. In the case of vaginal exams, for the first time in most women's lives they are "allowed" to see that part of their anatomy around which society has defined their lives and expectations.

Achieving the goal of realizing individual potential is dependent on numerous variables and quite difficult to measure. However, after participating in self-help groups, most women report feelings of strength, self-worth, self-confidence, and an ability to be more assertive. This feeling presumably originates from greater knowledge, but it is unclear whether this is from gaining basic factual knowledge, from knowing one is no longer alone or somehow negatively unique, from knowing that the collective experience is possible and women can interact with other women for their collective good, or from having enough knowledge to realize the right to ask further questions. Or, perhaps, it is a combination of all of the above.

There is, however, a dearth of documentation beyond verbal assurances as to the quantity or content of information and degree of self-realization which women experience from self-help groups, because studying the groups and obtaining socioeconomic data on which valid studies can be based is believed to be in conflict with the basic ethics of the self-help concept. There are, nevertheless, some telling comments in the medical literature about the increased ability of women to question their health-care providers and on the increased ability among "even the more docile ones" to challenge accepted stereotypes (Kaiser and Kaiser, 1974; *American Medical News*, 1974). An anguished American Medical Association asked in 1974:

> What is it that caused many patients—even the more docile, soft-spoken ones—to suddenly start questioning every procedure, every prescription, to come out with shocking position statements on pre-marital sex, lesbianism, and childless marriage, and to insist on using natural childbirth, breast feeding and diaphragms, when modern medicine has provided them with much less bothersome and painless alternatives? *American Medical News*, 1974).

Many other groups have evolved from the early gynecologically-oriented self-help groups; for pubescent adolescents; for elderly women; as nutrition groups; for rape victims; to deal with mental health; to encourage building body-strength; and for women with young children.

Because of the rapidity with which treatment is begun once a lump is discovered, mastectomy groups tend to be comprised of women who have already undergone mastectomies and are beginning rehabilitation. Women will share their surgical experiences and, if desired, may show their scars. They can challenge the social stereotype that a de-breasted woman is somehow not a woman. Much support can be derived from this process of realizing that there are others similarly situated and that these people are caring and sensitive to one's feelings. The group provides a safe environment for releasing anger and pain, for sharing disappointments and rejection from family or friends. The women can encourage each other to maintain the essential exercise regimen and can pool their abilities to locate the best prostheses. They may also develop appropriate reading materials for the use of other women faced with immediate choices over type of surgery (Alpert, 1979; R. Kushner, 1975). A similar process is followed in hysterectomy self-help groups.

In prenatal self-help groups, women in various stages of pregnancy will meet regularly to share both the physical and psychological changes being experienced. Women generally learn to weigh each other, to take blood pressure and urine specimens, and to assess externally their babies' growth. They will discuss and share information on nutrition, exercise, comfortable sleeping positions, sexual activity during pregnancy, relationships with other family members, and their own intimate feelings, fears, and joys about impending motherhood. As with other groups, women find tremendous support in knowing they are not alone and that their feelings are respected and understood. They are also in a position to compare standard obstetrical procedures as stated by their doctors and to help each other evaluate what procedures each woman will agree to.

Self-help groups for pubescent adolescent women follow the same basic format as does a regular gynecological self-help group but usually involve lengthy discussions on teen-age sexuality. In light of the high adolescent pregnancy rate and the negative effects early pregnancy can have on both mothers and children (Alan Guttmacher Institute, 1976), honest discussions among young women of their expectations, desires, and experiences of sex, away from the pressures of the media, young men, and peer conformity, can be invaluable in validating teen-agers' responses and setting them on a path of independent judgment.

Underlying the formation of all these groups is the basic principle that health-related knowledge is not just the domain of the health professional but can be beneficially shared among all who want it. Another underlying assumption is that those experiencing a particular health condition provide mutual benefits by sharing these experiences and that this cannot and should not be replaced by even the most empathetic care givers.

Self-help groups, regardless of theme, do not seek to replace the health-care professions but to help members use them more rationally. Women are encouraged to define what they realistically and preferably can provide for themselves, as compared with services on which they must remain dependent. They are also encouraged to evaluate medical facts and procedures. It is in this process of assessing preferred self-reliance and necessary dependence that the real power of the self-help group lies. By using the example of the health care system, participants become aware of how a social institution can control lives; women are easily able to translate this lesson to other institutions in their lives and to assess appropriate dependence and autonomy in these areas. The self-help clinic, regardless of its theme, thus has great potential for forging wider social change. Women recognize too that their knowledge and change in self-perception has come from a collective process, unattainable in the traditional isolation of capitalist competitiveness. The act of taking knowledge collectively and of supporting one another is seen as crucial in giving each woman a strengthened sense of autonomy in her life.

Although self-help has tremendous potential, it also can be quite easily co-opted. The last decade has seen increased attention paid to self-care, and even Blue Cross now advertises, "Good coverage is up to us, good health is up to you." By adopting some of the concepts of self-help such as using mirrors in the examining rooms to allow women to see themselves, or by facilitating family-centered care, sufficient minimal changes may be made in the doctor-patient relations to diffuse the need or desire for self-help participation. Providers can also deliberately presume too much knowledge on the part of self-helpers and can intimidate them with highly technical language.

Alternately, if people are viewed as being able to help themselves to all types of health care, an excuse can be made for cutting back organized services, particularly those which do not show an immediate cost benefit or which are directed toward unpopular groups. "For the good of the patient" people can be forced to assume responsibility and lose the option to assess appropriate self-reliance and dependence.

Adoption of a self-help philosophy can also be used to deflect institutional responsibility for ill-health such as industrial and chemical pollution (believed responsible for a high proportion of cancers). Knowledge of cancer's seven warning signals can only benefit an individual if it leads to early detection and treatment; but the underlying causative agents are still beyond individual control. Self-help can be a positive force, however, in promoting basic well-being by influencing personal habits such as smoking, diet, drinking, sleep, and exercise.

Self-help can also be co-opted by professionalization. Where groups have formed which share common concerns over child abuse, teenagers, alcoholism, or women's health, new experts have appeared, in part created by the media, in part self-appointed. Self-help is also fertile ground for research. If the findings and skills are shared to benefit the group, research can be constructive, but legitimizing the concept into the professional sphere tends to focus on the form and obscures the substance of society's responsibilities for the problem. Professionalization can also diminish the beliefs individuals have in their abilities to respond to their own needs. The fundamental ingredient in successful self-help is then lost and the cycle of intimidation and sense of helplessness and lack of power recurs. For women long accustomed to being "managed," this professionalization can be particularly insidious (Marieskind, 1980).

Despite the vulnerability to co-option, the self-help group is an invaluable concept. It is not just a personal solution for individual women's needs—although that alone is a valid reason for its existence. The self-help group is a tool for inducing collective thought and action, and radical social change.

Chapter 2

THE CHANGING NATURE OF LESBIAN AND GAY SELF-HELP GROUPS

Andy Humm

The main reason that lesbians and gay men have had to rely on self-help groups for personal growth is that traditional helpers have had an investment in preserving a negative view of homosexuality. Psychiatrists said we were sick, and did a big business in insisting we could be cured. Religious counselors told us that we were wicked, and insured that we would be seeking help to overcome this sin for the rest of our lives. Civil authorities held that we were criminals, and frequently scapegoated us when it was politically important to get us out of the way (and, ironically, into a prison with those of the same sex)! As a consequence of all this negative reinforcement, gay self-hatred was virtually inevitable.

There were scarcely any gay groups in the United States prior to 1950. Many people of my own generation—I'm twenty-six—grew up feeling that they were the only ones in the world who felt the way they did toward the same sex. We usually became familiar with stereotypical effeminate homosexual men and butch lesbian women because the media promoted such images. But these were not images with which many of us could identify. We were hard pressed to find others like us in our invisible minority and to share our experiences.

Locating those like yourself is a key problem for anyone attempting self-help. To identify themselves to one another, gay people in the past (and to a lesser extent today) have adopted stereotypic mannerisms, worn single earrings, frequented gay bars and clubs, and developed a set of "in" terms.

33

Havelock Ellis, in his *Sexual Inversion* study of 1915, describes how gay people signalled each other in his day:

> . . . it is notable that of recent years there has been a fashion for a red tie to be adopted by inverts as their badge. This is especially marked among the 'fairies' (as a fellator is there termed) in New York. 'It is red,' writes an American corespondent, himself inverted, 'that has become almost a synonym for sexual inversion not only in the minds of the inverts themselves, but in the popular mind. . . Male prostitutes who walk the streets of Philadelphia and New York almost invariably wear red neckties. It is the badge of all their tribe. . . Among my classmates at medical school, few ever had the courage to wear a red tie; those who did never repeated the experiment' (Ellis, 1936; Katz, 1976).

Despite obvious problems in associating with each other in those days, as early as 1895 there is evidence of gay men forming a group. Roland Reeves is quoted as saying at the time, "A score of us have formed a little club, the Cercle Hermaphroditos. For we need to unite for defense against the world's bitter persecution of bisexuals." (Lind, 1922; Katz, 1976)

The Society for Human Rights, unwittingly chartered by the State of Illinois in 1924, became the first homosexual emancipation organization in the United States. The society took far from a militant approach to gay rights. Its object was:

> ". . . to promote and protect the interests of people who by reasons of mental and physical abnormalities are abused and hindered in the legal pursuit of happiness which is guaranteed them by the Declaration of Independence, and to combat the public prejudices against them by dissemination of facts according to modern science among intellectuals of mature age. The Society stands only for law and order; it is in harmony with any and all general laws insofar as they protect the rights of others, and does in no manner recommend any acts in violation of present laws nor advocate any manner inimical to the public welfare" (Katz, 1976).

The group had guest speakers, put out a publication, advocated self-discipline among its members, and worked to educate the larger society about homosexuality. It was a true self-help group in a very hostile society.

The founder of the Mattachine Society, a group started in 1948 and still existing today, noted of the defunct Chicago Society, "My impression was that (it) was primarily a social thing. But just the idea that gay people were getting together at all, in more than a daisy chain, was an eye-opener of an idea" (Katz, 1974). Mattachine was originally called Bachelor's

Anonymous. It had social action and educational functions, but its primary purpose as stated in 1951 was "to unify those homosexuals isolated from their own kind," and to provide a principle from which "all of our people can...derive a feeling of 'belonging'" (Mattachine Society in Katz, 1976).

In 1955 lesbian feminists formed their own group called the Daughters of Bilitis. This began a tradition of separate lesbian and gay male groups which continues to this day, especially in urban areas. Some groups, however, have been able to maintain a mix of men and women from the beginning.

As early as 1961 these groups held that homosexuality is not a sickness and that gay people—not psychiatrists and sociologists—are the experts on gay life. The idea was revolutionary and became the basis for lesbian and gay self-help groups. Members are the classic case of an oppressed minority bearing a stigmatizing label, asserting that it is society which has the problem (homophobia) and that they themselves experience their difference as a positive force in their lives. (Indeed, through the educative efforts of the National Gay Task Force, homosexuality has been dropped from the American Psychiatric Association's book of mental disorders.)

In 1969, a gay bar in New York's Greenwich Village, the Stonewall Inn, was hit by a routine police raid. Rather than submit to this latest police harassment, gay people fought back for the first time in history. Three nights of riots ensued and the modern gay movement was born.

The groups which were organized just after the Stonewall Riots were strictly activist in nature. They included the Gay Liberation Front, the Gay Activists Alliance, and Lesbian Feminist Liberation. Their goals were to fight anti-gay discrimination with street action, education, and lobbying. The consciousness-raising that went on among their memberships was incidental to working for their goals, but it was also of a higher level than much of the formal consciousness-raising that goes on in groups today that are dedicated to that purpose.

As the movement has matured though the 1970s, specialization has become the key feature. Today there are such groups as Gay Teachers, Lesbian Mothers, Gay Fathers, Gay Youth, Gay People in Health Care, Gay City Workers, Gay and Lesbian Independent Democrats, Gay Conservative Alliance, Lesbian and Gay Male Socialists, Lesbian and Gay Blind, as well as groups for gay Latinos, older people, businesspeople, lawyers, psychiatrists, social workers and for members of almost every existing religious denomination (Dignity for Catholics, Integrity for Episcopalians, Lutherans Concerned, Gay Synagogue, Gay Atheists and many more). The latest addition to the roster is a series of neighborhood groups for lesbians and gay men. And for bisexuals who do not feel at home in either a gay or a straight setting, there is the Bisexual Forum.

Lesbian and gay male members of such traditional mixed self-help groups as Alcoholics Anonymous and Overeaters Anonymous have found it necessary sometimes to found gay chapters of these groups. These separatists felt threatened sharing the facts of their sexual orientation in the mixed group and as a result were not overcoming their addiction.

In today's lesbian and gay self-help groups we find the opportunity to stop fighting who we are, and to start becoming ourselves. The capacity for same-sex love can then be appreciated as a gift in a world where so many are incapable of any kind of intimacy. Just going to a meeting of any of these groups is a big step for most gay people—one in a long series of steps that constitutes the never-ending "coming-out" process.

The new sexual freedom may have provided a degree of sexual license to gay people, but the possession of a gay identity that we can present with confidence to the outside world is still a long way off for many who grew up in the self-hating confines of the closet. A whole generation of gay people is coming up who have not had to experience the isolation of being gay in the dark ages of only a few years ago. The majority, however, still need much encouragement to risk being who they are. Unfortunately, many will live out their lives without having worked up the confidence to be open about themselves to family, straight friends and co-workers.

Many groups deny it, but one of their primary functions is a social one. They provide a place to meet other gay people and an opportunity for friendship and possible romantic interest in an atmosphere that is not as sexually pressuring as the bar and street scene. In the past, groups feared indictment as places of solicitation, but now they routinely sponsor dances and socials.

But it *is* an indictment of some groups that they still foster a closet mentality among their members. Rather than helping each other to come out as the activist group members did in the early seventies, some members simply confirm each other in the insular safety of the closet. Because they are allowed to associate with each other in such groups, plans for liberating lesbians and gay men in the larger society are often relegated to small social-action committees. Staying closeted hinders the development of mature relationships among gay people because the quality of the relationship hinges upon openness and honesty as much as in non-gay relationships. Without a clear focus on the goal of liberation from the closet, lesbian and gay self-help groups risk become fragmented way stations for frightened homosexuals which do not serve to satisfy any but the most immediate needs of gay people for association. Some of this fragmentation is being overcome through the building of coalitions among the groups within a given city and nationwide. The National March on

Washington for Lesbian and Gay Rights on October 14, 1979 was a hopeful sign of how diverse groups were able to join together for a common purpose.

It is up to the members who have already been helped by the group to work with those just coming in and to serve as models for them by sharing their stories. Advocacy of an open and self-accepting lifestyle helps the older members to greater security in their own gayness. The help they give can also rescue newer members from feeling isolated or overwhelmed by the task of coming to terms with themselves.

Involved with the purest kind of self-help today are some of the groups with a more specific focus. The Gay Fathers group is composed of men who father children during their marriages. Most are divorced, some separated, and a few are still living with their spouses. They have several common emotional problems with which they deal in the group.

Most of these men knew they were gay before marrying, but because of social pressures (e.g., the pressure to be like everyone else) they tried to force themselves into traditional heterosexual life styles. While they often loved their wives, the relationships were sexually and often emotionally unfulfilling and ended in some kind of separation. The men then felt guilt over having married under less than honest circumstances, loss over the time that they wasted in their lives trying to be someone they were not, and even an additional sense of loss over breaking up their heterosexual relationship. Most of the men revealed their homosexuality to their wives at some point before or after the separation, with varying outcomes. Those who did not used other reasons for breaking up the marriage.

Then there are the children. Few of these marriages get very far along, so the children are usually young and incapable of understanding their father's gayness. The fathers rarely have custody of the children, but most have visitation rights. Those whose wives deny them access to their children are often afraid to fight for visitation rights in court for fear of their homosexuality coming out during the proceedings.

Even when the visitation arrangement is liberal and the divorced couple amicable, there remains the issue of explanation to the children. The Gay Fathers group can help with this problem through more than its weekly discussion group. They sponsor picnics and other group events where the men can bring their children to play with the children of other gay men. The father's gayness is then seen as less of an abstraction and the children get the chance to engage in more informal self-help of their own ("Your Daddy's gay? So's mine!").

In the past, gay fathers used to punish themselves for the mistakes they made and never found the courage to share the truth of their lives with those whom they loved in their non-gay past. Through the positive reinforcement of Gay Fathers, they are helped to live more positively as gay people and to reconcile themselves with the issue of their broken marriages.

Dignity, the lesbian and gay Catholic group, was founded 10 years ago as a haven for gay people in a church whose official teaching was and is that homosexual practice is a grievous sin. Dignity believes that homosexuality can be practiced in consonance with Christ's teachings. The majority of gay people left organized religion at about the time that they started to affirm their own gayness. Members of Dignity and groups like it in other denominations seek to maintain their religious identity and to celebrate their sexuality at the same time.

The efforts of lesbian and gay Catholics, as those of divorced and remarried Catholics, to engage in self-help mark a break with the rigidly hierarchical nature of the church to which they belong. They hold that spiritual truth is as much to be found among themselves as it is in the Vatican in Rome. It is that self-empowerment principle which the group helps its members to accept in order that they might accept themselves and be rid of the extreme guilt which often marks the life of the gay Catholic.

It is not easily accomplished. Sometimes it is only through the reassuring words of another member of the group who is a priest that a gay Catholic comes to accept him or herself.

While the group officially claims to have a mission to rid the larger Catholic church of homophobia and to integrate themselves with the larger Catholic community, it has turned in on itself at the present time. Through mutual support and reinforcement, Dignity hopes to produce a cadre of gay Catholics confident enough to change the face of the church as a whole. Probably they have more chance of helping to change the image of gay people in society in general where people are surprised to hear of a gay Catholic group. By maintaining an identification common to many members of the larger society, these gay people are bridging a gap between their subculture and the mainstream of society.

Most of the self-help at Dignity works in an informal way. The organization sponsors a weekly liturgy on a Saturday night or Sunday. The liturgy is not a self-help meeting *per se* but the members derive much more than they would from a service at their local parish church. At Dignity, they are spoken to as gay people, the priest himself is gay, they give communion to each other and they socialize with each other afterwards. They take part in performing the rituals practiced at any church, but with people who are like themselves. The therapeutic value of joining in a service such as this may never be equaled by the more cerebral sharing that goes on in a discussion group for gay Catholics. Nevertheless, Dignity sponsors discussion and consciousness-raising groups as well as peer counseling to supplement the informal self-help that goes on. Their Social Action Committee takes on the work of reaching out to the larger community with speakers and, if necessary, through confrontation with hostile church and civil authorities. Both types of outreach serve to spread the word about a group which, like most self-help groups, cannot afford large advertising budgets and must depend largely on word of mouth for new members. The professional establishment (in this case, the Catholic church hierarchy) is often of no help in advertising the services of a self-help group.

The growth of Dignity and other gay groups which have as their drawing card an association with a traditional institution (be it of a religious, occupational, or other nature), indicates that lesbians and gay men increasingly see themselves as less different from their non-gay counterparts in society. Indeed, eroticism is but one of the complex factors that determine the nature of an individual's sexuality. It has always been the oppression and repression of gay people that has made us seem and often act so different and hence to seek to band together in self-help groups. From this point of view, we may shortly witness the peak of the lesbian and gay self-help movement. As young people come up who have not felt the isolation of being gay, the emotional need for groups will wane.

At present, however, the self-accepting core of gay self-help groups must be aware that they are only the tip of the iceberg. There is a significant portion of the lesbian and gay community which has yet to be touched by the positive values of a self-help group. Thus it is imperative that existing groups maintain very basic self-help activities such as rap groups and peer counseling. Despite the fact that young people are coming along who are not burdened with self-hatred, there are older lesbians and gay men who have yet to be reached.

Groups also need to grow in their acceptance of people who fall in between on the spectrum from homosexuality to heterosexuality—and that means most of us. We in the movement should not set gayness over and against straightness, but rather provide an atmosphere in which people can be who they are. The goal of the movement should not be to gain acceptance for a narrow group of conventional homosexual people, but in opening up society to diversity itself in sexuality.

Recent developments such as the defeat of lesbian and gay rights bills in the New York City and New York State legislatures, the late response of government to the AIDS epidemic (because its early victims were primarily gay men), and the rise in incidents of anti-gay violence indicate that the lesbian and gay movement has a long way to go toward the education of the larger society and the development of our own. More has been accomplished in the last 14 years, however, than ever before. The outlook, therefore, is heartening for us all.

Chapter 3

DELANCEY STREET FOUNDATION:
A Process of Mutual Restitution

Mimi H. Silbert

Deborah was twenty-seven when she came to Delancey Street. A heroin addict at twelve, a street prostitute at thirteen, she had been "cured" by over a dozen other programs and hospitals. She had spent five years in prison, and had lived through numerous horrors, like having her baby drown in the bathtub while she turned her back on him to take a fix. She had tried to kill herself three times. Deborah left school in the ninth grade, was unskilled, and stated that she felt good "only with men and drugs." She came to Delancey Street to "beat a prison case," promised (as all residents must) to stay two years, and intended (as all residents do), to stay only a few months to clean up and then leave.

Deborah stayed at Delancey Street out of fascination and manipulation: she saw people she once knew as losers on the street living in San Francisco's most exclusive residential area, well-groomed, well-dressed. She believed, "There must be something 'dirty' going on at

Delancey Street," and planned to stay long enough to get in on it. Before she realized it, she had internalized enough of the processes she had been "imitating," so that she began to rethink her old values and attitudes. She worked long enough and hard enough in the tightly structured community to see herself gaining skills and work habits. She had been confronted about herself often enough by her peers that she had come to take responsibility for what she had done, and to exert some control over what she was doing now. In short, Deborah experienced something new: she saw a small hope for herself. Instead of playing the "cure game" while knowing secretly that she would always stay a dope fiend, Deborah began to believe that she could—and would—change. And then she stayed at Delancey Street for the right reasons: to redo her life.

Three and one-half years later, Deborah graduated from Delancey Street. She had an A.A. in business and a well-paying job as a sales manager in a nationally known firm. She traveled for the firm, received supervisory training, and was a respected employee. Aside from her career and well-balanced personal life, Deborah set up a program for paraprofessional volunteers to work with adolescent girls returning to the community from mental hospitals. Deborah manages to come back to Delancey Street often to serve as a role model for the new women residents who are coming in, giving their word to stay two years, and privately planning to stay a few months, clean up, and leave...

Delancey Street Foundation is described as a residential treatment center for ex-addicts, alcoholics, convicts, and prostitutes. It prefers to consider itself a recycling center where those whom the system has defined, and who, indeed, have defined themselves as society's garbage, can live, work, and learn together to return to society as productive citizens.

Delancey Street is a self-help center in the truest sense. The Foundation receives no government funds, so that its financial support depends upon its residents. It has no staff of experts, either professional psychologists or professional ex-drug addicts, so that its "therapy" also depends upon its residents. All too often, those of us involved in reform of one kind or another, define ourselves by our *goals* rather than by our *processes*. While by goal Delancey Street is defined as a drug/alcohol/crime treatment program, in its processes, Delancey Street has less in common with funded, staffed treatment programs, than it does with large families or small neighborhoods. In families and old-fashioned neighborhoods, as in Delancey Street, members are dependent upon one another as they grow to develop an identity and an independence which allow them to enter the world-at-large alone, while still maintaining a sense of continuity with the family and the old neighborhood. Delancey Street's self-help process of growth and change and interdependence is applicable to any group with varied goals who choose to pool their resources, rely on their own strengths, and help one another develop.

The residents of the Delancey Street family, like Deborah, are the hard-core helpless: those traditionally considered by society to be "unamenable to treatment." Over 85 percent have been heroin addicts for an average of 10 years; over 60 percent are multiple drug abusers; over 40 percent are alcoholics.[1] The average resident at Delancey Street has served an average of 7 years in prison and has been returned to prison between three and four times. This individual comes from a poor family, reads and writes at the sixth grade level, is unskilled, and never held a steady job for as long as a year. Given the population, the attrition rates are unexpectedly low. The overall attrition rate is 35 percent; of these, the majority leave in the first few months of their stay. Of those who leave, some return to Delancey Street and do well the second time. Some may survive well on the street. Some go to prison. Some die.

Begun in 1971 with four residents and a $1000 loan from a loan shark, Delancey Street currently has 350 residents earning their own way and living in several buildings in San Francisco, at no cost to the taxpayers. At a separate facility in northern New Mexico, started in 1977, there are about 95 residents living on a ranch located on the San Juan Pueblo. The population averages about one-third blacks, one-third Latins, and one-third Anglos, with an occasional small percentage of American Indians, Asians, and other racial and ethnic groups. Residents range in age from eighteen to seventy; about one-fourth to one-third are women.

Over one-half of the people who come to Delancey Street are referred by the courts through pretrial diversion, as an alternative to prison, or as a condition of probation or parole. The others come in off the street. There is only one criterion for entry into Delancey Street: the person in question must be the one to ask for help. No payment is accepted. No requests from

[1]These statistics total over 100 percent because they reflect multiple abuse for each resident.

concerned parents or lawyers can substitute for individuals taking the first step or accepting the responsibility for their own lives.

Social problems like drug addiction and crime are complex phenomena which involve the total *interaction* of the individuals within the system. In our zeal for quick cures to these problems, however, we develop simple definitions. There are those among us who consider crime to be solely the product of an unjust and inequitable society. These people tend to sentimentalize the criminal as a victim. The result, unfortunately, is legions of junkies and lawbreakers who, because they are stripped of the responsibilities of their pasts, are divested of control of their futures. Conversely, there are some who consider wrongdoing wholly the fault of the individual, be it through criminal inclination, biological defect, or psychological disease and personality disorder. These people tend to be "tough" on the criminal. But this attitude, while it engenders anger, bitterness, and hatred, rather than manipulation and guilt, leaves the criminal as void of options as the other extreme. We place people in prison, where, however horrible or however humane the conditions, the inmates are stripped of all interaction with society; they are also stripped of all responsibility, and are maintained at the taxpayers' expense. Thus they emerge with no sense of responsiblity or personal power.

Delancey Street cuts through this dichotomy to stress the interaction of the individual with the social system. Delancey Street's philosophy is that individuals must take the responsibility for their own actions so that they can exert a measure of control and create some viable options. Only from a position where individuals have some personal power over their own lives can they move to demand their due from society or work to change the inequities of its system.

Hundreds of people have graduated from Delancey Street with a high rate of success. Over three-fourths of the graduates are currently thriving in the community, with life-styles and occupations ranging from a deputy sheriff, a mortician, real-estate brokers, and advertising executives to contractors, truckers who own their own companies, engineers, medical and dental technicians, and lawyers.

The Foundation takes its name from the street in New York's Lower East Side where, at the turn of the century, Delancey Street came to symbolize the self-reliance of Old World immigrants who worked and earned their way into the mainstream of Americn life. In fact, the intake department at Delancey Street is called "Immigration," for the people who come to Delancey Street are like immigrants to the American system. They have never learned to live legitimately and sucessfully within that system, and that is what Delancey Street teaches them.

While this generation has been labeled the narcissistic "Me generation," where people struggle not to impose their own values on others, Delancey Street stresses traditional values: the work ethic, the importance of self-reliance, the dignity of earning one's own way in the world, and the value of helping others as a central means to feeling good about one's self. Unlike other organizations which develop alternative principles and life-styles, Delancey Street prepares its residents to live effectively in the dominant Amerian social culture. To "choose" to reject a society which has rejected them is a meaningless protest, for there are few alternatives. But the decision to work to change a system in which they have numerous positive alternatives, is indeed a viable choice.

The philosophy of change at Delancey Street is based on what I call "mutual restitution'." The residents gain the vocational, personal, interpersonal, and social skills necessary to make restitution to the society from which they have taken, illegally, and often brutally, for most of their lives. In return, Delancey Street demands from society access to the legitimate opportunities from which the majority of residents for most of their lives have been blocked. By living together and pooling resources, Delancey Street residents acquire enough strength and credibility that the demands to gain access to society's opportunities must be taken seriously. This process, of gaining the skills and abilities and self-concept necessary to make and receive social restitution, minimally requires two years. The average stay, prior to graduation from Delancey Street, is three and one-half years.

In order to accomplish this process of mutual restitution, there is a constant training and education process which begins on the day the new resident arrives. The first area of re-education is "school learning." Everyone who comes to Delancey Street is tutored in basic skills—reading, writing, and math—until they receive a high-school equivalency certificate. After that, residents can go on to various forms of education. There are currently over 100 residents in colleges and professional schools. One resident, soon to graduate, is now in his second year of medical school.

The second area is vocational training. Delancey Street maintains nine training schools which also serve as the businesses by which the Foundation maintains itself. These training schools include a restaurant, a catering business, a moving and trucking school, sales and production of terrariums and sand painting, furniture and woodwork, specialty-advertising sales, antique-car restoration, the operation of outdoor Christmas-tree lots, and a print shop. Residents who have traditionally been unemployable welfare recipients have started, worked, and managed these training-school businesses so successfully that they are the Foundation's primary source of working capital.

Vocational training is accomplished in three phases. The first is in-house training, where the residents are taught skills for application within the Foundation. The stress here is not only on learning basic skills, but on developing work habits and self-discipline. When residents have mastered the basic skills, they move on to testing these in work performed through a Delancey Street company for people in the community. After they have achieved a level of competence there, they are ready to move on to the third phase, which is to get a job in the community, where they must work successfully for 6 months before graduating from Delancey Street.

In the first few years of Delancey Street's growth, residents chose the field in which they wanted to be trained. However, the residents fell into the stereotyped roles they assumed society held out for them. The women chose paperwork jobs; the Blacks and Latins primarily chose physical labor and the Anglo males picked sales. Now, every resident is briefly trained in one physical-labor job; one sales-oriented job; and one paperwork job. After residents find they have abilities in areas beyond their stereotypic images, they can choose the fields in which they want to make their careers.

Everyone in Delancey Street works, and no one, including the two presidents, receives an individual salary. Any money received is pooled in the general fund. The general fund of the Foundation provides for the maintenance of all residents: housing, food, clothing, and entertainment.

Aside from the co-presidents, Mimi Silbert and John Maher, everone working in the Foundation is a resident. It is paradoxical to expect that a staff of experts can confer self-reliance and self-respect. Because there is no staff, there is no "we-they" division. The rules apply equally to everyone. For example, neither the presidents nor the newest resident can possess any drugs or alcohol or engage in or threaten any physical violence. Everyone is both a giver and a receiver. This process is much like mountain-climbing in a chain in which the person closest to the top is pulling everyone else along.

Despite long background histories of violence common to Delancey Street's population, there has never been one incident of violence in the 12 years of it's existence. This is accomplished with no external controls, without the armed security of prisons, without the drugs utilized for control purposes in many hospitals, and without the humiliation and shame-oriented punishments in which some programs engage. It is accomplished primarily through peer pressure. Punishments for wrong-doing at Delancey Street involve extra work, or loss of rewards. The most serious punishment is being asked to leave Delancey Street. Residents employ negative sanctions, as well as positive rewards and role modeling, with one another. This process of people working with one another rather than *for* or *on* one another, is fundamental to the family feeling of unity, as well as to the integrity of the model, and the ultimate success of the Foundation.

Residents are also trained in social-survival skills. Every morning and every noon at a daily seminar, they study a vocabulary word of the day and a concept of the day (for example, Emerson's "Self-Reliance"); they learn the basics of money management and of our economic system; of civics; of archaeology and cultural anthropology; of etiquette; of clothing, fashion, and style; of sources of energy; of consumer awareness; of ecology; of all the concepts and ideas that provide us with the tools to build a well-rounded life. These sessions are conducted in seminar fashion, where each resident speaks for a few minutes on the subject under discussion. In this way residents learn not only the matter but also the processes of addressing a group, of presentation of an idea, and of connecting a theory to a personal experience.

One of the central areas of education in Delancey Street is interpersonal relations. The majority of residents have a very difficult time interacting with others. This learning process is carried on informally 24 hours a day through communal living. For example, residents who were once members of racially oriented gangs such as the Mexican Mafia, the Black Guerrilla Family, the Aryan Brotherhood, live together in Delancey Street in the same dorms: Because residents work together, they must learn to accept authority and dispense authority to others. Developing friendships and sexual relationships are often painful and are always open to the scrutiny of others; feedback is constant at Delancey Street. While residents may become comfortable in relating to one another, it is most important that they develop skills in relating to those who are outside the Foundation. Delancey Street holds a constant open house where everyone in the community is encouraged to drop in and talk with residents on all facets of living. This open interaction with various elements in the community assures diversified opinions and buffers the intellectual narrowness to which all of are prone if we reinforce our opinions by talking only with those who are just like us.

The formal method for learning interpersonal skills is the group process in which residents must participate three times weekly for 3 to 4 hours a session. The emphasis in these groups (called "games") is not on the individual's problems, but style of relating to others. Here residents explore their feelings and their actions and behaviors toward one another. They learn how the impact of what they say can be brought into closer congruence with what they hope to communicate. These groups also allow for the release of hostilities verbally rather than physically. Perhaps most important the games allow for the development of a sense of humor about one's self, one's life, and one's problems. Unlike the "games" of other therapeutic communities, which are generally attack-oriented, Delancey Street games stress fun, humor, and interpersonal communication skills. In fact, the threads of humor and fun run through Delancey Street's entire fabric and their addition to its strength cannot be overstated.

Perhaps one of the most difficult areas of education in Delancey Street has to do with educating the self. The majority of residents in Delancey Street have been labeled "psychopaths" or "sociopaths," those who feel no remorse or guilt for their actions. In truth, Delancey Street residents are consumed and even paralyzed by guilt. For most of them, the horrors of the life in which they have been involved are so overwhelming, that the need to obliterate these memories is a life-saving defense. To force them to come to grips with some of the actions they have perpetrated against themselves and others, before they have any positive experences to mitigate the horror, could be a devastating process.

Residents are caught in an ever-downward spiral of self-destructive acts which destroy not only themselves but others; this leads to guilt, which leads to self-hatred; which leads to further self-destructive acts. In order to break the cycle, it is imperative to interrupt it with some countervailing experiences. In the tightly structured environment of Delancey Street, residents who follow the rules cannot help but succeed. They achieve success at work because others are counting on them; they achieve success in helping others, particularly those newer than themselves; they succeed in caring more for themselves in their personal habits, for example in their attention to cleanliness and clothing. Rather than enshroud the negative self-concept with "support" from others, residents replace the self-hate with self-respect by acting in such a way as to earn it, and earn as well some positive reinforcements from others.

Every reward, from moving from a crowded dorm into a semi-private room; or moving up a notch in one's job; or taking the responsibility and authority for more and more of one's decisions, must be earned through self-discipline, hard work, and caring for others as well as one's self.

At about 6 months we assume that the resident has achieved enough success and positive experience to look at the past for the first time in this stay at Delancey Street. This is accomplished in a weekend-long marathon session geared to dissipate the guilt of past behaviors. Here the newer residents, guided by the older, in groups of 15 review their past histories, reliving every act they have committed in the past, until they are able to rid themselves of the tremendous guilt which dominates their lives. The weekend is concluded with the other residents showing the newer ones how, in these past 6 months, they have proven themselves to be a new person, capable of a different kind of life. They now have a greater responsibility, because they've begun to see themselves for what they can be in the future.

The final area of education that Delancey Street stresses is one of the most critical: social or community training. Following the philosophy of restitution, Delancey Street residents, in addition to working, studying, and playing games, are encouraged to help others in the community. Since Delancey Street opened, there have been large numbers of residents who have worked with senior citizens, escorting them on errands and to the doctor's, showing movies, presenting plays. Residents work with juveniles from poor areas, taking them on cookouts, on tours of the city, and holding seminars on crime and drug prevention. By using their own experiences, by showing them that involvement with crime and drugs is by no means cool or exciting, residents provide a realistic assessment and hence potent deterrent.

Residents also do volunteer work with the handicapped and are engaged in police training. They help with fund raisers for the ballet and the opera. They are all encouraged to vote; and while, like any group, they don't accomplish full voting, several of the residents do go out and work for candidates or issues in which they believe. In essence, they work and donate time and energy to improve the quality of community life.

Social problems often are viewed as following the medical model, but often only one style of medical model: that say, of malignancy in which case the patient undergoes surgery which determines the prognosis. The social problems of drug addiction and crime are more comparable to a virulent infection like malaria. The disease is not one that grows inside the individual and can be treated within the individual. The disease breeds in the swamp and the swamp must be drained or everyone will be reinfected. In our society, the social, economic, and criminal injustices, are all elements of the swamp. Who better to take responsibility for draining that swamp than those of us who seem its likeliest prey?

At Delancey Street, impressive as our statistics are, we measure our success not simply by the number of individuals "cured," but by the impact we have had upon the breeding grounds. Delancey Street, for example, started the first federal credit union by and for ex-convicts, where poor people and those traditionally ineligible for bank loans and credit unions can raise the funds to get started in a legitimate enterprise. Delancey Street fought to get wine and beer licenses for ex-felons and for the right of ex-felons to practice law, and obtain real-estate licenses. Each of these has not only helped the individuals for whom Delancey Street secured the certificates, but has helped hundreds of ex-felons for whom many more opportunities have now opened. Delancey Street has worked with the handicapped in their fight for civil rights and has fought for the rights as well as the responsibility of labor groups to integrate their membership.

Delancey Street has been the subject of wide coverage by the media in this country and abroad. Articles citing its success have appeared in the *New York Times, The Los Angeles Times, People Magazine, Playboy, Playgirl, Time Magazine* and numerous others. Foundation residents have appeared on such programs as "Sixty Minutes," the "Merv Griffin Show," and "The Tonight Show." Residents have been requested by commissioners of corrections in several states to mediate prison problems, and they have assisted hundreds of groups around the country and in other countries in developing programs of their own.

Thus, while great numbers of people have succeeded in their task of giving up drugs and turning from crime, we feel that our residents have succeeded in more important ways. They have demanded of themselves that they make restitution to society; that they care not only about their own financial success, but that they care about honesty, integrity, and the values by which we remain more than a country of people living together—values which make us a society. Together they have pooled their resources to demand from society the restitution which grants them access to the same opportunities the middle and the upper classes enjoy. Ultimately, then, the success of the residents of Delancey Street is more than the hundreds of success stories like Deborah's; it is the dent they have made and are continuing to make in cleaning up the swamp which threatens to reinfect them, and perhaps infect us all.

Chapter 4

PARENTS ANONYMOUS
The Use of Self-help in the Treatment and Prevention of Family Violence

Leonard L. Lieber

A colleague from Great Britain recently traveled to the United States with a particular interest in studying the Parents Anonymous program so that she could better establish it in her community upon her return home. She asked for the names and locations of several P.A. contact people and we directed her to associates in several communities on the eastern seaboard.

When our British colleague was about ready to leave the United States, she called to reflect on her visits here. She commented on how the people she met presented a very similar "package" of feelings and ideas. She praised their openness, warmth, expertise, and willingness to share issues surrounding the success of their respective Parents Anonymous organizations. She said that she felt as though they were all part of the same family.

And now the P.A. family, numbering thousands of troubled parents, skilled and caring professionals, and even more lay citizens, has grown to a huge, loving, therapeutic family stretching beyond oceans, reflecting a much larger set of issues than how to treat and prevent abuse (Wheat and Lieber, 1979).

A Bit of History

The Industrial Revolution in Western Europe and the United States in the late nineteenth and early twentieth centuries not only focused on the excesses of abuse absorbed by children and their struggling parents, but also gave rise to a growing middle and upper-class of concerned patricians.

In the United States, these latter socially conscious persons became aroused at the number of "little victims" enduring inhuman living conditions produced by the combination of mass immigration, poor urban planning and uncontrolled corporate misuse of human beings.

The melting pots of large American cities rapidly became human wastepots of poverty, crime, and general misery. The patrician classes, imbued with puritan influence, saw the children of poverty as subjects of moral decay needing rescue. The powerlessness of these children and their families made it fairly easy for concerned citizens to break up such families by taking their jeopardized children to "islands of safety," i.e. foster homes, adoptive homes, and large child-care institutions far from their families and their roots (Chase, 1975).

The elite prerogative of knowing what's good for the powerless prevailed not only over the direct victims of industrial excesses, but in most recent years, the victims of child abuse and neglect. The philosophy of family separation has remained a principle tool for "therapeutic involvement" today but in spite of those who persist in practicing the rescue syndrome for any child in serious trouble, is gradually weakening in the face of a number of mounting pressures. Lack of adequate placement facilities, dwindling economic resources and, especially, knowledge from new creative family oriented programs in this country are forcing current generations of service providers to look seriously at their practices of child-abuse case management.

To digress for a moment, we should note that other events had taken place in the late nineteenth and early twentieth centuries in the United States. The mass migration and industrialization also produced population clusters in ethnic, religious, and trade groups that banded together to retain personal integrity and identity and avoid being swallowed up by the anonymity of the city.

These people were also part of an historic migration of dissatisfied citizens from other nations to the United States, struggling for upward mobility and freedom of self-expression. Out of this group came new entries into a growing middle class whose philosophies embraced a concern for the underdog, but not necessarily from the same puritanical spigot as that of the earlier patricians.

The work of Freud, viewing human behavior as other than morally based, gave rise to a broader view of the human predicament.

The concept of self-help, a blending of the radical breakaway from governmental control, more vital self-expression, emphasis on individualism and Freudian doctrine, began to make itself felt in the United States in the 1920s. Persons who chose to rid themselves of unwanted behavior, joined together in groups, aiding each other e.g. Alcoholics Anonymous; Recovery, Inc.; and later Gamblers Anonymous and Overeaters Anonymous (Sagarin, 1969).

After the Great Depression of the 1930s, the concept of self-help came even strongly to the fore when the public realized that governmental assistance had limitations—that individuals needed to use their own internal resources for problem-solving.

By the end of the 1960s emphasis was placed on openness and self-expression, to a degree the western world had never seen. Though tactics used in the free-speech movement of Berkeley may be questioned, what was evident was that the push toward breaking shackles on personal repression was well under way.

Though it became easier to admit to various unwanted symptoms, admitting to abusing a defenseless child still denoted an unspeakable moral failure, if not a criminal act, to contemporary America. Regardless of the fact that there are virtually no educational courses offered in the emotional aspects of parenting, and that we have a history rife with both ritual and casual child abuse in the western world, child abuse in 1970 was an unspeakable sin (Chase, 1975).

The causes of child abuse are many and intertwined. They include a lack of self-esteem, poor parenting models during childhood, a personal history of abuse during the formative years, mistrust of authority, social and emotional isolation, inappropriate expectations of young children—the list is long.

Of more importance is the issue of what we shall do with the abusing person, the child in the body of an adult who is deeply concerned for the future and for his or her child. Shall we continue to separate troubled parents from "at-risk" children? In a small percentage of cases, yes. Temporarily or permanently, in some parent-child relationships must be intervention. Yet several thousand persons today, in many parts of the world, are struggling to maintain their children's roots at their source—within the family group. In a rather modified, extended family setting, persons of diverse socioeconomic backgrounds who experience child-abuse problems, are finding the nurturing, acceptance, and support they need to become what their own children want of them—parents who can nurture and love in spite of their past failings.

Parents Anonymous began because of one abusing parent's own inability to find an adequate therapeutic setting. She finally made contact with a therapist who accepted her but not her abusive behavior. Although the therapist admitted lacking the capacity to stop her abuse, he involved himself with her idea of engaging the help of other abusers, and joined in bringing together socially and emotionally estranged, alienated parents who were seeking a solution.

Parents Anonymous began with three of us—two parents and a volunteer professional. The first P.A. group in Redondo Beach, California in 1970 became the model for the over 1,000 chapters which exist at this writing, along with scores of no or low-cost therapeutic groups for P.A. children.

For the first four years of its existence, the growth of Parents Anonymous chapters came mainly out of an informal interchange of ideas between parents and professionals. Most of the leadership came from Jolly K., the founding parent, whose kitchen table served as a base for our extended family. Following an important seed grant in late 1973 from The W. Clement and Jesse V. Stone Foundation of Chicago, the national office of Parents Anonymous slowly became operational. Then, in May 1974 when P.A. numbered some 50 chapters, the Office of Child Development, Department of Health, Education and Welfare, gambled on our premise, method, and optimism, and agreed to provide us with funding in order to develop a nationwide network of chapters and to provide technical assistance via printed material and on-site visits to serve the professional and lay communities.

THE P.A. FORMAT

In very simple terms, P.A. is a nurturing and teaching free therapeutic service operated by the consumer as a means to reduce and prevent further child abuse within the family setting. P.A. recognizes the following related forms of child abuse: Physical abuse, physical neglect, emotional abuse, emotional deprivation, verbal assault, and sexual abuse. Attempts to deal effectively with all of these are made within the parameters of the program. Persons coming to a P.A. group or chapter are self-referred or are referred by social agencies, courts, police departments, etc.

A group sponsor, a volunteer professional who invests time and energy in each P.A. group, serves as consultant, a resource for the parent-chairperson who leads the group, and, most importantly, represents a positive image of an authority figure—a service provider—who can acceptably refer to resources beyond the P.A. experience. This is a key issue for those P.A. members who may need additional services, such as individual therapy, family counseling, etc. Out of fear of rejection based upon past negative experiences in both childhood and adult life, they have never been able to reach out to an authority for help.

The group experience consists of a weekly two-hour meeting in a secure, cost free safe environment—a church meeting room, YMCA room, etc.—that does not impose the presence of an authoritarian agency. Members, new or old are not required to give identifying information. They're not even required to speak at meetings should they choose not to. However, the setting creates an opportunity that even the most frightened person truly wants—a chance to be touched and to reach out, in safety.

Meeting usually center on coping more effectively in the here and now, though significant segments of life histories are shared as a means to place individual circumstances in a revealing context. Members often exchange phone numbers, making supportive contacts and help with crises available during the intervening week. Healthy social relationships often result, ending a self-imposed exile with thoughts and acts too ugly to communicate. Feelings of "they understand" emerge.

Instant success is not common. The development of a greater sense of self and thereby more positive family relationships are the strived-for goals. Parents Anonymous is most familiar and competent with situations of physical and verbal/emotional abuse. Immediate alternatives are sought for members with physical-abuse problems, especially because of the risk of injury to the child.

P.A. parents as a group are militantly anti-child abuse. They react for other and themselves when they hear a group member discuss crisis issues. They will not take a wait-and-see attitude if a child and family are in danger, and a parent refuses to lessen a potential hazard. Reporting to authorities is done, though in very few circumstances.

A synthesizing approach is the usual style of P.A. group meetings. Many types of psychotherapeutic technique are adapted to the arising circumstances by P.A. sponsors. Training aids such as Parent Effectiveness Training, STEP (Systematic Training for Effective Parenting), etc., are utilized when a group believes that the time is right.

In his paper "Toward a Psychology of Healthiness," James G. Kelly observes that personal development occurs when there is direct expression, emotional involvement, and conceptual integration of the emotional experience. He suggests that we all learn more about the various emotionally supportive settings that encourage persons openly to test out values and acquire impressions for building a preferred role to develop commitments (Kelly, 1974).

In the Parents Anonymous program, a substantially healthy and corrective modelling process for the abusing parent takes place. As mentioned earlier, one of the dymanics of the adult and child caught in the cycle of family violence and child abuse is a lack of trust of authority figures and a lifelong sense of rejection by them. Within the P.A. model, the volunteer professional, by acting in a nonauthoritarian, egalitarian fashion, provides a troubled parent with the opportunity of experiencing authority in a uniquely healthy way never known before.

Thus the development of positive role modeling and a willingness to begin trusting a potentially helping world often results within the P.A. program. Ultimately, the cycle of family violence child abuse can be broken. The isolation, mistrust, and alienation is no longer passed down from the parent member to the child. Rather, hope for the next generation is a direct product of the self-help experience.

THE PROFESSIONAL AND THE SELF—HELP GROUP
NOT A PARADOX AT ALL

As one observes the Parents Anonymous approach, some questions may be raised over the critical involvement of professionals in P.A. and whether or not this compromises the program as a self-help effort.

Actually, the use of the volunteer professional who may come from the fields of child welfare, mental health, medicine, education, etc. enhances the consumer's effort, in P.A.'s case, to gain some control over life circumstances.

The volunteer professional lends skills to group members as they attempt to stem the precipitating factors in chronic family violence. It is also the volunteer professional, often making public appearances at various community groups and explaining the program and how it interfaces with the agencies legally charged to deal with family violence, who provides credibility for the P.A. program in the eyes of the community.

It is important to realize that the volunteer professional, the P.A. sponsor, serves at the discretion of the P.A. members. Through it is a rare occurence, sponsors are asked to terminate their participation in a P.A. group if their skills, style, or personality do not meet the needs of group members. Thus, the P.A. group is neither operated by an agency nor an individual professional. Rather, it is an outgrowth of a community's wish to provide consumers with an opportunity to develop a product that they may use to meet an urgent human need.

A LAUGH A DAY MAY KEEP THE VIOLENCE AWAY

Very early into the P.A. experience, those of us who were heavily involved realized the depths of despair of many P.A. members and also realized that it was necessary to learn how to laugh together, no matter how serious the situation. Though one may have difficulty finding any humor in proximity to a situation of family violence, it is nevertheless important to understand how crucial a role humor can play in developing a positive treatment situation.

Dewane notes that social workers (if not other professionals) have historically been taught "that to attempt to become 'close' to a client reflects the worker's need to be accepted by the client and signifies the worker's insecurity; to joke with a client shows an attempt to diminish the severity of the client's distress and demonstrates the worker's inability to handle the stress of the situation. Humor is seen, then, as an avoidance mechanism for both client and worker" (Dewane, 1979). But we have seen just the reverse in the Parents Anonymous program. As Roncoli observes, "when employing humor in therapy, the therapist takes the risk of appearing imperfect, fallible and human. But he also gives the patient license to behave imperfectly, fallibly and humanly" (Roncoli, 1974).

It is a very rare P.A. parent-chairperson or sponsor, indeed, who is not able to have a good laugh in the midst of the chaos which may prevail at a given moment. And it is a very rare P.A. group which can not laugh at itself as it means to leaven some of the pain and futility marking a family's past and present circumstances rooted in family violence. It is this quality, among others, that allows the P.A. professional—the sponsor—to provide a positive role model for a parent in distress who has never been given the "permission" or the capacity to laugh at anything.

SOME NOTES ON P.A. EFFECTIVENESS

It is hard to talk about "success rates" in statistics when discussing P.A.'s effectiveness. We can report that research done by Behavior Associates of Tucson, Arizona in 1976 indicated that participation in a P.A. chapter often enabled persons to stop physically abusing their children within a number or weeks. Emotional abuse and neglect were also dealt with effectively, but these usually took a matter of months.

P.A. isn't for everybody who has an abuse problem. In fact, the dropout rate for persons who join P.A. may be 20 to 30 percent during the first few weeks when it becomes clear that P.A. expects its members to work hard at changing their behavior patterns. For many persons it is very difficult to deal with the idea of change, and for that reason a number of people choose not to remain involved with P.A.

The thousands who remained with P.A. over a period of time have shown marked degrees of success in improving their parenting. This rate is often directly related to the amount of time they've spent in P.A. For example, someone who stays in P.A. for a year or more will probably not go back to abusing the children, either in the manner or with the frequency that brought them to P.A. in the first place. A parent who stays in the program for three or four years or longer actually ends up becoming a better parent than the norm in a community. In addition, such a member tends to become a paraprofessional expert on family violence and thus even more valuable to the community at large (Wheat and Lieber, 1979).

In another study of child-abuse treatment project, Berkeley Planning Associates noted a marked difference in the effectiveness of various treatment modalities for families troubled with child abuse. Comparing individual treatment, group therapy, and Parents Anonymous groups or peer group treatment, the research staff found that the most expensive and least effective method of intervention was individual therapy. More moderate in cost and with some more lasting value after treatment was group therapy. Heading the list as the treatment modality of choice was P.A. or peer group therapy (Berkeley Planning Associates, 1977).

GOVERNMENT AND ALTERNATIVE FAMILIES

Our belief has always been to place much emphasis on the service recipient as a person, to be an enabling force, rather than one of "therapeutic manipulation." An individual generally has the capacity to find the answers, given a healthy setting in which to do so. We find much support in the writings of Carl Rogers, who stresses the need for permitting the service recipient to be unfettered by controls, to sense a state or climate of acceptance, caring, and understanding (Rogers, 1977). In a nation fearing governmental control of family life, yet dazed by rapid change in the institution of the family, we have tapped the public treasure to establish another alternative to the family.

The intimacy of communication in P.A. groups, the growth of new permanent friendships and special, long-term relationships, suggests that we have tampered with the process of traditional family life. But have we?

I would offer that the American family basically is not in the throes of destruction. The *type* of family, perhaps. Preindustrial, extended, agrarian families, and twentieth-century nuclear families, have indeed changed, for a complex of reasons. A family group reflects the state of organization (or disorganization) of a society, and how it influences an individual.

In the case of an alienated, twentieth-century, abusing parent who experienced an unhealthy, extended, or nuclear family as a child, and who can find no solution to his own failure at nuclear-family living, a normal behavior pattern might include membership in a loose-knit "extended family." The need not be based upon blood ties, but upon basic human needs for identification, emotional support from others, skills in making positive social relationships, parenting, etc. In essence, we see this evolution of group members very reflective of healthy behavior seeking mechanisms on the part of P.A. members.

Where, then, does the government have a place in directly sponsoring, not controlling, but in enabling, alternative family groups to flourish?

Sol Tax, an anthropologist at the University of Chicago, notes that the United States Government has always professed its mission "to promote the general welfare." He sees public policy clearly served by strengthening self-help groups which are supportive of persons. His view is that groups which are supportive of people protect their physical and emotional health. And health strengthens the social and economic fabric of any culture.

Tax also states, "The fact that we have no public policy designed to strengthen the family suggests that it may be useful to get one for self-help groups in connection with the promotion of the extended family, which may well be the traditional self-help group of greatest importance" (Tax, 1976).

By the above comments, I certainly do not mean to suggest that any government be the total support of the family—therapeutic or otherwise. My experience as a public welfare worker in Los Angeles County during the 1960's and as a mental health worker in the 1970's taught me how angry the family group or individual adult can become when they realize that they are almost totally dependent upon others for sustenance.

My experience has also raised a number of issues over the long-term practicality of the classical psychotherapeutic relationship between "patient and therapist" which, in my opinion, has too often created as many "chains as keys to the locks." What is suggested here is a multinational policy designed to provide minimal support toward those life alternatives that enhance living in these perilous times.

Ralph Tyler, a behavioral scientist, offers that the "ways to encourage self-help groups without damaging their vitality are by favourable publicity, by the formation of nongovernmental organizations to aid them, and by making it easier for them to obtain professional and technical assistance when requested" (Tyler, 1976). In the case of Parents Anonymous, electronic and and print journalism have been our greatest source of spreading "the word;" organizations such as the National Committee for the Prevention of Child Abuse and Neglect (in Chicago) reflect an example of nongovernmental voluntary groups promoting our cause. P.A.'s use of lay volunteers from Junior Leagues, Junior Women's Clubs, Councils of Jewish Women, *et al,* in the involvement of professionals as P.A. sponsors, reflects the practical use of skilled community-service persons and "psychotechnicians." Not to be omitted, either, are the many individuals, foundations, and corporations who have tendered generous private capital to encourage program growth.

PARENTS ANONYMOUS STATE OFFICE PROJECT

With the assistance of the National Center on Child Abuse and Neglect in Washington, D.C., the national program of Parents Anonymous began to decentralize its functions in 1978. In this way, each of the 50 United States has an opportunity to work closely with state-level P.A. offices in providing P.A.'s "alternative-family/child—abuse treatment program" in a fashion which best suits the needs of a state but which is also formulated by P.A. parents, lay citizens, members of P.A. board of directors, professionals, and government officials.

The fear of distant centralized government control is hereby minimized, while the voice of the concerned populace is given an opportunity to share a task with local government and, ultimately, to gain self-worth and respect, as well as credibility in creating a service "for the people by the people"—a credo too seldom observed though often held as an ideal.

Rogers refers to the work of Finley and Hovet, who not that as part of a means to deal with serious global issues, "it requires that nations move beyond self-interest defined in terms of power and to concentrate on common interests defined in terms of realizing man's fullest potentialities." Rogers adds, "a desire for their citizens to develop their potentialities is one of the few items on which most of the nations of the world might agree. And it is precisely at this point that experience with a person-centered approach may have something to offer" (Rogers, 1977).

SOME CONSIDERATIONS FOR THE FUTURE

A look toward the 1980's tells us that this country's financial resources will be stringently limited for provision of human services to children, families, and the elderly—the financially and emotionally impoverished. We are now facing cutbacks in the public and private sector, or, at best, serious challenges in reallocation of funds that will not increase but which will be required to serve more persons identified as needing service.

As the decade of the 1970's ended, a national watchdog publication on children's services documented crises in human-services agencies throughout the nation: A state budget was rapidly being eaten up by soaring inflation, and protective-services workers were handling few other than crisis cases on a 15 hour daily agency schedule. Foster parents were reportedly difficult to recruit because the economy dictated that both persons in a family had to leave the home for employment. No longer were foster-care subsidies adequate to provide agencies with an historically critical tool to provide for children in out-of-home placement. Agency budget cuts and salary raises to keep pace with inflation were cancelling out the possible growth of required social-service labor necessary to meet the growth of agency services.

At a time when the stated philosophy in the United States is to keep families together and preclude the trauma of separation, no help is forthcoming to many families who might be kept intact with minimal assistance. Too often, agency people said, cases ended up in the courts where the cycle began again, feeding the demand for high-cost services that inflation was making increasingly difficult to provide (Child Protection Reports, 1979).

In the face of the financial dilemma facing human-service providers here and abroad, the following recommendations are proposed to heighten the utilization of volunteer efforts in human services and to implement more effective use of self-help programs in the entire process.

1) We encourage all communities to develop "block families" and co-op family centers to which parents and children within the neighborhood can turn for help in time of crisis. It has been, and remains, unwise to believe that publicly mandated and financed services or private-agency efforts can meet the needs of all families who are in need of extra nurturing and crisis counseling. Use of block families and co-op staffed centers would alleviate the pressures on established agencies to provide assistance, and they would also provide communities and neighborhoods with a greater sense of cohesiveness and caring than has been noted during the past several decades.

2) It is proposed that every community have attached to its public services agencies a cadre of trained volunteers to work with identified families in stress. The would free the time of salaried professional staff to expand their service potential by reaching out to additional families. It is belief that thousands of persons throughout the United States are eager and willing to become involved as part-time volunteers on behalf of families who are in need of their nurturing.

3) We ask that legislation be specifically developed to support the work of alternative family groups which provide nurturing outside the normal family group structure, including several hundred self-help organizations which provide "health maintenance" to individuals and families who can find it nowhere else.

4) We ask that legislation also be developed to support the beginning of a family policy in the United States which would identify various forms

of traditional and newly-established creative family groups which provide for the well-being of all citizenry.

Hundred of self-help groups have successfully provided their members with the nurturing support and therapeutic tools to deal with various problems. The trials of widowhood, obesity, child abuse, parenting a drug abuser, open-heart surgery, cancer, alcoholism, have been as effectively dealt with by participation in self-help programs as in more classic settings. This nation, as well as others, is challenged not only to accept self-help as a potentially useful tool, but actively to make it a companion service in almost every human-service setting. We must regard every one of ourselves—children and parents—as in jeopardy, needing mutual support and protection. This process will involve a partnership between government and its people—one in which mutual trust and support can elevate the social and political processes for all.

Chapter 5

OVEREATERS ANONYMOUS

Virginia Goldner

A little over 4 years ago I went to my first meeting of Overeaters Anonymous, or O.A. I was 50 pounds overweight, and to put it simply, unable to stop eating. A therapist friend of mine with the same problem had told me about the program, and after procrastinating in the usual ways, I finally took myself, skeptical, contemptuous, and desperate, to a dreary, ramskackle church where, as I had been told by recorded message, I found a "beginners meeting."

That was June 1976. By June 1977, I'd lost all 50 pounds, and in the process, had found, I believed, a new way of living. O.A. represented, as I wrote in report that fall, an alternative vision and an alternative a community for living out that vision that was comparable to some of the most dramatic and daring social experiments of the sixties.

From this distance, those analogies sound embarrasingly overdramatic—the excess of someone in the throes of a conversion experience. In this instance, it was a hypereducated, politically hip version of what they call in O.A. the "pink cloud" syndrome. For me, that phase lasted about a year after I'd lost the weight. And then things began to go a little haywire. I can only report what I remember—that I stopped going to meetings sometime in the spring of 1978, that I began compussively overeating in July of that year, and that by late August I was saying to my husband, "I can't stop eating."

The rest will be tediously familiar to anyone vulnerable to this particular compulsion. It had taken me years to put on that original 50 pounds. It took barely 6 months to gain it back. Then came another 6 months of diets, binges, and more diets, accompanied by the typical protestations of someone unable to face facts. I told myself daily that I was not going back to O.A., that I'd outgrown "that sort of thing," and finally (toward the end), that the scene there was just *too* depressing. I had managed, extraordinary as it now seems to me, completely to bury the reality of my own experience in the program, and to revive all of those grossly elitist distortions about "ordinary" people that keep professionals like me from places like that.

The source of those distortions was a complicated interaction of psychological defense and class prejudice. I didn't want to look at what I was doing with food, and as long as I pictured O.A. as barely one step up from an after-care program for pathetic, broken-down clinic patients, I wouldn't have to.

In the end, it was my husband who got me back to meetings. A therapist himself, he'd become convinced by my initial experience that managing compulsive overeating was a lifetime project, requiring the kind of ongoing group support that only O.A. could provide. The fiasco of the past year supplied the living proof. Eventually, his goodhumored, but implacable unwillingness to buy into any of my fruitless alternatives, coupled with my absolute failure to get my eating under control, propelled me past 18 months of denial and back into the program. It was almost 4 years to the day from my very first meeting.

My experience of re-entry was particularly vivid. Within 10 minutes I could feel reality colliding with the fantasies that had kept me from meetings for so long. Instead of seeing a huddle of misfits mouthing homilies to one another, I saw a group of people who had what I now realized I wanted—peace of mind and self-respect. Listening to them talk about their lives, and the struggles to keep food and feelings separate, I suddenly remembered that this was not a diet club. As one woman put it, "I don't have a problem with food, I have a problem with my——'n life!"

The message—now clear as a bell—was that as long as you were eating compulsively, your mind was cluttered with the debris of addiction—self-loathing, broken promises, aimless fantasies about the tomorrow-when-you-once-again-possessed-the-beautiful-body-that-would-make-everything-all-right, and so on. In a head filled with that sort of junk, there wasn't much room for sustained and serious reflection. Food and anti-food thoughts were a brain drain, making it impossible to be 'all there' for the real business of living.

It was true. As people were talking, I had a visual image of myself as a multiple personality living in a kind of time warp. The adult woman, my social self, living in 1979, was sharing a room in my mind with a stormy little girl from the fifties, who controlled my eating and all my thoughts about food. Each acted as if she were alone, which is why I could never recognize the body in the mirror as my own.

When I came home that night I knew that something was over. It was not my compulsive overeating, which has continued in fits and starts for the past 6 months. But that night marked the end of my relapse. Whatever I do with food now, I don't do it alone. The people in those meetings (almost all of them strangers) have insinuated themselves into the private regions of my head where the eating scenarios get launched. What was once a little girl's secret doings is now a subject for scrutiny by a Greek chorus of grownups.

In 6 months I haven't lost a pound. But this, I'm told by oldtimers, is to be expected. As one 7 year veteran put it, its the difference between the thrill of adolescent infatuation and the hard work of an adult relationship.

So the rest of what follows should be taken as an interim report on work in progress. It is not intended as an exhaustive analysis of compulsive overeating, nor even of O.A., but rather as an attempt to narrow the field and sharpen the focus by exploring the ideas and experiences that have been most central to my own fitful, but progressive, recovery.

GETTING THE DIAGNOSIS

The most significant rite of passage into membership in Overeaters Anonymous is the moment when one is shocked into a recognition that the shoe fits. Unlike alcoholism, which is no longer seen as an individual's moral failing but as a complex and progressive disease process, compulsive overeating is still viewed as if it were a defect of character. There are a number of consequences to this. First, by virtue of collapsing the distinction between the compulsion and the person, one can never analyze the compulsion on its own terms. It remains a stigmatizing and intensely personal experience, cluttered with fantasy and shame. This emotionally overcharged, socially isolating process couldn't be more counterproductive, since the real issue with an addictive disorder is longterm management, and that requires a cool head and lots of planning.

O.A. provides an antidote for this solitary psychodrama by taking an absolutely matter-of-fact, quasi-medical stance towards compulsive eating. While in no way minimizing the psychological aspects of gluttony (and therefore, the extent to which an individual must take responsibility for his or her eating habits), O.A. members argue that the compulsion to eat is, by definition, beyond the control of the individual. Once caught in its grip, willpower becomes meaningless. The trick, then, is to arrange one's life in such a way that the compulsion is not activated.

This deceptively simple line of argument immediately lifts one's eating out of the mire of value judgements and into the arena of management. The initial move in this process is to take the "first step" in a Twelve Step Program of Recovery" that O.A. has adpated from Alcoholics Anonymous. In the words of Step One, you must "admit that you are powerless over food and that your life has become unmanageable." This admission is not easy to make, especially after years, often a lifetime, of fighting against it. But with the willingness to accept complete defeat comes a feeling of great relief. It's settled. You give up fighting a losing battle about weight and start straightening out your life instead.

All this, of course, takes time—time to absorb the new ideas, time to test the rhetoric against the evidence. And evidence is what only groups like O.A. can provide. Here are people of all ages, from every social class, race, and ethnic derivation, and in all sizes and shapes, from the most horribly obese, to the most svelte, even anorectic. *All* of them consider themselves compulsive overeaters, no matter where they happen to be in the seesaw of weight gain and loss. Seeing people in various states of physical recovery (and seeing some relapse) underlines the notion that the compulsion to eat must be distinguished not only from the person experiencing it, but also from the body containing it: it is a disordered state of mind.

Once this idea becomes established, the task for the newcomer gets more focused. In a phrase, one stops looking at other people's bodies and starts looking at one's own mind. This change in fixation is accompanied by a change in mood. The hopelessness of the defeat dieter becomes the excited curiosity of someone beginning to think in a new way. The question is no longer, "How can I lose weight?" but "Am I a compulsive overeater?"

For many people, myself included, the answer comes leaping off the printed page in the form of anonymously written pamphlets published by the O.A. central office. What is written in these documents is startlingly intimate. Not since the early days of the women's movement (and that was the only other time) did I find my most private fantasies and impulses unraveled by friendly, nameless strangers, and spread out in print before me. With uncanny precision, these anonymous writers capture every dreary detail of compulsive overeating—the obsessive preoccupations, the humiliating binges, the dreamy romantic fantasies of being thin—*all* of it.

The voice in these essays is androgynous, steady, sane, and eerily accurate. It is the voice of *absolute authority*. Here is an example:

> you will recurringly...the sudden overwhelming impulse to take just one bite...(and)? the craving, not for food as such, but for the soothing glow and comfort just a bite or two once gave you.

The choice of words here is deliberate. This is not the language of ordinary experience, it is the language of addiction. The wish to eat becomes a "sudden overwhelming impulse," the experience of eating, a feeling of "soothing glow and comfort," and the inevitability of the eating compulsion taken for granted in one short phase, "you will recurringly experience... ."

Writing like this not only breaks through the barricade of isolation that surrounds this kind of crazy eating, but it is itself a weapon against it. By making concrete and particular what feels diffuse and total, the words provide a wedge between the obsession and the compulsion to act it out. To borrow a phrase from psychoanalysis, they create the possibility that "Where id was, ego shall be."

And finally, to assert the obvious: this kind of writing is entirely different from what appears in the trendy diet books that monopolize best-seller lists year after year. This is not only because these little pamphlets tell it like it is, but more importantly, because they have nothing to sell. There are no products to buy, no dues to pay, and obsolutely no pressure to do anything whatsoever. The message is simply, "If you find yourself in these pages, you belong with us."

GOING TO MEETINGS (JOINING THE FELLOWSHIP)

There is much to say about the details of the O.A. program—the use of a sponsor (a person one calls every morning to report the day's food plan); the utilization of prayer, meditation, and religious philosophy in general; the principle of "giving service" to the organization as a means of preventing a relapse; the central importance given to working on the "Twelve Steps;" and underlying it all, the implications of O.A.'s radical commitment to a single idea—that recovery from compulsive overeating requires a change in one's whole life, one day at a time. But all this awaits another paper, and a later stage in my own recovery.

At this point I simply want to share what it's like to live with a chronic disability. To begin, let me make explicit what is implied here. After almost 30 years of coping with being fat (I first cried about it when I was 6) I can state unequivocally that I *hate* having this addiction. It has interfered with my life for as long as I can remember, coloring my relationships with people, periodically limiting my social options, and constantly eroding my sense of myself. I now accept, but not without resentment, that I will probably have to live with this monkey on my back for the rest of my life.

But much as I hate all this, I can also say that I love being in O.A. and I expect to make it a part of my life for as long as I can. O.A. has enriched my life in countless, unexpected ways. It has brought dignity and depth to my struggles with food, a spritual dimension to my inner life, and the rare chance momentarily to get beyond the barrier of race and class, and encounter, on an equal footing, a whole world of people whom I would otherwise never come to know.

These serendiptious experiences are made possible by O.A.'s unique ideology and organizational structure, and also by the very nature of compulsive overeating itself. Unlike anorexia nervosa, for example, compulsive overeating seems to be a ubiquitous disorder that cuts across the usual demographic divisions of age, race, social class, and gender. Since all O.A. meetings are open and free of charge, and the only condition for membership is "a desire to stop eating compulsively," the social composition of the organization is extraordinarily heterogeneous.

At any particular meeting one can expect to find a cluster of expensively dressed, middle-aged women with 30 or 40 pounds to shed, a small collection of strange, often obese, socially isolated younger men who have probably spent the day at the welfare or unemployment office, a large contingent of vocal, working-class men and women in a variety of shapes and sizes, a somewhat smaller, but equally outspoken group of young professionals (mostly female), and invariably, a sprinkling or originals who resist all classification.

Part of the pleasure in going to meetings is, in fact, the element of surprise. I never know who will be there, and what slice of life will be served up for all of us to look at. Over the years I've catalogued innumerable tiny dramas—windows on a world closed to me by virtue of the social segregation that divides all of us. I've also come to expect that apart from the all-important experience of solidarity, I will usually discover someone who will capture my imagination, or challenge my ways of thinking—someone whom I can conjure up at those moments when eating seems inevitable.

I can't imagine another context in which all of this could be possible, since it depends upon people from every segment of the class structure coming together as equals. Moreover, having had this experience, I can't imagine a more straightforward challenge to the class prejudice that shapes social life for all of us. Here, I am partners in struggle with people twice my age and weight, and with a quarter of my schooling. Many of them are up against circumstances I can barely imagine: chronic unemployment, colossal debts, major illness. Most have lived with limitations I've never known; being stuck in low-paying jobs they hate, or being stuck at home with no break in the daily monotony. But while I may be more articulate, I also have less to say. These people can't afford to buy diet gourmet diet food, or to eat out if cooking at home is too tempting, or to take a cab to a meeting if it's too cold. They have to keep it together without the short cuts

I depend on, and they're tougher because of it. In the rest of my life, I may take my professional self-importance as a matter of course. In O.A., I'm just another addict.

Turning conventional status hierarchies on their head is remarkably effective in facilitating group process among this unlikely collection of people. There is very little cliquishness, virtually no scapegoating, and a consistent expectation of honesty, self-disclosure, and mutual support at O.A. meetings. At the same time, discussions are challenging, conflicts are not avoided (although they are "managed" in particular ways), and individual differences are respected. The effect is an experience that is often very moving—at once intimate and comforting, exciting and provocative.

Maintaining this delicate and lively balance requires more than good leadership and collective self-discipline. It depends, ultimately, upon an ideological consensus about the purposes of meeting together, and by implication, about the purposes of the organization as a whole. Here the O.A. literature is absolutely explicit—"O.A. exists for the sole purpose of helping its members abstain from compulsive overeating and to carry its message to other compulsive overeaters who still suffer."

Hearing this reminder at the outset of a meeting may appear to a newcomer like an overcautious constraint on discussion. But its real effect is to sharpen and deepen the exchange of ideas, since everything that is said is measured against a single standard: is it *useful* in the struggle against the compulsion to eat? This radical pragmatism not only keeps conversation focused, it creates a unique social structure for the group as a whole. Just as individual comments are evaluated in terms of a unitary standard, so are individuals themselves. In O.A., status is not won in the usual ways.

People come to meetings for ultimately one reason—they want to get through the night. This tangible urgency washes away conventional routes to the top. Physical appearance, money, social polish, professional success, or friends in power count for very little here. In this setting, you are what you eat.

Status within the group, then, comes only with seniority, since it is experience with the problem (and not necessarily success) that makes all the difference. This should come as no surprise to anyone with a knowledge of chronicity. Like many chronic disabilities, compulsive overeating is a syndrome characterized by relapse. Thus, "success," if one takes a long view, is probably a period of remission within a cycle of episodes.

To develop a sense of mastery over such a frustrating obstacle course requires a recognition that the rhythm is "one step forward, two steps back." No one knows this better than the old-timers who have seen the pendulum swing so many times that they can almost anticipate a change in direction. No matter how ordinary, or even invisible, these people may be in their daily lives, in O.A. they command absolute respect. When they choose to speak, I take notes.

Whatever happens in my long-standing battle with food, one thing is certain. My understanding of social reality and my vision of human possibility have been permanently expanded by the experience of being in O.A., and on its own terms—that of "helping its members abstain from compulsive overeating." I can think of no better alternative. Chronicity is, by definition, exhausting. Professionals don't have the time, and quickly lose interest in the tedious business of managing a lifelong disorder. The impulse, after a while, is to blame the victim, since relapses are practically inevitable, and progress, at best, is fitful. Moreover, the whole project is built out of small moments and trivial details. The victories are modest, epiphanies are rare—hardly the dramatic rewards that sustain a professional career.

Yet, for the individual client, success depends upon attending to the trivial, since staying on top of an addictive disorder is not accomplished day by day but, more often, moment by moment. And no one who hasn't been reduced to tears by the struggle against the impulse to eat (or drink, or shoot up) can understand what that means. No therapist, no matter how empathic, can identify with the handsome actor who described staying up all night trying to keep from eating by guzzling a giant bottle of diet soda. That kind of intimate knowledge is reserved only for those who've been there.

People in O.A., and groups like it, are experts in their disability. By sharing that knowledge and pooling those resources, they create the conditions to build an identity out of an embarrassment, and a lifetime support system out of a lifelong disability.

Chapter 6

"HELPING" IN MUTUAL HELP GROUPS FOR THE PHYSICALLY DISABLED

Phyllis Silverman
Diane Smith

INTRODUCTION

There is increasing interest in mutual-help groups on the part of health-care professionals. They want to know if these groups constitute viable, efficient, and cost-effective methods of helping people to cope with debilitating illnesses and the accompanying social and emotional changes. Observers of these groups come away with the impression that they are very effective. Not enough is known, however, about how these groups help, the impact of the help on the participants, and the participants' subsequent relationships within the health-care system.

This paper reports on aspects of a small study designed to explore some of the above issues. The respondents involved were participants in three mutual-help groups, the Cured Cancer Club of Boston (CCC) for Laryngectomees (LE's), the Kidney Transplant and Dialysis Association (KT/DA), and the Massachusetts Spina Bifida Association (MSBA). Members of these groups have chronic, and often life-threatening, conditions that necessitate long-term connections with physicians and other health-service providers. These three groups were chosen because they provided varied helping programs to their members that included written materials, monthly educational and social meetings, and outreach visiting programs. The outreach was of particular interest for its impact on newly ill people. Each group gave high priority to its visiting program, and invested in it a signficiant amount of organizational effort. In each group the visiting programs reached out to people soon after they became aware of their illness. The goal of the visit is to provide a personal view, from experienced members, of how it is possible to live effectively with their disability.

In some groups, such as Reach for Recovery, professional advisors, or the referring physician, determine what aspects of the illness visitors may talk about, and orchestrate the subsequent interaction they have with the people whom they visit. This study selected groups in which the mutual-help group members decided what to discuss and the type of help to offer. The visit was not a single act but the beginning of a relationship with afflicted individuals and their families.

THE GROUPS

The Cured Cancer Club (CCC) is composed of Laryngectomees (LE's) or people whose cancerous larynxes have been removed, and who no longer have normal voice function. LE's have a "stoma," which is an opening into the trachea through which they breathe. A stoma needs special care to keep it clean and protect it from infection and from the inhaling of toxic substances. LE's can communicate using an electronic amplifier or by learning esophageal speech, which is accomplished by swallowing air to reproduce sounds in the back of the throat.

The Cured Cancer Club of Greater Boston is 25 years old. The agenda of its regular meetings includes both social and educational programs. Several fundraising events, held annually, provide sufficient income for the group to meet its needs. The club is a member of the International Association for Laryngectomees (IAL), and an affiliate of the American Cancer Society (ACS). A visiting committee of 25 experienced members reaches out to people who are new laryngectomees. Referrals for this program are routinely received from six hospitals in the greater Boston area, from surgeons, and from the ACS. The group has developed an educational kit that visitors leave with individuals at the hospital or at home, after they visit. Members *never* visit anyone in the hospital without the physician's permission (there are some surgeons who do not permit their patients to have a visitor). In those hospitals where no formal relationship exists with the CCC, members sometimes know one staff person from whom they obtain permission to visit informally. Every patient is referred for speech therapy, and because many of the speech therapists are LE's and belong to the CCC, they see to it that their patients are told about the group, invited to meetings, and can be visited at home if there had been no contact until that time.

Visiting committee volunteers are members of the CCC chosen on the basis of their 1) desire to be a visitor; 2) good esophageal voice; and 3) personal ease at going into hospitals. Visitors must participate in a training program during which they learn how to listen and how to present themselves. There are also visitors who use a speech aid, a mechanical device that does not require learning esophageal speech. These people visit individuals more likely to choose a speech aid, such as elderly people who live alone and need to be clearly understood over the telephone.

The Massachusetts Spina Bifida Association (MSBA) is for children (and their parents and families) born with spina bifida, the second most common birth defect. This disease affects children's neurological systems, impairing their motor and intellectual abilities. A peculiarity in the condition of spina bifida is that the extent of the disability is unknown at birth; as the baby develops, signs that another of its systems may be affected may or may not become evident. Most of the children have motor problems; some are able to walk with braces, crutches, or canes, while others are confined to wheelchairs. Mental retardation is possible in some babies, but their potential both physical and intellectually is frankly unknown at birth, beyond a few generalizations made on the basis of the location of the spinal lesion.

When this research was begun, the leadership of the MSBA were in the process of organizing a formal visiting program to insure that all new parents of babies with spina bifida would be reached. Until recently, initial contact with another parent, usually the mother, occurred in the clinics where infants were seen on a regular basis. In the projected visiting program, the MSBA visitors would receive referrals from units in the hospital where children are treated. There are hospitals in the greater Boston area to which all infants with spina bifida are taken, immediately after birth, for their life-saving surgery. These hospitals have been somewhat reluctant to make referrals to the group immediately after the birth of the baby. The smallest service (that which sees the fewest number of babies) has been the most supportive. The staff has agreed to provide new parents with newsletters, and will make referrals when the doctors feel that the family is ready. Referral is made by telling parents that if they wish, contact is available. A second hospital has a nurse coordinator who routinely asks families if they would like to meet a member of MSBA and if an affirmative answer is received, they call MSBA to arrange a meeting. The hospital seeing the largest number of new babies is the most reluctant to consider a visting program. The staff in particular the attending physicians, are very cautious about who they will allow to talk with "their" patients.

The MSBA has regular monthly educational meetings, which provide parents with the opportunity to share experiences and resources. Parents are encouraged to bring their children. The newsletter, published several times a year, is full of vignettes of how families have coped with aspects of their child's disability. The Massachusetts chapter has several fund-raising events a year to support the activities of the local group, and belongs to the Spina Bifida Association of America.

The Kidney Transplant and Dialysis Association (KT/DA) is for people with renal failure who are on dialysis machines or are living with transplanted kidneys. Dialysis patients live on rigid diets with severe restrictions on the amount of their fluid intake. They do not urinate, and rely on dialysis machines to perform this essential life function. Approximately 5 hours, three times a week, is spent on the dialysis machine. Transplant patients are constantly on the alert for symptoms indicating that their bodies are rejecting the transplanted kidney; such rejection would return them to dialysis for survival. Before the KT/DA visiting program began three years ago, visiting was done on an informal basis when a member heard of a new patient who "could use some cheering up," or when a hospital nurse told a member about a patient who was "ready to talk to someone." The group cannot visit in the hospital without permission of the hospital staff. The committee notified all the social workers in dialysis units that thy were available to visit new patients, either in the hospital or at home, and asked for referrals. They have received only two or three referrals a month.

The group is not sure why the response is so limited, but speculate that the social workers feel threatened by the visitors' participation, or are afraid that since the visitors are not trained in counseling they may say something amiss. When the group hears of some one through its own informal network, members visit on their own without a referral by calling the person at home and asking if they may visit. If the person is in the hospital, they call the nurse or social worker to ask permission to visit. In one hospital, a member has developed an informal relationship with the head nurse of the renal unit who calls him when they have a new patient. In another hospital, a social worker does this. The hospitals which maintain large units, however, are not responding to the request for referrals.

The group also maintains an active mailing list of 1200 names. Any time members are dialyzed at a center and meet a new patient, they see to it that their name is put on the mailing list and that the person is invited to meetings. Groups seem to maintain their initiative in reaching potential new members in spite of the resistance they encounter from many health care professionals. The most frequent reason professionals give for not allowing visiting is that their patient is not ready. The concept of "readiness" will be explored in the presentation of findings.

Sample Description

A total of 18 people were interviewed: ten men and eight women. Nine out of ten people with renal failure and cancer of the larynx are men; therefore most of the members of KT/DA and CCC are men. The ten men interviewed were members of these two groups. One woman with renal failure was interviewed. Seven members of the MSBA were interviewed, all of them young women. Several of them were first-time mothers. One respondent was single and another divorced; the others were all married, and in most instances their spouses participated in the interview as well. A cross section of occupational and educational backgrounds were represented in the sample. Most members had no more than a high school education. But several had advanced degrees and taught at local universities. Such diverse occupations were represented as school teacher, car salesperson, bus driver, as well as firefighter and police officer. Families were clearly at different points in their life cycles. Most members of the MSBA were young, just starting their families and establishing themselves economically. Members of the CCC were for the most part much older, often closer to retirement. Members of the KT/DA varied in age. (Unlike cancer of the larynx which is primarily a disease of older men, renal failure can strike at any age.)

The respondents were not chosen on a random basis. Initially the leaders of each group were asked for the names of new people who would have received a recent visit. It would have been impossible to interview a new laryngectomee. Interviewing had to wait until they had begun speech lessons. However, all the groups had a similar protective reaction toward new people and were reluctant to expose group members, during this initial adjustment period, to a research interview. They preferred to have one of the researchers come to a meeting of their respective groups, present the project to the membership and ask for volunteers. Several volunteers were instrumental in starting the visiting programs. They provided retrospective data on how the group helped them. The chairperson of each group was also willing to suggest other people who were not at the meeting but who were "doing well, and might be willing to talk." Once the interviewing began and the group did not hear of any negative reactions, they were more comfortable supplying the names of people who had received their diagnosis more recently. Instead of following one person over the year to see how they coped, we were able to get a sense of the process by comparing the new people in their initial attitude to those who were "veterans."

Only three people received unsolicited visits. The remainder of the respondents sought out the group, or initiated the visiting program where none existed in the KT/DA group. There are several limitations in the findings of this study that must be cited: the smallness of the sample, the lack of a comparison group[1], and the fact that the leadership of the groups chose the respondents. (They were more likely to choose people their group affected positively.) Another limitation arises from the fact that we are joining in our discussion parents of handicapped children with adults who are themselves seriously ill. The issues for each group are very different. However, shortly after the birth, these parents feel as if they themselves are defective, as if their own lives are endangered. Therefore, their reactions are similar to those of the adults who are ill. In addition, we are concerned mainly with the *process* of help from a mutual-help group. This process can be the same regardless of the disability, and therefore these groups can be appropriately joined in this presentation.

In the face of a serious, life-threatening illness, the group of people who participated in this study have an "upbeat" approach. From these findings we can learn something about how they develop and maintain this attitude.

FINDINGS

The findings are represented in the form of a narrative to allow the reader to follow individuals' reactions 1) to their illness, 2) to the offer of help, and 3) to the impact the offered help had on their accommodation to their changed condition.

---

[1]A comparison group would have to be drawn from people with similar backgrounds and experiences who do not accept help from mutual-help groups. Lieberman (Videka, 1979), in a study of Mended Hearts found no difference in outcome for heart patients who participated in the mutual-help group and those who did not. Silverman (1973), in a study of women who refused help from the original widow-to-widow program, found that most of these women were copers who managed their lives and transitions well, using the existing resources in their family and in themselves. Often, they had a friend or relative who provided them with a mutual-help experience.

Reaction to the illness determines the initial reaction to the offer of help. Most respondents spoke of a sense of shock and disbelief as their dominant feeling when they first heard the diagnosis and/or after surgery. One man recalled his reactions to hearing the diagnosis of cancer of the larynx:

> It was such a shock. You think these things happen to people on TV or in books, but when it happens to you, it's a real shock.

A woman, after starting dialysis, said:

> I didn't want to know anything that I didn't have to. I wanted to take one day at a time. I didn't want to talk to anyone.

She was protecting herself from being overwhelmed by what she was facing. This extended to meeting someone else with cancer.

> I didn't want to see another laryngectomee. I wasn't ready for that.

He was not ready to accept himself as someone with a laryngectomee. He was trying to think of himself as whole, to deny the full meaning of what was happening to him. A mother of a child with spina bifida talked of the visit she received. She was holding back, not ready to acknowledge her situation and need.

> She came to visit us and was friendly, outgoing, and brought information. I didn't get too much into it. I still think I didn't want to know any more than I did. My husband wanted answers and talked with her.

To accept a visitor means at some level acknowledging you have the same problem as the visitor. As part of the effort to avoid facing this new reality, some people tried to prove they did not need help. A young mother recalls her reactions:

> The contact that was available to me in the first year did not work for me. I kept thinking I could do it all myself. Now, looking back, I could have accepted more help than I did, even if it was just to have dinner brought to me.

Some people actively rebuffed the visitor:

> When Charlie (a laryngectomee) came to my hospital room, I told him
> to leave.

People need time for the reality to emerge to consciousness. In some
families, the spouse maintained contact, as a linking agent and as a way to
get their needs met as well.

> Charlie stayed in touch with my wife and came to visit me at home. By
> that time I had taken the first speech lessons, so I could talk with him; I
> was ready to hear him.

Others delayed longer until they could no longer avoid the reality.
(Silverman, 1971)

> As it was, I didn't get into contact until my baby was 18 months old.
> By that time, the reality had hit. She wasn't going to develop normally,
> and I realized the ongoing nature of the problem. Even the first time I
> talked to another mother, it was depressing, although now we are in
> touch and have a mutually helpful relationship.

The burden on the visitor is substantial. One LE recalled how he had sent
the visitor away:

> Now I'm the first one to go out and visit when someone tells me that
> there's a new laryngectomee, because on top of whatever else people
> tell them, or the information they have, seeing me can give them hope.
> I don't get offended by their first reaction.

A mother of a child with spina bifida recalled:

> The first year, If you talk with someone else, you need real
> understanding. You need someone to ask, "How are you?" and then
> to ask again, "How are you *really*?" People need to handle it in their
> own way. If you are the one doing the outreach, it's real important to
> be sensitive to the emotional needs of the parents, and aware that they
> may not be willing to talk, especially at first. This is a club with a
> terribly high cost of dues. The emotional trauma is great.

The most outstanding feature in the respondents' behavior after they
were in contact with other similarly afflicted individuals was the sense of

relief. In retrospect, they recalled this feeling when they realized that another person existed with the same problems and that this person had accommodated to the illness. It helped to know that others had survived with the same problem. They valued the fact that the visitor maintained contact with them.

> It's really interesting, and reassuring, just to know that people are coping with it in their own ways. You feel close to them, somehow. You're not the only person. You're not a freak.

> The speech teacher was great. She inspired me immediately. She looked so good and could speak so well. She left me some pamphlets. When I read about survival rates, that threw me. Fortunately, my wife called the American Cancer Society an got more information. I was really glad for the information. As I got started talking, I felt better.

> There was a man at work whose niece had been on dialysis and now has a transplant. He had her call me. She told me about the Kidney Center and also about Jim, who called me and invited my wife and me to come and watch his dialysis at home. We had no idea that this was possible.

Respondents indicated that during this period, they did not relate to a group or organization. They were only aware of an individual who understood.

> The man I talked to, who was the oldest living non-twin transplant and one of the few transplanted patients in this area, was highly encouraging. He had the same symptoms I did, and had lived through the anguish of wondering if the kidney would take or if he would die. Another man, who had been transplanted 18 months earlier, came to my hospital room and cheered me up. It was important. I learned I could live a "normal" life.

Some people with prior experience in a mutual-help group anticipated their need to find others. One man on dialysis sought out the group because as a parent of a retarded child he had a prior successful experience in a local Association for Retarded Citizens. One young couple was presented with membership in MSBA by an aunt who had a retarded child. She knew they would need to meet others in a similar position. Only later did they appreciate what she had done for them.

People who have no contact with the groups seem to reach a point where they need to find someone in a similar situation.

> One day I was so frustrated with what was going on in the clinic that I said to my husband, "I have to talk to someone." I had seen a girl walking down the hall. Her baby was a couple of months older than mine. So I asked the social worker if she'd ask the girl to come and meet me. It turned out that she wanted to talk, too. We exchanged numbers and she came to my house, and I went to hers. It was wonderful, thank God, because I was at that point, really needing someone to talk to and someone who would understand. She was going though the same stuff.

The denial seems to diminish as does some of the anger and the feeling of helplessness. As people see there is hope for the future, which the visitor provides in person and in the material, their resentment and isolation are relieved.

> I was reading the article and immediately identified with that mother. I was reading about my own feelings of anger, even hatred, for other people who have a normal baby. I didn't want to have those feelings, but I didn't feel so guilty when I read about her. *You need to have some one else who's been through it.* My husband and I are close, and he helped to take care of us both, but you need some one else. I'm not strong, but I'm resilient. This is an experience not everyone goes through. It makes you stronger, and it helps to know (from another person) you can make it.

Meeting other people in similar situations has a far different impact from being told by a professional person or a family member, "You'll be all right. You can do it."

> I'm more relaxed now that I've been to some of those meetings. I saw that other parents with older kids are doing well. Along with the doctor telling me some hopeful things, the future doesn't look quite so bleak.

> My speech teacher told me about the group and when I went to the first meeting I saw all of them talking and functioning. I could see that some didn't do all they should, but others were right out there. The best thing I learned was that other people had lived 8, 10, and 12 years as laryngectomees, so I knew there was continuity to life.

Respondents indicated they needed someone to model themselves after who was living an acceptable life and whom they could be like.

> At first, I was really upset. There are all these doctors around saying, "This is your future." I have a family. How am I supposed to spend 5 to 8 hours on a machine, three times a week? You never dream it could happen to you. After a while I was starting to give up, until, for some reason, I started learning about it. I felt a little better when I got to understand more. One day at the hospital I finally had the courage to go and look at a machine. Of course, after visiting Jim and seeing his setup at home, seeing how well this guy is doing, it's a lot different. I still wonder, but I feel better now that I know more. After all, there he was, relaxed, sitting in a chair, talking with us for hours. It was like nothing was happening to him. He and his wife told us how they travel. I know I could take my family to Florida and not have to worry about missing dialysis.

People need to feel "normal again," and to feel less isolated. The family with a mentally retarded daughter recalled what they had learned from that experience, and from the KT/DA.

> That experience taught us about the value of groups. You know, when you have a health problem, you tend to ask yourself, "Why me?" Your friends are all "normal." We went at first to meet other people with the same condition. We found out that others put up with more than we do. It sometimes makes you feel lucky. I also wanted my wife to talk to another wife who was dialyzing her husband at home, and to ask things like, "Did you have a problem with such and such?" You find out that others deal with some of the same things you do. The more we went to the meetings, the more we liked it. We liked what the group was doing and saw that it really was patients helping other patients, all on a volunteer basis.

Once they relaxed and were able to recognize their common problems, our respondents talked about what they learned from the groups. They needed to learn how other people did things. People's reactions appeared to be logical responses to the many unknowns with which they were dealing. A major illness makes one question, "Will I live?" As the adjustment process continues, people become more aware that life is possible, and begin to ask, "*How* will I live?"

Even though the doctors told me my baby's meningiocele wasn't as severe as it could be, I still wanted to be in touch with other mothers who had kids with special needs. I wanted to share information. I spent a long time, for example, looking for shoes that would fit over the braces. It was frustrating not to be able to do something as simple as buying a pair of shoes. Another mother at the brace shop finally told me where I could get them. That kind of frustrating experience could be avoided.

Some people are not interested in ongoing group activities:

I'm not a social-function man, but I read everything I can get my hands on. I like to read about other people, about the progress they're making, the pros and cons of transplant and dialysis, the adventures of people and how they travel, etc.

They also needed to learn to talk to health professionals who treated them.

It gave me confidence. I would talk to them and they would tell me to ask questions, to ask why and not just go along with what the doctors were saying. I realized it wasn't just that I was being emotional, but that I had a right to be depressed and confused. I could always rely on the nurses, but it was the doctors. I'd come home ready to strangle some of them, and then call someone from the group, and we'd be able to laugh about it. I just have to find some way of dealing with the doctor's personality.

Typically, the respondents were people who were intimidated by professionals. They were accustomed to deferring to the doctor.

I talked with them (the group) to find out *what my rights are.* You can feel very intimidated by doctors. They're sort of like gods. They've been through a lot of training, but they're not gods, really. They can be wrong. I'd like to know if I can say, "No, I don't want this procedure done," and still not have him be offended, especially if I have to deal with him for the next 20 years, and depend on his help.

One woman was afraid to ask questions, fearing they would think she could never understand.

> It was no good for me. Every time I went to the clinic, it seemed I would see a different resident, who had a different story, and I couldn't get it straight. I realized it wasn't just me, the reason I was overanxious and crying all the time. Part of it was their problem, about communicating, and I didn't know who to trust.

The group pointed out to this woman that she could choose her physician, and was not obligated to stay in the clinic. Members gave her the names of several physicians who had worked out well for people with similar problems, and she chose the one she liked best. This was a new experience for her and for her family.

People also learned practical things about how to manage their everyday life.

> I learned a lot of practical things. They told me where to get the Medic-Alert Bracelet, and the shower bib. They were so enthusiastic about the International Group for laryngectomees and the annual convention, that my wife and I are planning to go to it. They also reminded me about the way to eat. It's important to eat slowly.

Since the whole family is affected by the illness, spouses were involved not only as linking agents but in the group itself, which provided them with support and information.

> My wife goes to the meeting to talk with others who are doing home dialysis. She learns a lot, but mostly it's just talking to someone who is doing the same thing. She feels more comfortable about what she's doing. When I went to my first meeting (of the CCC), it was 8 months after surgery. Ann (the speech teacher) asked me to speak to the group. I liked it, and kept going back. My wife went along, and found that other wives were supportive to each other.

Overall, the following remarks summarize how our informants feel about being contacted by a member of a mutual help group.

Everyone should have a visitor. I would visit, even if there is that denial. I would keep in contact with the spouse, like C. did in my case. I would tell them I'm willing to share my story, because whatever else you have, information, magazines, stories about other laryngectomees, it's not the same. They've seen me, heard me, and let me tell them what I've done. If you have the desire, you can have the hope that I have. I'd tell them, "You're not somebody with a disability. You just have a voice that's different."

Acommodation for most of these respondents was facilitated by being involved in some kind of helping experience. The group of respondents who were 3 to 10 years away from the acute phase of their illnesses all communicated a sense of confidence derived from having lived through those early stages, and discovering they were able to achieve a satisfying life. In part, they attributed their success to affiliation with and involvement in the group.

Most of us feel so grateful to still be around that we're willing to share whatever we can. I took part in all kinds of medical studies after my first transplant. I just felt I owed it after what had been done for me. We seem to take every day as it comes, maybe because at one time we thought we didn't have many days left. That's one reason why people in this organization are willing to work for each other. There is a certain trust among us. We're not selfish. Even though we have different opinions, we basically agree that our most important task is to turn around and help others. That's where my satisfaction is. Most kidney patients are optimistic and appreciative. Out of gratitude, we are willing to help.

There was evidence of newcomers taking on the role of helper. As Riessman (1965) observed, by helping others, they in effect helped themselves.

As soon as we get settled (we're moving in the fall), I'd like to be more involved with the group, because I think my husband and I both have something to give. We can reach out, like some of the others have reached out to us. It would also be an outgrowth of our personal philosophy. Also, they have things to offer us—the fact that they have children who have already gone through the stages that P. will be going through. We're also excited about the newsletter, because J. has edited a newsletter and I've been an English major. He has written four poems and developed a slide presentation about the baby's birth. We

would enjoy submitting poetry like other parents have, and maybe help
with editing.

> At first, the meeting site seemed to be too far away, but we went
> because we wanted to share information.... At the picnic, it was
> encouraging to see other kids running around wearing sneakers.
> You're always looking for encouragement. I'm excited about the next
> meeing because it's on genetics. B. asked if I would be corresponding
> secretary. I want to do something, but not something that takes a lot of
> factual knowledge. I'm better at contacting parents, congressmen,
> fund-raising, and publicity. I'm getting more self-confidence about
> reaching out to other parents. They need the information and support.
> I have the name of a new mother and I'm going to contact her in case
> she might be afraid to call me.

> I feel good, now. I don't feel like I can't handle this. Everybody
> has their days, I guess, and I have mine, too, but they don't come as
> often. Being able to keep busy and belonging to something helps. They
> asked me to serve on the professional advisory board, and I'm glad,
> because I can be a link between parents and the doctors. I encourage
> mothers to ask lots of questions. There's so much to keep straight.

People do not have fewer problems. They seem to cope with them
more effectively.

> The bank kept my job open so I went back after the transplant. Seven
> and a half years later, when the transplant failed and I had to go back
> on dialysis, they kept it open again. I went back within a few weeks
> after re-starting dialysis, even though the shift was 11:00 P.M. to 4:00
> A.M. Eventually, I got onto the 7:00 to 12:00 P.M. shift, which
> allowed me to keep working at my job and also keep up with the
> JayCees, and with the KT/DA, which was just getting going at that
> time. My life is very active.

People involved in groups have discovered ways in which to live
quality lives. One man and his wife traveled extensively, once they learned
he could be dialyzed in foreign countries as well as in the United States. All,
except one participant who at the time of the interview was recovering from
a complication of dialysis, have returned to their jobs and are maintaining
their incomes, supporting their families, and feeling productive.

As the groups matured, they became more and more concerned with
outreach. They also provided programs to educate members at meetings
about diet, the latest in technology, new treatments, and so forth. In
addition, they involved some of their members in public education, so that
they could tell others about their illness.

We've really grown, from the first "Kidney Patient Appreciation Fund." We've raised money from raffles and bake sales to buy equipment for the lab, an ECG machine for the kidney unit, and patio furniture for patients to use outdoors. Then we built the lounge. By that time, we also were writing a newsletter and holding dinner dances. We had a real bond, an empathy. After all, there were so few of us, and we really cared. One member recently suggested we publish a flyer to make the group known to more patients and families as well as to "the public." I designed the logo. We are getting up a panel discussion to educate more people about kidney disease. We may have a softball game between KT/DA and a local radio station to help that cause. We're also trying to decide on a kind of scholarship fund for patients and their children, a "continuing education" fund that would cover trade school as well as college.

The written word is also important. We have been working on a manual for patients written by R. and others in the group. It will be published in the spring. It has articles on diet, symptoms, and coping with the disease on all levels. We tried to hit every aspect of renal disease, *from the patient viewpoint*. We wanted to cover the financial, physical, and mental components and promote the welfare of these patients on all levels.

I like seeing the group do more of the encouraging, helping people to mainstream. I think it's a way that I cope. Somehow you need to give back what you've been given. All I sought after in other ways has come to me through this medium.

What's best about it is that it's patients helping patients. We do for each other what the doctors and our wives and families cannot, whether it's money for groceries, or hearing someone say, "This is what I did when I had those symptoms, too. You might try it."

Experienced helpers in the groups refer to the delicate sense of timing needed by the outreaching or visiting member. When is it appropriate to intervene so that the newly diagnosed people can make use of their innate, protective denial? What does the visitor say, or which approach works most effectively, in communicating an offer of help? Several respondents described how they did outreach and what they hoped it would achieve.

I think the time to see new patients is right after surgery, because that's the time you're the most down and when you ask yourself, "Why me?" like Bill Gargan. They need the uplift. After a severe operation, they need to know that things get better. When I visit, I'm casual. I try to size up people, and I use humor, as a way of encouragement.

Before I started dialysis, the doctors suggested I go to see a patient on the machine in the hospital. However, I don't think that's the right way to do it. They (hospital dialysis patients) are usually *really* sick. I did what they suggested, but thought, "That can't be what it's like. Am I going to be that sick?" I think that's what made me suggest to the KT/DA that we visit people so that they can see how well we're doing. Then, they can come to my home and see the setup, see that I still have my job, that we enjoy travelling, and that kidney disease doesn't have to interfere with one's life.

We can conclude that for the respondents in this study, meeting someone else with the same illness was instrumental in helping them cope. It helped them accept the new reality of their physical limitations. Their feelings of anger, of frustration, and of despair were legitimated. They were able to identify with other people in the group and, as a result, they were more hopeful about the future and could see a way for life to continue on worthwhile terms. Some talked about a particular person to whom they felt closest, who was their role model. They reported feeling less unique, realizing that their experiences and reactions were typical. They also got practical information. In addition, many people got continuing help from reading the group's newsletters and any other articles they could find in popular magazines on how people cope. The group was sufficiently important to them that they paid dues to remain on the active mailing list. Mutual-help exchanges took place over an extended period and in many settings, such as clinic waiting rooms, on the telephone, and in each other's homes.

For many, the opportunity to be a helper in turn was very important to their ongoing sense of well-being. As a result of the mutual-help experience, people focused on developing competency rather than on retaining a disabled image.

Participants in a mutual-help experience seem to utilize the health-care system to better advantage. The groups help people understand and negotiate with the system and to use it more appropriately. Recognizing the limits of formal professional help, the groups provide people with personal attention and understanding in another context. Members of mutual-help groups, as evident in this study, are more knowledgeable consumers, have a different attitude toward their condition, and are less beholden to the health care system for their *total* well-being.

DISCUSSION

Robert Kahn (1964) defined "coping" as "dealing with both the objective conflict and with the affective reactions to it." Different behaviors often contribute to the same end: controlling the meaning of the problem the individual is facing. These different behaviors may include counting one's blessings, finding a positive attribute about a given situation, or assuming that hardship is a necessary part of life. Pearlin and Schooler (1978) found that coping is multidimensional, and that no one method/mechanism accurately describes the process. A highly efficacious coping behavior may be less effective than a *collection of responses* to life stresses, and successful coping depends on *how much* we do as well as *what* we do.

They go on to suggest that when coping responses fail, they do not necessarily reflect the individual's shortcomings, but may represent the failure of social systems in which the individual is enmeshed. Therefore, in looking at the adjustment patterns of people who are faced with the crisis of chronic illness and disability, it is apparent that the afflicted individuals must rely not only on their own capacity for adaptation, but on a larger ecological and social network that can either help or hinder the adaptive process. The adaptive process cannot be understood unless it is viewed over time. People's needs and reactions vary the longer they live with a condition. For example, the denial observed above was functional initially (Weissman, 1973) but it could not continue indefinitely if the individuals were to be involved in life-saving treatment. Our respondents talked about accommodation, not as a final state which they achieved but as an ongoing process. They were, in effect, in transition and any help offered had to enhance their ability to develop appropriate coping strategies for each new phase of the transition. People do not inherently know how to cope with trauma and unanticipated change. Opportunities need to be created for them. Mutual-help groups seem to be uniquely qualified to help to supplement the resources of the individual in his/her social network.

Silverman (1978) observed that mutual-help groups are most effective for people in transition. Using the work of Bowlby (1967) and Tyhurst (1958), she states that most transitions can be characterized by at least three identifiable stages. The first stage, *impact*, is a time of disbelief that a change has really occurred. For example, when individuals learn they have a disabling and life-threatening illness, they may feel numb, act reflexively, and be unable to acknowledge the seriousness of the news. The second stage, *recoil*, is characterized by a growing recognition of the reality of the change, and simultaneously, a mounting frustration at the inability to live life as before. The final period, *accommodation,* is a time when people will find a new direction and a way of integrating the changes into their life.

The help provided by mutual-help groups responds to these stages. In the impact stage when denial is most apparent, individuals need help in accepting their new situation. The ability to acknowledge this new self-image and thus lessen the impact of the denial is facilitated by meeting someone with a similar problem who is coping. (We can only speculate why the hospital staff seemed reluctant at this point to make a referral. They may have recognized the process of denial that people go through initially, but may not have understood how a mutual help experience could then be of value, in spite of people "not being ready.")

In the next stage people begin to develop a sense of common cause with the group; to recognize that they can *learn* ways of coping which will lighten their burden. They begin to feel less alone or deviant as they share their common experiences. They find a role model, someone with whom they can identify and from whom they *learn* alternate ways of dealing with their disability. Finally, in the accommodation stage, some people change roles from beneficiary to provider of help. The fact that recipients can change roles and become helpers reinforces their sense of competence, giving additional meaning to their previous experiences, and enabling them to make a successful accommodation. Overall, this is an educational process. Different information is needed and can be assimilated at different stages. People with handicapping illness need to learn a new set of skills as well as to deal with an altered self-image.

What facilitates learning in a mutual-help group? Schachtel (1959), reporting on a study of affiliative tendencies in college students during periods of anxiety, observes that subjects chose to be alone under stress rather than be with people who had not shared their experience. He concludes that:

> ...under conditions of anxiety the affiliative tendency is highly directional.... Whatever the needs aroused by the manipulation of anxiety, it would seem that their satisfaction demands the presence of others in a similar situation.

Schachtel's findings help to explain the appeal of mutual-help groups to people in times of stress. There is a need to find someone like themselves so that they no longer feel alone or unique. Schachtel suggests that it is easier to learn in a setting with people who are having the same experience. In every mutual-help group with which we talked, members expressed the relief they felt in finally being able to share what they were feeling with someone else "like me."

Bandura (1977) has described three approaches to learning: modeling, vicarious learning (seeing others perform threatening activities without adverse consequences), and verbal persuasion. He notes that people can be persuaded that they possess the capability to master a difficult situation, but, unless they are provided with effective aids for action, they are unlikely to learn. Modeling provides the opportunity to learn, from other people's experience, that changes are possible and subsequently to learn how to make similar changes.

That people may develop models for themselves from their own prior experience is a further observation of Bandura (1977). However, people in transition often do not possess this experience. He suggests that with role models and effective aids, learning and change take place for people who have no prior experience in coping with the situation in which they now find themselves. Mutual-help experiences provide the opportunity to find a role model in "someone like me" and to learn vicariously what is needed to make necessary changes. Mutual-help groups can be successful where others, such as members of the formal health-care system, cannot, because these conditions are inherently present.

As the health-care system struggles to solve its problems, many authors have suggested it meet some of these by incorporating successful aspects of mutual-help groups in its practices. For example, Gottlieb (1976) suggests:

> The lay treatment network consists of informal caregivers who substitute personal involvement for the professional style of distance and objectivity, and spontaneity of self-expression for standardized techniques. Lay treatment has prolifereated, suggesting that health professionals might profit from an examination and adoption of the self-help movement objectives and practices.

While both groups do have similar goals (i.e., promoting the well-being of their constituents), the means of achieving these goals are dissimilar. The most important component of mutual help is the fact that the helper has had personal experience with the problem and is using this experience as the basis of the help offered. The recipient of help can become a helper in turn. Further, since the group is autonomous, it determines, based on member's experiences, the help to be provided as well as who does the providing. The very essence of this help may be lost if it is integrated into another system with different operating rules (Silverman, 1979).

Along with the all-important practical advice and suggestion-giving, it appears that another person "like me" is the only one who, in the end, can thoroughly understand the initial feelings undergone, and who can be patient with the necessarily gradual process of accommodation. Regardless of the competence and expertise of the attending physician and other professional staff, and the support of available family members, there is nothing quite like the person who, from personal experience, can say, "I know how you feel. I've been there, too."

The authors believe that service providers and mutual-help groups have much to learn from each other's expertise and experience, and that the growing mutual respect they have for each other is of immeasurable value to the individuals and the families who rely on them. We would support efforts at increasing both systems' knowledge and understanding of each others' work. Rather than wanting professionals to emulate the groups' system of helping, our participants indicate that they respect the professionals' style of helping within their own sphere, as well as the mutual-help group for the specific assistance it offers. It would be dangerous to co-opt this person-to-person movement and eliminate its function as critic and educator. The two systems should be autonomous, aware of each other, and able to work together. Comprehensive care needs to include services from many systems.

Chapter 7

SELF-HELP GROUPS FOR CAREGIVERS OF THE AGED

M. Joanna Mellor
Harriet Rzetelny
Iris E. Hudis

The self-help group has become an increasingly popular form at a time of diminishing resources in the 1970s. The concept of self-help is not a new one: such groups have been described by Kropotkin (1972) as arising in primitive times; but beginning with the turmoil of the sixties when dissatisfaction with traditional social institutions was vocal, the self-help group concept began to gain popularity as an alternative to the institutionalized service agencies. A rich diversity of self-help groups has since proliferated.

With this growth an interest in self-help has developed among both sociologists and social-work practitioners. The self-help group concept is now well-established and must be understood by practitioners for its potential strengths.

Alfred Katz and Eugene Bender (1976) define a self-help group as a "voluntary small group structure for mutual aid in the accomplishment of a specific purpose." Very often social workers have viewed the growth of self-help as undermining the social-work profession, and, indeed, such groups often emerge in direct response to a gap in service provision. Another perspective is that the nature of professional social work itself hinders the development of self-help within a group setting. This argument rests on the premise that self-help cannot develop under the auspices of professional, formal leadership. In our experience both these viewpoints are untenable. Self-help need not lead to professional redundancy, nor should professionalization hinder self-help.

Self-help was pioneered by groups encountering very special problems such as mental retardation, drug addiction, and alcoholism. But today our understanding and definition of self-help has widened to embrace any group of persons sharing a similar concern or outlook. The self-help group is a natural and beneficial extension of the philosophy which undergirds the social work profession. Social-work practice is based on the principle of helping the client to determine personal goals and to implement a plan of attainment. A self-help group embodies this principle in that its members come together in pursuit of agreed-upon goals and in response to their own perceived mutual needs. Although self-help groups can form spontaneously, impetus from professionals is not uncommon.

The self-help group approach, so defined, is seen as a vital and integral part of our service program. To explain why this is so, it is first necessary to describe the Community Service Society's Natural Supports Program.

In recent years appreciation has grown for the vital role played by family, friends, and neighbors in providing support for the aged in the community and as a means of maintaining them outside institutionalized settings. Studies show that approximately 95 percent of those aged sixty-five or older live within their own communities and rely for help when needed on this informal network.

The myth of the isolated older person has been repeatedly questioned by findings in a variety of studies (Shanas 1977, Mayer 1976, Cantor 1975). Cantor (1975), in her study of the urban aged, has identified the presence of an extensive social-support system defined as "those informal and formal activities as well as the personal support services required by older persons so that they can remain independently in the community." This social-support system provides for three central needs of the aging—socialization, aid with the tasks of daily living, and personal assistance during illness or crisis.

For the aged, bureaucratic organizations under governmental and private auspices deal routinely with the provision of income, health care, food, housing, social services, and so forth. However, at every service connection between the aged and the formal bureaucracy, the support network plays a significant role in mediating needs with available resources and supplementing organizational provision. Litwak and Meyer (1974) note that greater interdependence of tasks between bureaucratic organizations and the primary-group structures means that the two support systems cannot be kept isolated from each other without detriment to their respective goals. Modes of coordination are necessary between the formal and the informal social structures. Because of this need and because of the complexity of responsibilities and the stress experienced by the informal support network, the Natural Supports Program of the Community Service Society came into being.

The Natural Supports Program is designed to supplement and strengthen the informal care-giving supports of the older persons, whether these informal caregivers are family members, friends, or neighbors. Since 1976 the program has provided individual services to families caring for older persons. These services include the provision of home-care to provide respite for the family care giver, counseling to alleviate stress incurred in the caring function, escort service, assistance in systems negotiation, and advocacy towards obtaining entitlements.

In 1978 a proposal for developing community-based group services for caregivers of the aged was funded by the Administration on Aging under the joint auspices of the Community Service Society and the Brookdale Center on Aging of Hunter College. As a result, group programs have been offered in specific target areas throughout New York City, beginning with four communities and now expanding into two others. All six communities were chosen to represent differing racial, socioeconomic, and family variables. Whatever the community, we are finding that there are similar service needs which can be met through group programs. These needs are for education about the aging process, skills training, peer support, and mechanisms for crisis intervention.

Group services are planned on a community basis. It is the practice of the program to work closely in each target area with agencies which are serving the aged and may already be helping their caring families.

The group meetings may be communitywide, providing information and opportunities for discussion, and linkages between the formal and the informal support systems of the aged. Or the meetings may be small, of six to twelve members who assemble on an ongoing basis or for a predetermined number of sessions. These groups determine their own agendas, frequency of meetings, and type of group format. The gatherings may be socioeducational in nature with speakers invited to share their expertise. Areas of interest are the psychological and physical aspects of aging, how to care for the chronically ill older person, and the range of entitlements and services available for the aged.

Meetings may also be mutual-aid/peer-support group get-togethers in which participants learn from each other and provide each other with recognition and support in their caring roles.

The most frequent topics are methods of coping with the stress involved in caring for a disabled older person, and with the guilt experienced by caregivers, frequently middle-aged women who need to balance the care they give with the demands of their own families. In no way do the group programs attempt to substitute for the caring role of families or neighbors, but seek always to supplement and to strengthen the caring network.

A self-help group approach appears particularly appropriate   for groups of caregivers of the aged for a number of reasons. Caregivers of the elderly are a recently identified population, whose needs, the professional service network is only just beginning to recognize. Caregivers themselves possess the necessary expertise and hold many of the solutions to their own problems. Group meetings can be a conduit for this knowledge between care givers. The professional ethic which emphasizes the importance of clients formulating their own goals and directions is most evident here. This self-help approach also translates into greater investment on the part of the group members by virtue of their sense of ownership.

In addition, caregivers of the aged are not members of a deviant group but are enmeshed into chronic, long-lived situations which may worsen over time. The chronicity of the older person's situation creates a need for continuing aid and support by the caregiver. A self-help group approach enables the group's duration. This in turn sets the stage for the development of a self-help network of caregivers to which people can turn in times of crisis and on an "as-needed" basis. The self-help format is also attractive because the Administration on Aging grant is for a three-year period only, and the involvement of our Natural Support Program is time limited. It is our desire to build continuity into the program, enabling group services to continue after the program's funding is terminated.

For these reasons the Natural Support staff determined early to enable groups for caregivers of the aged to move towards a self-help model, though it is recognized that not all groups will desire to become self-sustaining and self-help oriented. Also, for some group programs, such as the large socioeducational meetings, the self-help approach is not necessarily appropriate. Therefore the project also involves sensitizing the local communities to caregivers' needs.

In order to provide a scale against which to measure the movement of each group towards self-help as we define it and to evaluate our own attempts in promoting this movement, a self-help continuum was envisaged. (See chart.)

At one end of the continuum appears the traditional, structured, professionally led group in which members are dependent upon the leader for direction. There is a lack of interaction and little commitment to the group on the part of the individual members. At the other end of the continuum is the pure self-help group with no professional leader; the members plan and expedite their own activities, recruit their own members, provide each other with peer support, and engage in social action and personal change. Each member identifies strongly with the group as an entity and a force in itself. These two extremes are hypothetical concepts.

SELF-HELP CONTINUUM FOR GROUPS

Professionally led group	Professional leader	Professional leader is resource person and facilitator	No professional present but reliance on professional contact	Non-professional lead or no leader
Dependence on leader	Peer support	No formal leadership	Social action/personal change	Members plan and expedite activities
Lack of sharing	Mutual aid but only within group setting	Mutual aid within and without group setting	Peer support, mutual aid	Social action/personal change
No commitment to group	Leader recruits members	Peer support	Recruits members and accepts referrals	Mutual aid, peer support
Passive	Members defer to leader in decision making	Some social action	Ego reinforcement	Recruits own members
		Recruits own members and accepts referrals		Ego reinforcement

NO SELF-HELP   SELF-HELP

Natural Supports Program

All groups fall somewhere along this continuum.
Groups may move in either direction or back and forth over a period of time.

Community Service Society/Natural Supports Program
Funded by a grant from the Administration on Aging.
H.E.W. Grant #90-A-1609(01)

It is in the "middle area" that peer support may be greater or lesser, the leader more or less dominant, and it is in this "middle area" that our groups of caregivers may be found. Against this diagrammed continuum each group can be measured, and the role of the leader adjusted in an ongoing effort to move the group towards self-help.

A self-help approach may not always be chosen or even be appropriate; but when it is, the function of the group leader as an agent for self-help has a distinct bearing on that role and requires distinct terminology. We have chosen to use the term *facilitator,* rather than leader, following the example of the National Self-Help Clearinghouse. The term facilitator, selected for its connotation of *enabler,* in contrast to *leader,* clarifies, and suggests the specific skills necessary to guide a group towards the self-help pole of the continuum.

Some case histories illustrate the utilization of the continuum and the role of the leader/facilitators:

Group A consists of six to eight women in their late fifties and sixties, Black, White, and Hispanic, who are caring for a parent, relative, or spouse.

A series of six communitywide meetings were planned in the spring of 1978 entitled "Caring for Older Relatives." Outreach for the meetings consisted of fliers and publicity to the service agencies. As a result of the first few topical informational meetings, several women indicated that they would like to continue meeting on an ongoing basis. A professional social worker facilitated the first meeting at a community senior center, stating that she would be available for four meetings, after which the participants might want to continue alone on a self-help basis with her assistance as a resource person. After the first introductions, the facilitator explained that the group was convened in response to members' needs ("This is your group") and asked the participants how they wanted to used the sessions. Two members immediately responded by requesting information about entitlements for the aged so that they "might better help" their friends. The facilitator promised that in addition to providing information, she would teach the participants how they could gather their own information and emphasized how they might help each other by pooling their knowledge. Throughout, the facilitator encouraged participants to offer suggestions to one another, and asked one member to gather information about services to share with the group at its next meeting. The next three meetings followed much the same format, with the facilitator underscoring and encouraging mutual aid between members.

At the fourth and final meeting, the leader recognized the group's interest in continued meetings, and facilitated discussion of time, place, and frequency. One member volunteered her home as a meeting site. Then the leader asked whether the group wanted to be open or closed. The group chose open membership, at which point the leader requested permission to refer appropriate care givers. As another way of transferring leadership, the facilitator gave resource booklets to the group for future distribution to members. She clarified her future role in relation to the group, reminding the members that she would no longer be meeting with them regularly, but that she would be available to help them as needed. She has since maintained a regular phone contact with one member, providing technical assistance around resource information and group technique. Although the professional facilitator was invited to attend whenever she could, she chose to remain physically distant from the group and has only once returned since this time.

Attendance at the meetings was and is still aided by the provision of financial aid for transportation to the meeting place and, occasionally, for the provision of home care for the older person while the caregiver is away.

This group has moved from left to right along the continuum, and is close to our pure self-help extreme. Individual members are involved in publicizing the group and the needs of caregivers, taking an active part in public testimony. The group is unwilling to sever completely the contact with the professional network. This contact is seen as a lifeline, providing support if professional intervention is needed. In addition, several members also attend socioeducational group meetings at a local senior center where they can hear informed speakers on topics of interest to caregivers of older persons. The need for peer support, satisfied by the self-help group meetings, is supplemented by the educational opportunities provided by this latter group.

Group B is made up of eight to twelve Hispanic women, neighbors who have been meeting since the spring of 1979. They live in the same housing project, and interact between meetings on a social basis. Low-income women in their mid-fifties, most of them receive some form of income maintenance and are Medicaid recipients. Members of close-knit families, their caring relationships are to spouse, to sister, or to mother.

This group originated from three communitywide meetings held in the winter of 1979. General presentations were made at these meetings and the participants then divided into small discussion groups, one of which was led by an Hispanic paraprofessional, and caregiver to her husband and sister. About five persons attended the first small discussion group, which was conducted in Spanish, and participants returned to the following two sessions bringing friends, and two of the relatives. The members expressed a desire to continue meeting. However, tentative plans had to be abandoned when the paraprofessional returned to Puerto Rico for an extended stay to care for her sister.

A month later, a meeting was arranged with an Hispanic professional staff facilitator. He introduced himself, explained the possible objectives of the meetings, and asked how the participants would like to use the group. It was agreed that the meeting would be a source of information concerning entitlements for the aged, and would allow for some mutual aid to evolve. Meetings were planned for every other week. The following few meetings saw an increase in attendance and followed the pattern of informal discussions. Members were encouraged to talk of their care-giving roles, and were thankful to find "somewhere to talk about (their) feelings." Requests for aid in securing entitlements were brought to the facilitator, who provided technical knowledge. A resource directory listing services and eligibility requirements for the aged in this specific community was found to be a useful tool. Its translation into Spanish was undertaken by the group facilitator. Between meetings, the members keep in touch with the facilitator regarding entitlement advocacy. He, in turn, encourages them to provide peer support to each other in their caring problems. The members accompany each other to clinic appointments, help each other as interpreters, and keep in telephone contact as needed. As the immediate entitlement needs have been met, participants have begun to identify specific topics on which they need further information.

The group initially moved towards the mutual-aid, self-help end of the continuum, and then for a while moved back towards the other end with requests to the facilitator that he arrange for speakers to address the group, and continue to attend their monthly meetings. Members have spoken at local Hispanic churches, at a popular bingo club, and have brought notice of the meetings to a Spanish theatre in the area and other comminity centers. In this respect the group at the present time, falls about midway along the continuum.

Group C consists of white middle-income caregivers, male and female, who live in a semi-rural area, where social services for the chronically ill aged are scarce. Individual names of caregivers had been secured from a communitywide meeting held in the fall of 1978, and after personal outreach to these people, a group meeting was set for February, 1979. The first meetings were conceived as socioeducational and the facilitator scheduled speakers for a series of four weekly meetings. Only three persons attended the first meeting and they arrived at different times. No formal contracting with the group towards self-help was attempted. The second meeting, after renewed outreach, was attended by nine persons. A presentation on "How to Help a Mentally Impaired Older Person" led to lengthy discussion of each participant's concerns, which the members agreed was "most helpful."

Future directions of the group beyond the four-part series was discussed at each meeting. At the final session one member declared, "What's the use of talking more. We know what our problems are. We need help." There was general agreement that the overwhelming problem in the community was a lack of resources for the frail elderly, and the group agreed to continue meeting twice a month, as an action group, publicizing the needs for care givers and working as a catalyst for social response. For the next three months the group met regularly with the facilitator, identifying the specific service needs and gathering information. Articles were written and published locally, and the facilitator arranged for group members to join a planning committee of service professionals to coordinate efforts to meet service needs. By summer, attendance was fluctuating due to seasonal shift in routines, and the introduction of new members, while interjecting new life into the group, caused it to focus chiefly on peer support. The group members relied on the facilitator for planning and outreach, but with his help took responsibility for providing each other with resource information. Individual service needs were expressed and the facilitator encouraged members to turn to one another for help and information.

This group thus moved back and forth along our continuum. Although still dependent upon the leader/facilitator for information and meeting arrangements, individual members have taken social-action initiatives and been instrumental in causing the local-service network to address service needs. This action has brought the care givers into a collegial relationship with the professional service network—a relationship sought by the group members themselves.

At the end of the summer the staff facilitator left the project and ended his involvement with the group. It was hoped that his departure might provide an ideal opportunity for the group members to subsume his role, moving the group closer to the self-help conceptual model. This was not the case, and the continued professional facilitation was requested. The group falls to the right of the midway point on the continuum.

Group experiences over the past year, and efforts to trace the movement of groups back and forth along the self-help continuum, indicate the skills required by a group facilitator to move a group whatever its composition or evolving cause, towards self-sustaining status.

These skills, or "Principles of Action" for the facilitator of a self-help group for caregivers can be enumerated as follows. A facilitator will:

- enable caregivers to define direction and content;
- encourage mutuality;
- teach caregivers advocacy and problem-solving skills;
- identify and foster shared leadership abilities;
- model and teach group-process skills.

Once these principles of action for facilitators are identified, a training format can be devised. The training covers five major areas and is suitable for adaptation at all levels of expertise; but it is specific to the program of providing group services to caregivers of the aged.

A. *Sensitization to the Caregiving Situation*

An introduction to the training series outlines the role informal support-systems play in maintaining an older person in the community. From this overview, discussion is encouraged on the particular caring patterns of older persons. This elicits deeper understanding of care-giving relationships and of some of the problems and stresses involved. The following simple diagram is used to illustrate how any problem may be broken into these three elements and how increased strains in any one of the elements tax the caregiver's ability to continue in a caring role:

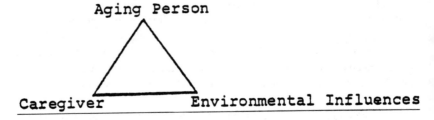

B. *Group Development Skills*

This phase centers on two areas—the importance of personalized outreach and the organization of the first meeting or series of meetings. Since the care-giving population is generally unrecognized by society, care givers generally do not recognize themselves as a distinct group with unique problems and needs. Initial program design and outreach has to serve the dual purpose of helping caregivers establish their common identity and motivating involvement in a group. A format that has proved successful for these two purposes is a large topical meeting, or several meetings, with speakers who provide education and information, followed by small group discussions. Methods of outreach are them examined and critiqued, and trainees form subgroups to plan hypothetical community meetings.

C. *Developmental of Facilitator Skills*

Since philosophy of the program is based upon belief in self-help, this aspect of the training has provided the greatest emphasis. The continuum of self-help is explored, using examples. As a method of demonstrating our facilitators'principles, traditonal group leadership functions are presented. The principles of action for the facilitator of a self-help caregivers' group, as previously outlined, are then examined in this context, using examples from the three case histories noted in this paper. Participants are asked to play out the various ways these facilitating skills might be utilized.

D. *Sensitization to a Caregivers Network*

In keeping with the attempts to build continuity through the growth of self-help, and in response to caregivers expressed needs for acknowledgement, and the legitimization of their role, a network of caregivers has been initiated by the Natural Support Program. This network also serves as a vehicle for policy recommendations and social action. The concept of this network is introduced, and participation by the trainees' own group members is encouraged.

E. *Documentation*

As one of the caregivers stated: "Talking about our problems is not enough. We need action!" Present national and local policy does not support caregivers. Recent legislative hearings on home care underscore the need for documentation to support caregiver's expressed needs for new and improved services, both for older people, and to enhance care givers' efforts. In addition, the Group Natural Supports Program is a federally funded program with documentation and evaluative components, and trainees are asked to participate in this facet.

This training series is easily adaptable to the skill level of a varied group of people. Since most professionals, paraprofessionals, and volunteers participating in training have worked directly with older people, the emphasis of this training refocuses their attention on a new consumer population and on how the needs of this population influence the development of group programs. In addition, introduction of a self-help continuum and the pinpointing of facilitation skills that enable a group to move along its course, has proved a useful conceptual tool, no matter what level of group work skill the trainees bring with them.

Trainees have also responded favorably to the idea of a caregivers' network. Besides providing a ready forum for the social action needs of care givers, it is also seen as a way of providing continuity and as a natural linkage between groups.

In summary, it is our belief that self-help is not an alternative to professional social work but that the two forms can readily complement each other and establish a partnership. The self-help group maintains an essential link with the institutionalized social services, necessary in times of service crisis, and the professional social worker learns much of value from the direction and input of the consumers. This partnership is particularly well suited to planning programs for care givers of the aged. Self-help is a vital group form and the profession of social work must be prepared to meet its challenge.

Part II

PROFESSIONALS AND SELF-HELP

Chapter 8

PARENTS ANONYMOUS
The Professional's Role
as Sponsor

Mildred L. Willen

Professionals frequently are anathema to self-help groups. The very idea of a self-help experience seems to rule out the need for a professional. The theoretical asumption is that the group itself holds the key to its own goals. Why then in Parents Anonymous (P.A.) is a professional built into the structure.

Parents Anonymous began 10 years ago with the collaborative effort of a parent and social worker. After many false starts, Jolly K., a frantic, abusing mother made contact with a professional who understood her crisis. They devised the model which continues, that of the parent as chairperson and the sponsor as back-up, resource, and trainer of the chairperson. The sponsor's manual states, "P.A. asks that whatever the sponsor's professional background and experience, he makes the commitment to the parent-as-leader model. Without this there can be no P.A. chapter. It may be therapy... but its's not P.A."

The sponsor does not have to be a social worker or a mental-health professional; background may be in other disciplines. What the sponsor should or should not do is spelled out concretely in P.A. position papers. "The sponsor is emotionally supportive of the chairperson, helping the chairperson to grow and to realize his/her own potential as a group leader...this is not to say that the sponsor does not interact in the group. The sponsor relates in group on a feeling level, making it okay for the parents to share and express feelings. His/her professional aura's left home, enabling all involved to interact on an equal level." The sponsor is to assist and help the chairperson to develop, and to be a fully contributing member of the group. These are the major commitments set down: no easy task! Most social workers are trained to be professional, objective, and essentially nonrevealing of their own lives. The professional is encouraged to allow clients' needs and feelings, to flow but not to participate by sharing personal hurt and pain. How does one begin to shed an aspect of the professional role while maintaining another?

In my three years as a professional P.A. sponsor I have grappled with these and other issues, and there are new ones each week. The loose structure of P.A. does not invite a dogmatic approach. There is no accountability expected of a sponsor, no investigation or overseeing by any supervening organization. One can be a P.A. sponsor and have no more contact with the central organization than an initial receipt of basic materials and an occasional newsletter. What a variety of sponsorhip emerges! This open, loose, and flexible system invites delights and disasters. From the nurse who chided and scolded her members for bad behavior to the super-clinical psychoanalyst who intimidated them, anything is possible. According to members of the New York State Parents Anonymous resource office, inept sponsors eventually drop out, but in the process usually cause the disintegration of the group as well. My own sponsorship, I hope, has been benign.

In examining my own experiences and in identifying the issues I see as crucial to the self-help area, I hope a more cohesive network of sponsor contacts can develop, so that we can share with as well as train one another. I work at a large, well-respected community mental-health clinic in Suffolk County, Long Island, New York. I am a social worker, trained and practicing as a psychotherapist both at the clinic and in private practice. In 1978, I was asked by the administrators of my clinic if I would be the professional sponsor of a recently-formed P.A. group. The group had functioned for one year and had a meager membership. Another P.A. group had just disbanded because the sponsor herself encountered personal difficulties. That sponsor was a professional person not affiliated with any accredited agency; when she could no longer continue, the group disbanded.

A citizens' committee interested in children had started a group which my clinic had agreed to sponsor. For the first year a psychologist was the sponsor. When he left the clinic I took over his position. The value of agency back-up is readily apparent. There will always be someone to sponsor the group as long as the agency continues to be responsible for it. It is not dependent on the whims or destinies of one person. A group in another community was sponsored by a counselor, the wife of a local physician. The group was vital and close but as the sponsor's need for her own professional life took precedence, she had to leave the group. The group subsequently disbanded.

For my own group, the mechanics of finding a place, setting, time, and appointing a chairperson had been taken care of by the previous sponsor and the childrens' committee. The regional P.A. representative had helped to set up the group, but when funding by the national P.A. was stopped, she could not function on the same terms, although she continued as an unpaid volunteer.

In the ensuing six years I found a range of ways to work as a sponsor and have identified some of the besetting issues. Certain of these are personal in relation to my own background and training, but since so many sponsors are social workers I will assume that my experiences are often paralleled.

SPONSORS OR AGENCY VALUE SYSTEMS

People are coming to the meeting. The chosen chairperson is perhaps reluctant, certainly fearful. I know this is not group therapy. I know what my role is supposed to be. But here I am with seven group members looking to me for leadership, advice, sustenance, love, parenting, fairness, understanding—wait a minute! I'm not supposed to do that: try again. They are looking to me, so that I can back up the chairperson. But why is the chairperson looking to me for leadership, advice sustenance, etc... Try again. Be quiet. See what happens. Okay.

Someone starts to speak. She says she has had a terrible week. Her four year-old and six year-old boys were squabbling. In the process they left a mess on the living room floor. She can't stand clutter, mess, or dirt. She screamed at them, called them monsters. The six-year-old was sassy, and she hit him, not as hard as she used to but still hard enough. He ran to his room.

Breaking off, she turned to her husband sitting beside her in the group and said, "It's your fault, Dick, If you'd let them know they can't mess up, it wouldn't happen." Her voice rises, she starts to assail him, blaming him for all their problems. He sits ashen-faced, watching her without speaking.

I clench my hands and my teeth to keep quiet. The chairperson, earthy, sloppy, direct, intervenes (Whew!) "Mary, Dick isn't the problem. Now, what are you yelling at him for." Mary, on the breath of a tirade, slows down, begins to come to, and listens. The chairperson tells how when her boys do something that upsets her, she's learned to remove them or herself from the room. She will call her husband in to handle the situation. It doesn't matter how he handles it, at least she is out of the room and away from her own violence. Mary says that Dick is too passive. He wouldn't do anything. Again she begins to rage at him. I say, "Mary, what happens when Dick is with the children?" Mary bursts out with her frustration at his inability to speak or move quickly, his passive acceptance of anything that goes on, and her enormous discomfort at her abuse of him and the children, and her terror that nobody will help her to control herself. Many in the group understand that frustration. The chairperson picks up the theme and tells a bitter but funny story about throwing her husband's pajamas down the basement stairs and putting nasty notes in his lunchbox.

Nobody interprets, nobody analyzes, nobody offers any "insights." Essentially, at this point, sharing situations, acceptance of hateful aspects of one's self, and some laughter seems to be enough. We all feel a little better than when we came in. I can see that the chairperson's graphic descriptions, easy-going personality, and humor set a tone for the group.

Somebody asks me about my own family. I tell them my children's ages, a little about adolescent problems. This group all have young children. Some months later some parents with teenagers come in. I feel lucky that my kids have almost grown past the teen years, with their crises. At the group's beginning they were fourteen, sixteen, and eighteen. I had learned something by living through these times.

Unlike a group therapist, my role is not just to be true to my character, which is part of psychotherapy, but specific in my information about my own life. To be a P.A. sponsor is to be knowledgeable, but not a remote authority, to be resourceful but not bossy, to be helpful but occasionally helpless. My awareness of transference and resistance can't be dismissed, but I do not use it as a therapist does.

One young woman saw me arriving in my 1975 Chevrolet and said, "I thought you'd be driving a Mercedes." She also asked if I did my own food shopping. The transference, the fantasies she had woven about me would have been interesting to explore had we been therapist and patient. Instead, I kidded her about my living in a palace and complained bitterly about my chauvinistic son's reluctance to do any work about the house.

The reality is that I do have a better-paying job than most of the group members, that I do go on vacations and sometimes miss the meetings, and that sometimes they feel envious. Most members of our P.A. group are white, working-class people. We have had some nurses, teachers, a school administrator, and a college teacher, but the core of the group seems to set a particular tone and style. Most are in financial straits, which, or course, exacerbates the family problems.

This opens up other issues for the sponsor and sponsoring agency, which are value questions. What about the cost of being a chairperson? In a large community such as ours, phone calls from one town to the other can be very expensive. Driving half an hour to a meeting and paying a baby-sitter all add to the cost. Yes, it is a self-help group but does that mean that the chairperson, who should do most of the telephoning, pays for it? One chairperson was living so carefully that she could not pay these costs without cutting into her food and transportation budget. We then set up a small fund at the clinic to help defray some of these costs. I will discuss later some of the clinic back-up services. Here we are concerned with the roles of the sponsor, the chairperson, and the group.

The sponsor's role as a back-up to the parent-as-leader model is now clearly compatible with our therapeutic philosophy. I work as closely as I can with the chairpersons, who are a couple, and who shift leadership at various times. Sometimes tension in the marriage emerges. Then what? Neither wants to be referred for therapy or marriage counseling. Both have had negative experiences in the past (a common theme with many P.A. members, who have had contact with agencies and/or psychologists and have been turned off). In another community, a P.A. day-group forms and the wife becomes chairperson there. The husband, attending college at night and aiming at a degree in social work, is referred by me to the clinic for inclusion in our paraprofessional program. He gets training and supervision, and obtains status and recognition. She often comes to our meeting as a member, but has her primary position in her own group. This works. My role was to help steer them in appropriately helpful ways. They left our group when they moved to another community in order for him to attend graduate school. While there they started a P.A. chapter. Developing resources in order to facilitate changes clearly seems to be my proper role.

Another couple in the group called me privately, admitting a sexual problem which they feel they can't share with the group. A group of therapists at our clinic had formed a private sex-therapy clinic. They offered a few low-cost scholarships to clinic patients. We got one for this couple who spent a year in sex therapy, reporting small but discernible improvement. The couple stayed in P.A. through this time and became better able to deal with problems with children as they found ways to become closer to each other.

Other people are referred to the clinic for individual therapy. For some, the P.A. contact softens their fears of agencies and make it easier to engage in therpeutic experience. Some, after finding they can work with their therapist, no longer need the group. Some have gone for private therapy or used other agencies. P.A. is a complementary experience.

Many P.A. members have been so terrified, and are so hostile that they cannot handle the slightest hint of bureaucracy. A referral to the clinic, with the usual forms, questions, and necessity to wait, even briefly, will trigger enormous rage. We had one family who lived and played "earthquake" all the time. Moments of uneventful tranquillity goaded them like unsupportable boredom. The father and eight year-old daughter screamed and abused one another. The child would tear up her room, write on the walls, rip and gouge her mattress. She would threaten the younger siblings, the father would threaten her, the mother would moan and faint; but they all kept the scenario going with enormous vigor.

Breaking into that cycle, which was not intolerable to the family, was tough. We tried to get the child into therapy, seeming to go along with the parents on the idea that the child was "the bad seed." However, when the therapist suggested that the family be involved in the therapy, dismay was great. P.A. was used as a sounding board for the father's rage. It was extremely helpful to the wife, who said she had a few days of peace after every meeting. If he could yell at our meetings, with no bureaucracy, no consequences, no condemnation, he could calm down a little. The child, with fewer attacks from him, provoked less, and the mother felt a bit more alive. The child was amazingly sturdy, as were the younger siblings, for when the family left the group, having moved to another community, they were all heartily yelling, but less abusively than before.

The fact that many people will not or cannot use therapy is clear. We then use whatever resources we can besides the group itself. AA is a close relative of ours, not administratively or nationally, but for our group members. At one point everyone in the group had an alcoholic association. One was the daughter, one the wife, and one the sister of an alcoholic. Some have gone to Al-Anon groups as well as P.A. One member calls herself a self-help "groupie." The formerly abused wife of an alcoholic husband, she came to us when he stopped drinking and yet continued to be abusive to the children. She functions in the group primarily as a supportive, encouraging person, hardly expecting any specific help with her own problems. The affection the group feels for her "motherliness" gives her the nourishment to keep her going a little longer in the face of an uninterested husband and essentially indifferent children. In our group her giving is rewarded. To deal with her masochism would have been inappropriate. Insight therapy is not what she came for.

We also have contact though rarely, with the Department of Social Services (DSS). Surprisingly few referrals come to us from Child Protective Services (CPS), although they should. The one couple referred to us are now our chairpersons. A young couple, they have the backgrounds' one reads about as typical of child abusers. Abused themselves, physically, sexually, economically, verbally, this young couple have two little children and an inability to handle the daily stresses without resorting to violence.

Referred by a Child Protective Service worker after they were reported for child abuse, they came to us apprehensive, defensive, and frightened.

The group's acceptance and concern emerged immediately. We suggested foster day care for the children, giving the mother a chance to work and help ease the financial struggle. Susie, the mother, a fast-moving and charming woman with a vibrant sense of humor acted upon our suggestion immediately. The next week they reported on the relief of having the kids away during the day. Violence, however, erupted in terms of wife-beating and husband-berating. We received calls between meetings and within a few weeks saw an abashed, miserable husband reporting that his wife had taken the kids and run away. She subsequently put the children into foster care, stayed with friends, and then came back home.

The children came home on weekends, the husband and wife both obtained jobs and they now lead our group. They still fight, and abuse is a constant issue, his of her, his of the children, hers of him, hers of the children, usually short of the danger point. My contact with these chairpersons is almost daily. The dual role of group leader as well as person called upon in crisis seems to be efficacious. Susie, effervescent and appealing, now loves coming to community meetings, speaking before groups of strangers about herself and P.A. To be chairperson, to have a title, she finds thrilling. The intelligence and vitality that have had no outlet are being used. She has good ideas about publicizing P.A. and she follows through, calling the director of social services and setting up a meeting with him, putting up posters and generally "yacking it up."

These issues of values and the definition of agency back-up are fundamental to the forming of a sponsor-group relationship. I have an active nature, so my sponsorship is lively—that's my style. It doesn't have to be. Each of my three chairpersons have had a different relationship with me, and have led the group differently. We have utilized any available resource as necessary, from our own clinic to other agencies, from private therapy to sex therapy, AA and Al-Anon, CPS, and foster care. We are not dogmatic. We essentially believe in the corrective value of the group process with the help of a back-up person and agency.

THE MECHANICS OF SPONSORING A P.A. GROUP

The place for a group meeting should be neutral and free of specific identifying factors so that anonymity is maintained. A church or synagogue, a Salvation Army building all make good meeting places. The space must be donated since P.A. has no funds to pay any kind of rent. A family-service agency or mental-health clinic could be used but it would be better to have no mental health "stigma" attached. We meet in a community center and are called a parents group. The center has easy access—people come for ceramics classes, basketball, and various meetings, so that there is no identifying who is there for what. In publicising the group, no street address may be given. The local newspaper or *Pennysaver* carries ads that give only a telephone number.

We give my number, and now the toll-free number of the statewide P.A. group. It takes a few phone calls to be sent to the right person and it would be better if initial contact could be immediate and direct. However, we have found no way to do that. When I receive a call, I try to refer it to the chairperson immediately. Sometimes I can't. The chairperson may not be available, or the crisis is hot and the person needs an immediate ear. The correlation between a "good" phone conversation and attendance at the group is nil in my experience. I have had long, intense discussions on the phone, have sometimes been called twice or three times; but the caller has not come to the meeting. We consider the phone calls an integral part of P.A. work and understand that some people may not wish nor even need to be in the group. There are many calls and nowhere near that many new members. Nevertheless, it works fairly well. People screen, consult, and test before making a physical plunge into a potentially frightening experience. After getting information on the phone, some people will come to their first meeting. Many never return, some come a few times, some come spasmodically, every few weeks for a long time, and some connect and stay with the group.

When they come in to the meeting, mutual introductions are made by first names only, and then most people listen for a while. At some point, the chairperson asks if they would like to talk. Most people do. But the glue that ultimately holds the group together is the telephone and the personal-contact network. We exchange phone numbers. People are invited to call any one of us. Before erupting, call! Sadie, one member, told of how she would force her hand to reach for the telephone on its way to a child's head.

The people who remain as group members have usually found an identificaion with at least one person there. With that one person, there is a connection. When one connects, the feeling of isolation is lessened and a bond begins to form. The phone contacts from another member or the chairperson help to cement the bond. Sally, a deeply unhappy Southern woman came in over serious difficulties with her fourteen year-old daughter who was hostile, drug-involved, and sexually active. She and her husband came to the first meeting together and it was clear to the group that the air between them quivered with tension. She somehow related to Nancy, an impeccable housekeeper, shy, frightened and somewhat agoraphobic. Nancy hardly ever left her home, spending her days depressed, and endlessly cleaning (walls, radiators, doorknobs, everything shone!). Sally, also housebound with a handicapped child, found in Nancy a potential playmate. Both had very hard-working, serious husbands. Both needed to have some fun. They had lunch and occasionally went to a movie or a dance together. The group was enlivened by their playfulness and laughter. We all benefited. When Sally moved because of her husband's business relocation, Nancy found no friend to replace her. They still correspond, but Nancy has found a job, is calmer with her kids, and has left the group.

In this kind of free-entry arrangement, unlike its therapy counterpart, resistance is not considered a problem and people can stop coming at any time. If they have a friend, feel accepted, get specific help, or just feel better for coming, they will stay with the group.

AGENCY RESPONSIBILITY AND BACK-UP

The agency then is responsible for paying the sponsors' time, helping when possible with publicity, making therapy available as quickly as possible to any P.A. members. Somehow, that begins the process, but the involvement grows deeper and more complex. The child-abuse issue is of profound community concern. As a P.A. sponsor I felt the need for more community involvement. I was asked to serve on the County Advisory Committee for Child Abuse. That necessitated freeing more clinic time. Then issues such as the handling of child-abuse cases at the clinic arise. For instance, when we report cases of child abuse to the local Child Protective Agency, who better to be called upon than the P.A. sponsor?

We developed a Child Abuse Screening Committee. This involved more time donated by the clinic. We arranged to meet regularly with our local Child Protective Service unit, to ensure that families in treatment with us do not lose contact with agencies if CPS drops their case after referring them to us, and if the families don't follow through with therapy. One family we worked with consisted of a mother and two children. Mrs. Long lived in constant turmoil with her twelve year-old son. Her fourteen year-old daughter had aligned herself with her mother. The mother was referred to CPS by neighbors because of her constant fighting with her son. CPS insisted that she come to therapy, something she does not want and uses only sporadically. However, the son did see his own therapist and I worked with the mother, more on an emergency basis than in any way resembling real therapy.

When the mother would explode frequently at Charlie, the son, his therapist and I were able to work together to protect him. At one point CPS was reactivated (they had closed the case) because of the real physical danger to Charlie. Grandma Long came into the picture and a plan was evolved to get Charlie into her home. He is still there, still in therapy, but in much better shape than before. I still see the mother to keep in touch with all sides of the family. With the mother's permission we keep CPS aware of what is going on. A family has been kept together as a result of our liaison policies.

We have also developed a teen-age volunteer big brother/big sister program. We have recruited high-school seniors and are training them to work with neglected and abused kids. While the parents are seeing their therapists, or before or after the child's therapy, the teen-age volunteer talks to, play with, or tutors the child in a room we have set aside, filled with games, toys, a record player and a tape recorder. We are supervising the volunteers and beginning a liaison with the local high schools. Though this is in an embryonic stage, with lots of knots to unravel, this might turn out to be another in our network of family support systems.

We are also setting up a small fund for recreational activities, summer camps, or any other unique need of a child. This money is coming from local service groups, (i.e., Elks. Lions, Rotary) and is not part of the regular clinic funding. Part of this fund is also used as needed for P.A., i.e., phone calls and transportation as warranted.

THE RELATIONSHIP OF P.A. TO THE LARGER COMMUNITY: RECRUITMENT, PUBLIC RELATIONS AND ISSUES OF CONFIDENTIALITY

Publicity is undertaken sporadically. We have sent letters, (typed by the chairperson, mailed by the clinic) to local hospitals, pediatricians, and other social agencies. We get some ads into the service column of the local newspaper. Otherwise, we rely on local hot lines and an occasional plug in an Ann Landers column. We have a phone listing in a social-services section of our local telephone directory.

The issue of confidentiality is a crucial one. In the clinic we constantly evaluate at what point we are mandated, by New York State law, to report to Child Protective Service. At P.A. there are somewhat different considerations. People come to us because of the promise of anonymity. If we do not know their last name, how can we report? We have never had to do so in my group. However, there is general policy which states that if there is known and continued abuse by a group member, the group itself will confront the member with the danger, and explain that if the situation does not improve, they will be forced to report. We received one call from a local health group asking P.A.'s advice on reporting a case on which they had received a call. We called the person in question, heard a baby crying, and the mother distraught and confused. She refused a visit from us, a referral to our group, to the local family-service agency, or to any alternative. The danger appeared real, and we suggested that the health agency report the situation to CPS. They did.

With the heightened community and legal awareness of the importance of a sound reporting system, the issue of mandated reporting is a continually complex one. Therapists are highly (and appropriately) sensitive to any incursions into the therapist-patient relationship of confidentiality. The New York State Child Abuse Law clearly states that reporting of abuse supercedes confidentiality. When we understand more clearly what CPS does and how the system operates we are able to make decisions more intelligently.

The more I know, as a P.A. sponsor, about all the agencies such as CPS, DSS, and the rest, the more of a resource I become to the group. The more the community knows about us, the more referrals P.A. will get. It is hoped that this will cut down the work of the other agencies, since we can do a great deal by ourselves. For the number of people who have been helped, encouraged, and have used the Parents Anonymous group, the cost has been very small and the rewards great.

These have been my experiences, carved out with no precedents and replete with errors. To anyone wishing to underake the task of sponsoring a P.A. group I say, *do it*. It's satisfying, enriching, at times even fun and, I believe, useful to many families.

Chapter 9

MUTUAL SUPPORT GROUPS IN A SUBURBAN SETTING:
The Opportunities, the Challenge

Bill Claflin

MUTUAL SUPPORT GROUPS IN A SUBURBAN SETTING:
THE OPPORTUNITIES, THE CHALLENGE

During recent years both the professional literature and the popular press have focused increasing attention on the effectiveness of mutual-support, self-help systems, and their rapid growth in many countries. This presentation will examine the support and utilization of self-help groups in a community health and mental health center in a suburban county in the New York metropolitan area.

When legislation was passed by the United States Congress in 1963 creating the first community mental health centers, the beginnings, without precedent, were modest. At first, traditional methods of counseling and psychiatry were made available to populations not usually served by therapists, psychologists, and psychiatrists. It soon became evident that the people initially receiving treatment were largely those who presented serious mental and emotional disabilities. Increasingly, thought was given to ways of intervening in order to reach larger numbers and provide counseling and treatment at earlier stages—prior to the onset of serious dysfunction and the need for emergency hospitalization, medication, etc.

Outreach and public-information efforts were initiated, and referrals increased from a variety of human-service care providers and various community agencies, including the police.

As referrals materialized from these sources, it became clear that some individuals were seeking help in meeting particular life crises—death of a spouse, loss of a job, an alcoholic parent, etc. Although the individual presented symptoms such as anxiety or depression, in many cases it did not appear practical to initiate psychotherapy to deal with the life-situation related symptoms; and in many cases the symptoms were a normal reaction to the stressful event. Brief, intensive intervention and counseling often proved effective with no need for long-term treatment or hospitalization. But citizens still sought help in dealing with a variety of difficulties. A typical situation is noted in the book, *DISTRESS IN THE CITY*, edited by William Ryan: Bill Claflin was formerly the Coordinator of Alcohol Education at the Rockland County Community Mental Health Center, Division of Consultation and Education, Pomona N.Y. He continues his work in addiction education with Ericksen Associates, Box 623–Union Station, Endicott, N.Y. 13760.

> ...consider the case of a depressed and defeated working-class housewife turning to someone for help with a multitude of problems that are overwhelming her: an alcoholic husband who disappears for days at a time; the piling up of pressing debts; an eviction notice from the landlord; two children in diapers and a third who is enuretic; a sickly daughter and a neglected oldest son whose school work is worsening daily; headaches and stomachaches; increasing trouble with her neighbors as she becomes more and more short-tempered; and a growing sense of guilt as she finds that she herself is turning more and more to liquor for consolation.
>
> If this woman were to be viewed in a narrow mental health context, it is possible that she would be diagnosed as suffering from depression; and, if she were so diagnosed or identified, it is likely that she would be referred for psychiatric treatment. Possibly she would be identified as a person with marital problems and then be referred for marital counseling. the question that comes to mind is: How logical would such a narrow identification be? It is likely that this woman would *not* be viewed as a suitable candidate for psychotherapy; and this judgment would probably be correct, since she is neither introspective nor verbal, nor does she consider herself 'mental.' Most important, she would tend to perceive talking to someone once a week for a long period of time about her feelings, her thoughts, and her many worries as a totally inadequate method of helping her solve her problems. Aside

from the probable futility of referring such a client for counseling or therapy, however, one must consider the question of whether it is even appropriate to make such a referral—to abstract, as it were, a 'disease' from this complex of problems. Her 'depression' is a condition that might seem quite natural in view of what is happening to her. To call her situation a marital problem seems, not only to her but to most people, a rather glaring understatement.

It is suggested, then, that in this woman's situation the strict application of the usual system of referral is not suitable. Her emotional disturbance, her marital difficulties, are discovered in the context of serious social disturbance and are only parts of an interlocking system of problems. It may be that these realistic problems should be considered and dealt with as they exist—that is, as a total unit, without any attempt artificially to pull out one or another of the problems for separate treatment or to squeeze a complex situation into a diagnostic mode which does not fit it.

Regrettably, this author was not aware of two peer-help programs that could have offered support, knowledge, and a repertoire of coping skills. I refer, of course, to Al-Anon and Alateen, fellowships for families of persons with alcoholism, many of whom are encountering the types of problems just described.

Nine years ago, the division of consultation and education in The Rockland County Community Mental Health center became convinced that people could often be aided by peers in dealing with stressful life events troubling otherwise adequately functioning individuals. Distressed persons thus could receive effective help without the need for professional intervention. Steps were taken to initiate and enable a peer-support group for widows and widowers. Despite periods of uncertainty, the widows' self-help group flourished and over 700 individuals attended the weekly meetings in a period of five years. Only a few have needed to seek professional therapy for depression, anxiety, etc., during the difficult period of bereavement and adjustment. Staff from the Center provided the group consultation and support as needed, and also arranged a location for the meetings.

The division of consultation and education 7 years ago assembled a directory of mutual aid groups in the county (population: approximately 250,000 within 160 square miles). To everyone's surprise, after many hours of effort, it was determined that 40 peer-help groups were active in the county, ranging in size from a handful to over 500 active members in two mutual-aid fellowships. The directory was distributed to the groups listed and to a cross-section of human-services care providers. In additon, a substantial amount of publicity was carried by the local radio station and several newspapers.

After the directory was distributed, the division of consultation and education attempted to enable the formation of a council or asociation of the local peer-help groups. Several meetings were held, but despite the substantial publicity efforts only a small number of the groups were represented. The feeling among those in attendance was that an association of the local peer-help groups might be desirable and useful; but none of the representatives attending the planning sessions believed that they had the time to devote to this effort.

Another possible inhibiting factor could be the nonspecific, open-ended prospct for a newly created council of mutual-aid groups. Members of the existing groups were accustomed to participating in programs with a very acute focus. Unquestionably, an opportunity offered without clearly stated objectives and methods can be unsettling for many individuals, particularly if they have little organizational experience. After six planning sessions, the organizing effort was discontinued.

Subsequently, some staff at the community mental health center raised the possibility that more extensive use of peer-help groups could help reduce the time on waiting lists for non-emergency mental health services, and also possibly shorten patients' stay in treatment programs. Educational programs were offered to the staff at the center. A large orientation seminar on peer-support was held for staff and other human-services programs and a training session for therapists on one treatment team was arranged. Attendance at the large meeting by therapists was disappointing and the small group-training experience revealed a high degree of skepticism about the effectiveness of peer-help systems—at least as they applied to mental/emotional health.

Interestingly, most of the care providers readily conceded that Alcoholics Anonymous (AA) was singularly helpful and successful for individuals with drinking problems; and the effectiveness of peer counseling for individuals having disfiguring surgery did not appear to be debatable. Perhaps significantly, two therapists indicated that a referral to a support group for an individual with a physical health problem might be desirable; but it was their feeling that this should be left entirely to the treating physician.

Also, there was a prevailing and persisting perception that use of peer-help groups, at least for mental-health problems, would be an either/or proposition, despite efforts to indicate otherwise. Patients might be referred *after* treatment, but not during therapy, in view of most therapists. To my knowledge, only two clinicians were willing to refer people to peer-support programs while still in therapy. And this writer can still recall vividly a staff meeting during which he mentioned Schizophrenics Anonymous. The immediate comment from a psychologist was: "I can't *conceive* of such a group." And this perhaps focuses on a key issue for many therapists: how can troubled or disturbed individuals help each other with emotional-health problems?

Here, perhaps, is a central point in professional resistance. There is a prevalent assumption that peer-support groups practice group therapy. And, at least in some cases, it appears almost impossible to explain that self-help groups do *not* diagnose or treat. Most often there is a great deal of sharing, and the focus is almost entirely on feelings, and symptoms, and their management. How do you handle depression, anxiety, or rage, etc. *Hope* is perhaps the key ingredient that attracts people to mutual aid groups—and keeps them involved after the initial contact. Other essential ingredients are action and change.

The various mutual-aid groups teach very concrete methods for dealing with symptoms. Recovery, Inc. teaches their membership that "symptoms may be distressing but they are not dangerous." And as long as the individual can control the muscles, he or she can control the situation. Alcoholics Anonymous (AA) teaches the membership that "Nothing is so bad that a drink won't make it much worse." And AA discovered 48 years ago that the drink that got the alcoholic drunk was the first drink—not the last three or four. So the newcomer to AA learns that it is the primary objective at *all* times to avoid the first drink, one day at a time (or, one hour at a time during difficult periods). And tremendous, concerned support is always available to the members, just for the asking. Several of the mutual help groups teach people symptom management by simple observations such as, "feelings are neither good nor bad (they just are)—what you *do* about your feelings can certainly be good or bad."

Looking to care givers outside the mental-health network, it has been my experience that there is a different perspective on mutual-aid fellowships. In recent years, for example, many hospital nurses have been only too glad to call on volunteer counselors to speak to patients who have had mastectomies, ostomy surgery, laryngectomies, etc. They have seen the devastating emotional impact of these procedures, and they appreciate the hope and practical suggestions that come from individuals who have made a good adjustment following surgery. Nurses are accustomed to working as members of a treatment team and rarely have the primary responsibility for treatment. In the mental-health field, however, the therapist is usually a solo practitoner (although she or he may be perhaps a member of the clinical team in a particular setting). Not every therapist is willing to share treatment responsibilities, and the concept that individuals in distress, or suffering from emotional problems, can assist each other therapeutically is difficult to entertain.

Those care providers dealing with disrupted and troubled families quickly note the changes taking place when family members participate in fellowships helping families distressed by alcoholism, compulsive gambling, child-abuse and/or neglect, etc. Family members learn how to refocus family attention away from the disabled individual, and they come to understand that their primary responsibility is effectively to meet their own needs. They cannot, for example, make the alcoholic stop drinking or the compulsive gambler give up the obsession. But when the troubled person reaches out for help, the family is more likely to respond and help *if* they have been properly meeting their own needs and maintaining an acceptable level of management in family life.

The last few years have seen an explosion of groups adapting the AA program of "Twelve Steps to Recovery." Fellowships have been initiated to deal with compulsive overeating, having a family member in prison, compulsive gambling, unmanageable emotions, abuse/dependence on medication, etc. And to the extent that these programs are known, it may be logical to assume that some individuals would be attracted to membership, although they might not see themselves participating in psychotherapy or other mental-health services. And, indeed, many destructive behaviors have proven highly resistant to mental-health treatment.

Probably the most extensive use of the self-help directory in Rockland County has occurred among the groups listed in it. Hundreds of residents have become familiar with the enormous range of mutual-aid activities represented by groups such as: Parents of Twins, the Ostomy Association, Foster Parents Association, Overeaters Anonymous, Recovery, Inc., Gamblers Anonymous, the Heart Club, etc. I know of several cases in which members of a fellowship acquired information that made it possible to identify a serious but overlooked problem with alcoholism or compulsive gambling.

Anonymous, and are excited to learn that there are similar programs to assist people, for example with emotional or mental problems. Perhaps I should comment here that the national headquarters of at least two mutual-aid programs have noted, for reasons that remain obscure, that they get far fewer referrals from professionals in the metropolitan New York area than in any other areas of the country.

In closing, two further points require comment. Unquestionably, the human-services field, and mental-health services particularly, will face increasing demands for service during the period of economic uncertainties and social readjustments that we face in the years just ahead. And it appears that at least in the United States, there will be serious limitations on the availability of traditional mental-health professionals to meet these needs. It seems clear to this writer that a virtually untapped source of assistance for large numbers of individuals experiencing unusual stress or troublesome dysfunction can be found in mutual-help programs. All too often, however, in the various conferences I have attended over the last 15 year, educational and training seminars are being utilized by those care providers who are already at least partly convinced of the effectiveness and success record of the self-help field.

It seems absolutely essential to me that major efforts be undertaken to include course material at the undergraduate and graduate levels concerning the nature, effectiveness, and limitations of mutual-support systems. Most urgently this material should be included in the basic course work for students in nursing, medicine, social work, psychology, and other related fields. Students should come to understand that these resources exist in most communities and *must* be included in every inventory of human-service programs. Also, greater emphasis must be placed on effective prevention programs and thoughtful attempts to de-stigmatize the whole area of emotional and mental non-health.

I'd like to share an experience I had not too long ago at a meeting of a mutual-aid fellowship. Shortly after the meeting began a young couple joined the group. When it came their turn to share, we learned of a tragedy they had just experienced—watching their home burn with an infant in the bedroom, inaccessible to rescue efforts. They had lost everything—the child and all their material possessions. And they came to a place where they knew, somehow, help would be available. After the initial shock, and a brief silence as all of us contemplated the tragedy, there was a spontaneous outpouring of emotion that is impossible to describe. A number of those present had experienced the death of a child; all had lost someone close and understood the despair being experienced. One or two of those present had lost all their possessions in fires. But everyone had something to contribute that offered comfort, empathy, or hope. When the meeting ended, practical help was there immediately—a place to live temporarily, clothing, small sums of money, and numerous modest items of aid. But most important, however, were the feelings that all shared. And here, perhaps, is the key to the truly unique value of peer-help programs. Assistance is offered, not by a professional specialist, but by individuals who are concerned, committed, who understand the value of mutual support and of sharing with others during times of stress and difficulty. Spontaneity and intimacy are characteristic of the group's activity, and empathy is the product of common experiences. The individual in difficulty is not viewed as sick, but as a friend needing help. And since all of us at times need the understanding and support of others, there is a substantial element of universality that forms the common bond linking all together.

Chapter 10

MAKE TODAY COUNT
A Collaborative Model for Professionals
and Self-Help Groups
Richard Wollert
Bob Knight
Leon H. Levy

Within the last 35 years the number of self-help groups (SHGs) has increased steadily (Tracy and Gussow, 1976). The scope of these groups also has expanded, so that many now deal with problems having a significant psychological component. Although their effectiveness has not been determined empirically, several writers believe that mental health oriented SHGs have helped their members (Bumbalo and Young, 1973; Hurvitz, 1970). The proliferation and increased scope of SHGs, coupled with the belief that they are effective sources of help, has led to the suggestion that appropriate collaboration between clinical psychologists and SHGs could lead to a powerful approach to mental health care (Levy, in press). This seems reasonable since SHGs might take advantage of the organizational and consulation skills of professionals (Caplan, 1974), while clinicians might benefit from observing innovative techniques applied in SHGs (Levy, 1976).

A survey of the literature, however, suggests many obstacles to collaboration. For example, SHGs have been observed to have a strong bias against professional help (Barish, 1971) and to distrust professionals (Back

---

[1]Techniques used by self-help groups have been discussed by Levy (1976) and Durman (1976).

and Taylor, 1976). This antipathy, together with the emphasis many SHGs place on anonymity, would seem to make entry difficult for professionals. Even if they were admitted, members' fears of co-optation (Kleiman, Mantell, and Alexander, 1976) could militate against acceptance of professional help. Finally, professionals might alienate members by expressing opinions counter to the ideologies of the group (Antze, 1976).

In spite of these obstacles, three observations suggest that collaboration may be possible. First, the readiness with which our research team was received by SHGs suggests that entry difficulties can be reduced. Second, our interviews with members indicate that many believe professionals could be involved with their group. Third, several reports show that professionals are becoming involved with SHGs on a variety of levels (Caplan, 1974; Dumont, 1974; Levy, 1976).

In order to realize substantial benefits from their involvements, it is important that professionals and SHGs develop positive working relationships. We believe that many difficulties continue because no model exists to guide the establishment of such relationships. This, in turn, may be due to the lack of published reports of successful collaboration.

This paper presents a case history of a 2-year collaborative effort between our research team and one chapter of Make Today Count, a SHG composed of cancer patients, their spouses, and health-care professionals. On the basis of data obtained from several sources, we see this involvement as having been highly successful.

History and Structure

The national Make Today Count (MTC) organization was founded by Orville Kelly (Kelly and Murray, 1975). The chapter we became involved with was organized in 1974 by a physician and a medical secretary who became interested in MTC after watching a television interview of Kelly. Both professionals believed that many residents in their area could use MTC to work through adjustment difficulties associated with life-threatening illnesses. With no formal guidelines, they organizd the group by "going out and getting people together."

We contacted the MTC chapter in 1975 through a telephone call to one of the chapter founders. We explained that we were involved in a federally-funded research project studying SHGs, and expressed a desire to learn more about MTC through nonparticipatory observation of the group. Two members of our research team attended MTC meetings in August and November 1975. Before the first meeting we introduced ourselves, and mentioned our research involvement and our conviction that there was much professionals could learn from SHGs. During these first meetings we listened quietly, and did not take notes.

ASSESSMENT OF GROUP FUNCTIONING

Although evaluation was not our primary purpose, some assessment of the group's functioning was unavoidable. The chapter appeared to have several strengths. Several charismatic and outgoing individuals were group members. Warmth and friendship characterized the members' interpersonal relationships. Finally, the members seemed very determined to establish a permanent SHG. In spite of these assets, our observers agreed that numerous signs reflected weaknesses. For one thing, a low percentage (about 20 percent) of the group were cancer patients. From members' comments, we concluded the group had little success in recruiting new members. Meetings lacked a cohesive format. Organizational questions, such as the group's target population, were frequently discussed but not resolved. There was little discussion of adjustment difficulites. Ominously, the frequency of meetings had been reduced from twice to once per month. These observations led us to believe the group was not fully meeting the members' needs.

In August 1975, we attended the national MTC convention. More than an hour was spent discussing difficulties faced by the chapter we were observing. Questions raised by chapter members included how new members might be recruited, and how meetings should be conducted. Members therefore shared our concern for the group's functioning.

CONSULTATION PROCEDURES

After the second meeting, we made interview appointments with specific members. Our first interview was with one of the founders. She expressed concern over the group's operation, particular disappointment at the disorganization of meetings, and felt that the real goals of the group were not being met. At the end of the interview, we discussed meeting formats and interaction styles of other groups, and offered to share this information. She was enthusiastic about this offer and, after consulting with other members, requested that we discuss SHGs and moderate a group discussion of organizational alternatives.

At the February 1976 meeting, we presented an overview of the purposes, techniques, and strengths of SHGs. This presentation was made relevant through a discussion of how various SHGs dealt with problems similar to those facing MTC. We then facilitated a discussion of these problems, intervening mainly to keep the discussion focused and to present pertinent examples from other groups.

During the discussion, a consensus was reached that the group's purpose was to help its members "lead more fulfilling lives, and to make every day count." The members also decided the group was open to "those who have a life-threatening illness, and to others involved in coping with life-threatening illnesses." These were important developments, since these issues had often been discussed without formal resolution. Members also expressed a desire to devote more meeting time to personal issues, and to improve the meeting format. To achieve these goals, members were willing to consider reorganization along lines suggested by our research team. After this meeting, we drafted a letter to MTC summarizing our understanding of the discussion. We also offered to formulate, at the group's request, guidelines to enhance group organization and facilitate personal discussion. We were again informed that the members were interested in our suggestions.

We presented written guidelines, consisting of three sections, at the April meeting (Wollert and Knight, 1976). These suggestions were based on our observations of organizational patterns in other SHGs, and on interviews with members on how they had been helped by their group. In an opening section, we stressed that a viable SHG needed to have a clear purpose, and be open to new members. We noted that the decisions made during the February meeting met these criteria. The importance of maintaining group unity while providing opportunities for self-expression was also emphasized. Toward this end it was recommended that debates be avoided about what were the "best" attitudes or coping strategies.

In another section, organizational topics were discussed. A format was presented, consisting of: (a) an introduction which welcomed members and guests, and restated the purpose of MTC; (b) consideration of business matters; (c) a session for sharing in which each member brought up recent events of personal significance; (d) formal presentations such as outside speakers or discussion focused on a specific topic of concern to the members; and, (e) closing. It was observed that responsibility for chairing the meetings could be rotated among members if such a simple format were adopted. It was also suggested that committees be formed to handle matters of meeting content and member recruitment.

In the final section we presented several techniques which members could use to help others in group discussions. These included disclosing personal difficulties, accepting others' viewpoints without argument, providing support in the form of encouragement and reassurance, and communicating to others that their concerns were understood and that they were not alone in experiencing negative emotional reactions to the stress of coping with life-threatening illness. The stated purposes of these techniques were to: (a) reduce feelings of isolation; (b) reduce feelings of being different or abnormal; (c) avoid arguments; and, (d) increase tolerance of different points of view.

Th way in which the guidelines were presented stressed that they were not the only lines for reorganization, but might be considered useful alternatives. We also recognized the group's final responsibility for their implementation. Within this context, our presentation was received enthusiastically.

RESULTS

We did not attend the next meeting, but were in contact with the group by telephone to ascertain what steps towards reorganization had been taken. A planning committee was formed to determine the content of meetings, and a decision made to have members alternate as chairperson. A meeting format similar to that which we outlined was also adopted with minor alterations.

These changes had some immediate impact. Members believed that the new format led to better organized meetings. Several potential new members commented that they were impressed by the group's organization. Because positive changes were brought about through the efforts of the group as a whole, members identified more fully with the group.

We attended the June and July meetings, and our observations were consistent with these telephone reports. We also noticed that more members attended these meetings than previously, and that the percentage of patients had increased to about 50 percent. These changes may have been due to the efforts of a "publicity and recruitment" committee which made media appearances, placed ads in the local newspaper, and met with interested groups to discuss MTC. Another major change in the group was that members displayed a greater readiness to discuss events of personal importance.

From a global standpont, we noticed a great change in the meeting "atmosphere." Earlier meetings were disorganized, restrained, and somewhat dismal. Later meetings were organized and open, and showed some of the warmth and enthusiasm of sucessful SHGs.

FOLLOW-UP

We observed the group for another 9 months, discussing our observations with some members after meetings in a free exchange of ideas about group processes. While some new ideas emerged, our input consisted largely of support for the leaders' ideas. We emphasized throughout that our role was consultative, and resisted requests to assume roles as discussion leaders. This stance was based on our conviction that the group's interests were best served by helping members to attain higher levels of competence and self-confidence rather than to loan them, temporarily, our own competence.

In this period MTC consolidated the changes which had taken place, attributing improvement to their efforts and our support and helpful suggestions. The group increased the frequency of meetings to twice per month, continued to recruit new members, became active in presenting seminars on death and dying, and moved from a ''problem-child'' status within the national organization to that of a model for other groups. In fact, the group received requests for assistance from other chapters referred by the national organization. Chapter members requested that we prepare a general version of our guidelines for them to distribute to other chapters. This reflected the cooperative nature of the relationship we established with this SHG.

DISCUSSION

The potential for cooperation between professionals and self-help groups has been the topic of much discussion, ranging from optimism (Levy, 1976) to the conclusion that some alliances are not workable (Kleiman et al., 1976) or simply unproductive (Hurvitz, 1970). Noting the diversity of professional contacts with SHGs, a few observers have called for a more systmatic exploration of possible styles of interaction (Lieberman and Borman, 1976).

This case history suggests several conditions which increase the likelihood that profitable collaboration may occur between professionals and SHGs. The first is adequate professional knowledge of the workings of SHGs. Through our observations, interviews, and readings, we developed a framework for understanding self-help patterns (Levy, Knight, Padgett, and Wollert, 1977) and different types of SHGs. This enabled us explicitly to formulate organizational alternatives and guidelines for effective group interaction. Since SHGs do not typically provide members with formal training in self-help techniques, these were definite strengths we brought to the collaborative effort.

It is also worth noting that SHGs do not embrace the treatment model characterizing most therapy groups (Hurvitz, 1970). A professional who enters a SHG with expectations based solely on clinical experience is therefore likely to be disappointed. This could lead to attempts to change the group so that it conforms more closely to a professional model, with the probable outcome being the group's rejection of the professional. With an adequate knowledge of SHGs, the chances are reduced that such failure-producing expectations will be adopted. On a number of bases, then, there is no substitute for a thorough-going familiarity with self-help phenomena as a condition for collaboration.

An effective rapport-building approach is a second precondition for collaboration. In our approach, we conveyed respect for the group by not taking notes or offering gratuitous opinions. We conveyed acceptance through our repeated assertions that we could learn a great deal about helping others from our SHG observations. The professional-member status differential was de-emphasized by maintaining informal contacts with members, openness about our research project, and recognition that SHGs have their own domain of expertise. Our lack of interest in formal evaluation also underscored our acceptance of the group.

A final condition which enchances collaboration is application of an appropriate consultation model (Caplan, 1970). Much of our consultative work was based on an extension of our approach to the group. For example, we offered assistance only when it was obvious that this was desired by the membership. We also expressed a willingness to work collaboratively with the group. In structuring the relationship, we explicitly stated that we saw our role as facilitating discussion of organizational difficulties and presenting alternative solutions. We saw the group's role as implementing our suggestions as the members saw fit. While we considered ourselves friends of the group, we would not become members or leaders, minimizing the destructive role conflicts that could arise.

The goals and methods we adopted in our work are also worth noting. First, our goals were limited. We were not interested in the group's becoming a model of therapeutic efficiency. Rather, we hoped that the group would become self-sustaining and achieve a style of interaction which met the members' needs, as they saw them. Second, we worked in a pragmatic fashion, developing our intervention in a series of steps. Third, the group assumed responsibility for determining issues and taking action. Within this context, we frequently contacted the members to insure that we fully understood their desires and decisions.

OBSERVATION OF OTHER PROFESSIONALS

During the 2 years of our involvement with MTC, a number of other professionals (doctors, ministers, nurses and psychotherapists) passed through the group. A description of their interactions serves to highlight some of the critical differences between our approach and theirs. These differences may also explain why our relationship was successful while these other relationships were, on the whole, unrewarding.

The typical entry approach of most other professionals was quite different from ours. They often took up much time citing their professional credentials. They also generally stated an interest in helping the group or finding out how the group could assist them. This approach calls attention to professional/member differences and implicitly asserts the professional's superiority. It also precludes the professionals learning about the group, since the time for group work is reduced and much of the meeting is spent resolving the professional/group interaction. A more productive approach would surely be to listen throughout a few meetings, to build rapport, and to determine whether the professional and the group have anything to offer one another.

Many professionals also tended to practice their profession in the group; in effect, they acted in their first contacts as counselors or leaders. This alienates the members and undercuts the group process. In contrast, we operated primarily as organizational consultants. It therefore seems that professionals involved in SHGs must often de-emphasize the idea of directly helping others in favor of providing assistance which allows group members to serve this purpose.

Finally, a number of professionals engaged in open evaluation of the group. The implicit criterion and judgment was often "what you're doing is different from what I do therefore, you are wrong." This stance, quite naturally, antagonizes the members, and generally leads to unproductive arguments. It seems more useful to recognize that SHGs have a unique style, and deal with many problems professionals help their clients resolve. Where a decision has been made to rely on self-help rather than professional approaches, that decision should be respected.

Overall, our observations of other professionals' contacts with MTC indicated that they were often hurried and evaluative, focused on the professional, and asserted the professional's superior status. Our own contact was long-term, nonevaluative, group-centered, and characterized by a respect for the group's right to accept or reject our input.

COMPARISON WITH CANCERVIVE

A comparison of our experience with that of Kleiman *et al.* (1976) is especially interesting in that they also were involved with a group for persons with life-threatening illnesses (CanCervive). Working for a highly professionalized agency, they sought to use the group to provide counseling to hospitalized cancer patients. After 2 years of contention between professionals and members over issues of competence and control, the group was dissolved. Their negative experiences led Kleiman *et al.* to assume a pessimistic stance about the potential for collaboration among professionals and agency-sponsored SHGs. They concluded that such collaboration is not possible since the group surrenders autonomy, egalitarianism, and its sense of urgency, whereas professionals find their identity, power, and control questioned.

Our disagreement is not so much with the conclusion of Kleiman *et al.*, which fits not only their experiences with CanCervive but also our observations of the interactions of many professionals with MTC. What is questionable is the generality of their experience. In short, while conflicts often characterize the interaction of professionals and SHGs, there are other modes of relating which can avoid these pitfalls.

The key to a successful professional-group relationship appears to be the adoption of a consultative role (Caplan, 1970) by the professional as opposed to a therapist role. This role allows the professional to respect the autonomy and egalitarian spirit of the group. Since the professional is consulting with the group rather than joining it, status-differential problems are minimized. This also allows the professional to avoid control conflicts, since the consultee retains the right to reject advice.

In summary, our experience with MTC suggests a model for collaboration among professionals and mental health-oriented SHGs. Our proposed model is consistent with Tyler's (1976) suggestion that professionals should encourage but not regulate such groups, and is entirely harmonious with Lieberman and Borman's (1976) suggestion that the way to find out what assistance a group desires is to ask the members. It is hoped that our experience will serve to suggest to other professionals that collaboration is possible, and will represent a step towards explicating some ways in which SHGs and professionals can assist one another in meeting mental-health needs.

The authors are indebted to Pat Kennedy for helpful comments on this article. Portions of this article were presented at the annual convention of the Southeastrn Psychological Association, Atlanta, 1978.

Chapter 11

THE MENTAL HEALTH PROFESSIONS AND MUTUAL-HELP PROGRAMS
Co-optation or Collaboration?

O. Hobart Mowrer

In inviting me to contribute a chapter to this book, the editors suggested, as a title, "Training Professionals to Work with Mutual-Help Groups." But such an assignment immediately raises some perplexing problems. Do professionals *wish* to be trained to work with mutual-help groups (cf. Mowrer, 1977)? Where and by whom is this type of training to be done? What direction and form should it take? Should the training consist mainly of the gleanings of indigenous workers' experience in various types of mutual-help programs? Should it consist of knowledge and skills which certain professionals have acquired informally or by chance? Should professionals make a point of specifically informing themselves as to the origin and operation of various types of mutual-help groups, and then decide where their prior expertise equips them to make the most innovative and useful contributions? Or does reciprocal instruction and "training" offer the best model?

HISTORICAL PERSPECTIVE AND CONTEMPORARY PROBLEMS

For a long time the relationship between professional and indigenous mental-health workers was predominantly one of mutual disregard and distrust, with the possibility of constructive interaction receiving scant consideration. This polarization stemmed largely from the fact that members of mutual-help groups, before finding acceptance and constructive change in such groups, had unsuccesfully sought help from professionals; and the latter had found that trying to work with such persons along traditional lines was singularly unrewarding, both because of their apparent untreatability and, very commonly, their inability to pay even minimal professional fees.

However, within the last decade or so various developments have, for better or worse, brought professionals and indigenous helpers to increasing propinquity. It has long been recognized that the recovery program of Alcoholics Anonymous is more effective in the achievement of "contented sobriety" than any other approach; and alcoholics who have recovered by this route have commonly been offered and sometimes accepted jobs as alcoholism counselors in state or private mental hospitals and local clinics. Here there was usually formal or informal pressure on such persons to "upgrade" their training by participating in seminars or courses conducted by mental-health professionals, with the result that they gradually began to feel "better qualified" than ordinary A.A. members and frequently decided they had, in fact, outgrown Alcoholics Anonymous. At this point these persons often stopped going to A.A. meetings and, in a good many instances, were soon "drinking socially"—and then not so socially. This problem has been sufficiently prevalent and serious that the question as to whether it is wise for A.A. members to become "paraprofessionals" has been actively discussed at both the local and national levels of Alcoholics Anonymous.

I have also seen the process operate in the reverse direction. Sometimes local A.A. groups have pooled resources and bought or rented a small house to serve both as a sort of social club and as a temporary residential facility for persons who were not yet able to work the A.A. program on an ambulatory basis. This supplementary support for alcoholics was often quite successful; and the sub-regional office of the state department of mental health would sometimes offer both commendation and financial assistance. If this support, both moral and financial, continued for 2 or 3 years, these local semi-residential A.A. programs would expand, only to discover that they had, in effect, "sold their soul to the company store" (i.e., the state department of mental health), which would then begin to insist that mental health professionals be introduced into the program, under threat, that without compliance, now essential funding would be withheld. In this way a lot of people who had never before heard the word "co-optation" learned its meaning, the hard way. Fortunately, A.A. as a whole is a self-sustaining, "outpatient" type of operation and has been able to maintain its overall autonomy. The same has been true of other organizations which have patterned themselves after A.A., such as Gamblers Anonymous, Neurotics Anonymous, Overeaters Anonymous, etc.

Unfortunately, effective rehabilitation of "hard-core" drug addicts usually requires residential facilities; and here the problem of financing becomes crucial. The first of these facilities, Synanon Foundation, sensing the danger of co-optation by municipal, state, or federal funding agencies under the control of professionals, remained grimly self-sufficient (Yablonsky, 1965)—in fact, eventually became disastrously so (Bassin, 1979; Deitsch, 1979); but virtually all of the 300-plus residential drug-rehabilitation programs now operating in this country are largely dependent upon "tax dollars" and/or "third-party payments," and as a result are being increasingly pressured to "meet standards" in order to be accredited for the receipt of such funds. Many of these facilities continue to do a certain amoung of "hustling"; and parent associations contribute some financial support; but very few, if any, of such programs are able completely to pay their own way.

Between 1964 and 1968 I had considerable contact with several residential drug facilities, particularly Daytop Village, Inc. (Bassin, 1968; Sugarman, 1974). During this era funding agencies made very little attempt to influence either the philosophy or programs of these facilities. The discovery that drug addicts could, contrary to assumption, be rehabilitated was such a "miracle" that outsiders were willing to leave well enough alone. But in September 1979, I attended the Fourth International Conference of Therapeutic Communities (held in New York City) and was sorry, though not surprised, to hear a lot of talk, especially on the part of American drug-facility directors, about powerful forces now being brought to bear upon them to modify their programs in certain ways in order to meet the certification requirements of the Joint Commission on Hospital Accreditation, the now semiofficial accreditation organization for drug-rehabilitation programs. At the conference a common lament was: "We are *not* hospitals, and we do not operate according to the medical model, yet this is a medically oriented commission which now has the power of life and death over us" (cf. O'Brien, 1979).

Some residential programs seem to have been able to get funds without materially modifying what they regard as the heart of their program; but deep inroads have been made in other instances. Not long ago I was invited to give an address at the "graduation" ceremonies of a residential drug facility which has high morale and is functioning quite well; but the staff configuration and the language used in connection with the program reflect some striking changes. It was particularly strange to hear residents speaking about their "counselors" or "therapists," terms that were never used a few years ago and could have come into currency only because there are now staff members designated by these terms. In the "good old days," residents had "role models" and talked about "going through changes," but they *never* spoke of "therapy." They had already had too much of that, without benefit, before they got to the program now really transforming their lives.

The Therapeutic Communities of America has appointed a committee to deal specifically with the impact which the accreditation procedures are having on rehabilitation programs and the types of staff personnel they are being required to employ, either on a full-time or consultant basis (Kerr, 1979). At this juncture there seems to be no consensus as to what sort of compromise, if any, may eventually prove possible between the drug facilities and the Joint Commission; but some facility directors report that the commission has shown an inclination to make certain concessions to drug facilities. However, there is a general fatalism with respect to the ultimate loss of operational autonomy as a result of the accreditation process.[1]

The basic difficulty arises from the fact that there are now so many facilities requesting financial support that the funding agencies must have stipulated criteria of some sort for granting or withholding funds; and the most convenient monitoring organization to ask for assistance in this connection is the Joint Commission. But this is not necessarily the only feasible or best possible procedure. When, shortly after World War II, the National Institute of Mental Health was authorized to disperse millions of dollars helping academic departments of psychology to upgrade their training programs in clinical psychology, standards obviously had to be established and applied to determine which programs were or were not ready to be approved." However, Dr. Robert Felix, then Director of NIMH took a very consistent and statespersonlike position in this connection: he insisted that psychologists themselves should set up and administer this certification process. Accordingly a special, revolving committee for the evaluation of clinical training programs was established and still operates under the jurisdiction of the American Psychological Association (APA). During or after the period that I was chairperson of this committee, I never heard any complaint about loss of autonomy or co-optation of these programs by NIMH. For better or worse, these programs were fashioned and have functioned according to the best judgment that academic and professional psychologists, acting through the agency of the APA, could bring to bear on the situation.

For what it may be worth, it would be my urgent suggestion that the 300 or so residential drug-rehabilitation facilities now operating in this country act as quickly as possible to establish the capability for the self-discipline and self-regulation with respect to the problem of accreditation and residential drug-rehabilitation programs according to criteria based upon *their own history and experience*, rather than upon considerations derived from other sources which may or may not be entirely relevant to the task at hand. Informed and concerned members of the established mental health professions should, by all means, be invited to participate in this process; but the locus of power and policy should remain essentially indigenous to a committee or commission consisting of facility staff members who are the most competent and most trusted by their colleagues, with special expertise acquired, not by virtue of academic investiture, but by the route which has led to the conception and development of the type of programs and facilities here under consideration.

APPROACHES TO POSITIVE INVOLVEMENT OF PROFESSIONALS

The preceding pages may not seem to bear obvious relevance to the suggested title, "Training Professionals to Work with Mutual-Help Groups;" and this is indeed the case. But relevance they do have, of a significant, albeit subtle, nature. Before one can realistically address the specified topic, it is necessary to appraise the *political* situation as it regards the mental health professions and mutual-help programs and facilities. As has already been pointed out, Robert Felix, a psychiatrist, did not permit his own professional affiliation, or "party," to impede or distort the development of training programs for clinical psychologists in the late 1940s. As far as he and his staff were concerned, the situation remained beautifully apolitical (although a committee of the American Psychiatric Association in 1954 tried strenuously, but unsuccessfully, to grind a political axe at that time).

But the funding, and thereby the ideological and practical control, of residential drug programs has become pervasively politicized in the foregoing sense; and this is why I have been at some pains to suggest at least one way that this situation may be depoliticized. At present, other mutual-help groups are not making large demands for financial support; but it is vitally important at this juncture that professional and nonprofessional forces come to amicable terms, if at all possible, before this problem arises.

Certain other historical, as against political, considerations are also relevant here. It is a common assumption that peer or mutual-help groups have always had grassroots rather than professional origins. However, as Lieberman and Borman (1979) have noted, there has, in fact, been appreciable professional input in the formation and encouragement of several mutual-help groups (See, for example, *Alcoholics Anonymous Comes of Age,* anonymous, 1957; Silverman, 1968; *GROW Comes of Age,* Sprague, 1979). But, as Lieberman and Borman point out, there has been a distinguishing characteristic of many of these professional contributors: they have nearly all become disenchanted with the dominant orthodoxies of their respective fields of specialization and thus are in a more or less refractory frame of mind. Therefore, the first form of "training" which seems to have induced professionals to become interested in mutual-help groups or "the strength in us" (Katz and Bender, 1976) has been professional defection of one kind or another. Professionals were, in short, looking for a better way to help others, at a time when laypeople were trying to find ways of helping themselves.

A related consideration is that sometimes professionals have had to look for a way to get better help *for themselves* than their own specialities provided. There are quite a number of physicians and psychiatrists who are members and staunch supporters of Alcoholics Anonymous for the reason that it, alone, has proved successful in helping them overcome alcoholism, in themselves or in members of their families. I do not happen to know of any psychiatrists, social workers, or clergy who have sought help in residential communities for drug addicts; but I am sure their number is not insignificant. This is another way—perhaps the very best way—in which professionals "get trained" to understand and work with or in mutual-help programs. And professionals may also become interested in Compassionate Friends because of the loss of a beloved child, or in Parents Anonymous because of child abuse.

Sensing that the profession most naturally attuned to the approach of mutual-help groups would be the clergy, this writer in 1961 obtained a generous 5-year grant from the Lilly Endowment, Inc., which made it possible for seminary professors, chaplains, and pastoral counselors to come to the University of Illinois (for varying periods of time) for a combined psychological and theological study of the problem of guilt, and for a *practicum* experience in integrity groups (Mowrer, 1961; 1964; Mowrer et al., 1975; Mowrer, O.H. & Voltano, 1976).

In one sense, the Lilly Fellowship program was a success in that it clarified the congruence between the Judeo-Christian ethic and the ideals and principles upon which mutual-help groups are usually based; and from this program three significant books emerged: *Guilt: Where Psychology and Religion Meet* (Belgum, 1962); *Integrity Groups—A Christian Evaluation to Mental Health* (Drakeford, 1962); and *Competent to Counsel* (Adams, 1970). But neither these nor my own two books seemed to have had much influence in stirring conventional churches to make the small-group experience a part of their total program of worship and service. However, for reasons not entirely clear, mutual-help groups have recently become an integral part of "community" or "covenant churches."

In any case, the immediate result of the Lilly Fellowship program was discouraging, and the writer and some associates instituted an academic graduate course entitled "Seminar and Practicum in Clinical Group Work," (Mowrer, Vattano, Baxley, and Mowrer, 1975), which at first attracted students from clinical psychology and educational counseling, but is now taken chiefly by social workers. We conjecture that during the period that this course has been given, psychotherapists and counselors have had to rely increasingly on private practice for both individual and group therapy (cf. Yalom, 1975) which is at variance with the mutual-help approach; but there has always been a strong emphasis in social work on "helping others help themselves," which provides the basis for much greater compatability. How extensively social workers have established mutual-help groups in the domain of community mental health is not known; but the main impetus in this connection still seems to come from grassroots sources, as it has in the past. Paradoxically, the clergy are now occasionally forming mutual-help, or "share and care," groups for themselves, even though they may not have such groups for their congregations. This may be the way the small group movement is eventually to become established in ecclesiastical contexts. The training in "pastoral counseling" which most clergy have received in seminary has usually not provided either the theory or practice most relevant for the establishment of mutual-help groups; and it may be that the clergy are starting to educate themselves along these lines.

Although textbooks in clinical psychology and psychiatry are beginning to make token reference to mutual-help groups, the latter are still largely neglected; but the small-groups movement is gaining such momentum that it is drawing attention from scholars outside the mental health specialities and in the popular media.

Then there is the sociological, historical, and humanitarian route to professional interest and involvement in the mutual-aid movement. Here we are talking not about mental health professionals exclusively but also professional scholars and researchers, especially in the social sciences. In 1965 Lewis Yablonsky published an excellent book on the first residential drug facility entitled, *Synanon: The Tunnel Back;* and in 1974, Barry Sugarman did an equally competent job in a book called, *Daytop Village: A Therapeutic Community.* Significantly, both of these authors are sociologists. Reference has already been made to the Katz and Bender book and the one by Lieberman and Borman; and others will presently be cited. In passing, mention may be made to Glen Evans's *Guide to Self-Help* (1979). Government has taken its initial cognizance of mutual-aid and natural support groups in the *Report of the President's Joint Commission on Mental Health* (Bryant, 1978); but no provision is suggested here for implementation or funding of the report's recommendations (Vol. I, p. 15). However, the National Institute of Mental Health has authorized and funded the preparation of a booklet entitled *Mutual Help Groups: A Guide for Mental*

Health Workers (1978). The author is Dr. Phyllis R. Silverman, lecturer at the Laboratory of Community Psychiatry, Harvard Medical School. It is instructive to examine the conclusion of this document, which is quoted in full:

> This monograph is a guide for mental health professionals to help them expand their networks and links in the communities in which they work, thereby enhancing the nature of their effectiveness. At the outset, this monograph discussed the need people have for each other—a basic human interdependence. This interdependence affects the nature of human psychological experience and its accompanying problems as well as the complexity of the helping process. The goals of all psychological help are to give people tools which enable them to cope with and alleviate distress they are experiencing. In the service of these aims there are many helpers and many modalities of help.
>
> This monograph focuses on the modality of mutual help, a powerful and constructive means for people to help themselves and each other. This modality is especially effective during periods of critical transition when people must seek a new role definition for themselves in their social network. Through mutual help individuals learn a set of behaviors appropriate to their new role and increase both self-reliance and the ability to take charge of their own lives. Mutual help further enables them to maintain connectedness to their world as they build new links and networks. Mutual help groups represent an opportunity to find new solutions to problems, to enlist new helpers, to utilize the life experience of their members, as well as new collaboration between people in general and with the professional community in particular.
>
> The basic dignity of man is expressed in his capacity to be involved in reciprocal helping relationships. Out of this compassion comes cooperation; only then is it possible to build a community. The quality of life of any individual is affected by the nature and quality of the helping networks or exchanges in which he participates. By facilitating and enhancing these networks it may be possible to prevent or alleviate psychological stress and improve the quality of life in any community (Silverman, 1978, p. 56).

On an earlier page, under the heading of "Why Mental Health Professionals Should be Concerned with Mutual Help Groups," Silverman also says:

> In spite of the obvious tensions that often exist between mutual help organizations and the formal mental health system, the two systems cannot ignore each other. While each system may not arrive at its goals in the same way, each shares the goal of promoting human well-being. Further, both exist in the same communities and often try to reach the

same constituents, sometimes sharing constituents. The purpose of this monograph is to enable the mental health professional to increase his awareness of the wide range of helping modalities in which people participate. In so doing, he can begin to analyze the components of effective help from other systems or networks, available to individuals in times of stress. In the long run, these systems complement rather than compete with each other (Silverman, 1978, p. 9).

One might wish to know how well Dr. Silverman's classes have been received by professional mental health workers. It is hoped that they find many enthusiastic and dedicated members.

An essentially similar orientation is described in the Gartner-Riessman 1977 book, *Self-Help in the Human Services*. Under the heading of "Roles for the Professional," these writers observe:

> The new spreading interest in the self-help approach on the part of professional groups could lead to a positive combination of the aprofessional and the professional. However, there is also the danger that the professional will attempt to dominate and socialize the self-help groups to professional norms, co-opting them and making them appendages of traditional agencies. As Antze (1976) points out, "Whenever outsiders try to support or cooperate with one of these organizations, they run the risk of tampering with its ideology.... Sometimes the mere involvement of a professional can weaken the meaning of certain teachings (for example 'Only a drunk can help another drunk'). Matters become worse if the observer should point out that a given belief runs against medical knowledge, or if he counsels changes to increase the group's acceptance in professional circles. If the view developed here has been valid, then meddling of this kind woud do real harm to the therapeutic process." The professional orientation, however, can also lead to concern for systematic evaluation and increased accountability. Evaluation could improve the outreach approaches of the self-help groups, so that they would attract individuals currently not drawn to them (p. 128).

A Venture in Reciprocal Education — The Eagleville Model

Both of the books just quoted, along with several others previously cited, certainly represent attempts to *educate* mental-health professionals as to the nature and potential of mutual-help groups. But something more is obviously needed if they are going to be "trained" to participate harmoniously and effectively as staff members in therapeutic communities, such as those available to alcoholics or drug addicts, or to be maximally helpful to nonresidential mutual-help groups. An individual who is unusually well-prepared to speak with respect to this problem, both from the theoretical and practical standpoint, is psychiatrist Donald J. Ottenberg, Director of the Eagleville Hospital and Rehabilitation Center, in Eagleville, Pennsylvania. The following quotations are from a 1977 paper entitled, "Traditional and Nontraditional Credentials in Addictive Problems—A Dispatch from the Battlefield."

> The first assumption is that having been an addict or alcoholic necessarily equips one to be an effective counselor or therapist in this field. I think that most experienced workers, including recovered alcoholics and addicts, probably would agree that some people aren't suited to this type of work, even though they have had the experience of personal recovery from addiction. And yet, very little has been said about how to select candidates appropriate for work in this field. . . .
>
> Another assumption is that having an earned degree, say a master's degree in psychology or a master's in social work, necessarily qualifies a person to work with addicts or alcoholics. Here, a tricky word, "qualifies," can have two meanings. My degree may satisfy a bureaucratic office, perhaps the State Civil Service system, that I am qualified to be a counselor or therapist, but, looked at carefully, the academic degree is no more certain proof of my ability to work effectively with addicted people than was the mere fact of being a recovered addict or alcoholic. In both cases a true test of my competence in the field of work has not been applied. . . . The usual training of physicians has not included sufficient education for this type of work, and many physicians seem attitudinally unsuited (Ottenberg, 1977a, p. 56).

Early on, Ottenberg takes the position that in the working situation of an actual facility, the "training" has to be reciprocal, mutual, and interactive. The indigenous staff worker is not uneducated, it is rather that he or she had a different kind of education and done a different kind of "research" from that required for academic or professional degrees. Typically, Ottenberg notes, the indigenous worker who is coupled with a professional is likely to say:

> "I don't begrudge him the opportunity to learn these things from me, but I do question why you say that he is training me, when I am training him just as much, if not more."
>
> It isn't so easy to contradict a statement like that, because it contains much that is true. We may have to revise our concept of what goes on in so-called training relationships. . . . As radical as the idea may seem, perhaps some kinds of training must always be a two directional interaction, with both participants understanding from the outset that both are trainers and both trainees.

If this idea has merit, I merely ask the question: In the revised relationship, where both parties train and both are trained, will they be paid equally?

This carries us to another asumption demanding careful, yet courageous, examination. It has to do with money, in many places spelled e-g-o, so we know in advance we will have difficulty with it.

We want to be a truly interdisciplinary program, and keeping all recovered nondegreed staff at the same level and degreed staff at other levels tends to perpetuate elitism based on academic credentials which is the very inequality we are trying to escape from.

So far I have heard a good deal of rhetoric and many angry charges based on stereotyped accusations. We still await a reasonable statement that begins to address in an honest and courageous fashion the true advantages, disadvantages, potentialities and limitations of both degreed and nondegreed professionals and which begins to work out mechanisms for assessing competence and assigning value to competence without regard to the way in which the competence was achieved.

Although it is hard to hear the truth when people are wildly shouting, anyone familiar with the arguments on both sides may believe, as I do, that there is some truth in what is being said in both camps (p. 62).

We can agree, I would hope, that neither side has a monopoly on knowledge and wisdom, however obtained, and neither on sensitivity, empathy, compassion, or the necessary generosity and courage to make these commendable human traits useful to other people.

Can we, also agree that it is foolish to think that people learn nothing in schools—or to take the corollary, that the only way to become educated is on the street? . . .

My plea is for a reasonable, rational and generous approach to understanding and alleviating a difficult and painful issue. I hope we can begin today (Ottenberg, 1977a).

In a succession of other provocative and cogent papers, Ottenberg (1974b; 1976a; 1976b; 1977a; 1977b; 1978a; 1978b;) continues to balance theoretical and practical considerations, and arrives at two provisions for dealing with the question of how both professionals and nonprofessionals can get the kinds of training that seems likely to make them, in their own special ways, optimally useful and mutually amicable in the setting of a therapeutic community.

For the indigenous, and often academically unschooled worker, Ottenberg and his staff have established a master's degree program jointly designed and administerd by Lincoln University and the Eagleville rehabilitation facility to lessen the discrepancy in the area of formal education between indigenous and conventionally trained workers; the latter have been encouraged to become involved in the program, as learners as well as teachers. Professionals who are able to make this transition gain certain human qualities and commitments which make it much less necessary for them to "pull rank," as they might originally have been inclined to do, without this in-service type of experience.

The lesson that has emerged from the Eagleville experience would seem to be that professionals cannot be "trained" to function with maximal effectiveness and satisfaction in (or outside of) therapeutic communities in which the mutual-help principle is emphasized unless an effort is also made to improve the academic and professional sophistication of the indigenous staff members. In other words, it looks as if a new amalgam or alloy of knowledge and skills is being forged which may soon be recognized as a new, specialized type of profession. This, as we have seen, is not without difficulties and dangers; but as of this point in time it seems to be the most promising and constructive alternative available.

EPILOGUE

In the *APA Monitor* December 1979, an article entitled "Made for Each Other," by Ian McNett presented an exciting and highly informative joint interview with Frank Riessman and Alan Gartner on the thesis that "mental health pros and self-help groups could be a perfect match." This supposition is elaborated thus:

> Two pioneer activists in the self-help movement currently are using the seeming collision of lay and professional interests to articulate a new notion of helping, and possibly, to design a new approach to service delivery that would strengthen and capitalize on the strengths of both camps.... Gartner and Riessman are currently establishing an "urban brokerage" to bring together self-help groups and professionals to help them learn from each other (McNett, 1979, p. 6).
>
> So one of the ways that the formal health care system, if it wants to assure its survival, can deal with the question of unserved people is to try to use itself more efficiently and effectively. Reaching out to enlist people who can do certain parts of the activity is an important part of a strategy for the human service system to increase its own areas of responsibility.....
>
> Indeed, Riessman and Gartner argue strongly that self-help groups and professionals need each other. They contend that cooperation enhances the effectiveness of both, in most cases. "The professionals know they're under attack," says Riessman. "They know they have to expand the resources and the energy in the system. I think the professionals are burned out. Self-help groups are not burned out. There's a lot of energy and a lot of wanting to do something, of wanting to help. They get a kick out of helping (McNett, 1979, p. 7).

But the full significance and impact of this article can be experienced only by reading it in its entirety. So far as the writer is aware, this is the first time the small groups movement has received major attention in any APA publication.

That the mutual-help phenomenon is receiving serious consideration in at least certain university departments of psychology is indicated by an announcement from the Interpersonal Process Research Group, Department of Psychology, UCLA, with a covering letter dated August 6, 1979. It reads, in part, as follows:

> We've developed a program which works within existing self-help traditions to make people better at sharing and listening without violating the ground rules of an ongoing program. Our programmed series of audiotapes are a breakthrough for teaching major communication tools. They are a clear complement to a self-help group's need for individual responsibility, strong helping skills, and acceptance of others without judgment (Burstein, 1979, p. 1).

The complete announcement is well worth reading, and reflects a growing interest which probably exists on other campuses but has not yet become widely recognized.

A manuscript which this author has recently been asked to evaluate for possible journal publication, entitled "Multi-Modal Behavior Therapy: Use of Professional and Paraprofessional Resources" (Anonymous, 1979), speaks of "the unique contribution of the paraprofessionals working in the real-world setting on a variety of social-skills problems." (p. 3). A "case study" is then presented in which a "paraprofessional" (volunteer) helps another young man, after prolonged hospitalization, to learn to "get around:" order a meal, use the subway, etc. This paper begins with the following summary paragraph:

> Recent developments in behavior therapy include the realization that comprehensive treatment necessarily extends into the client's social and cognitive environment. The multimodal behavior therapy approach (Lazarus, 1976) emphasizes that the generalization and longevity of a particular therapeutic intervention is partially dependent on the degree to which that approach covers major modalities of the person's functioning (p. 1).

A striking description of constructive interaction between a mental health professional and paraprofessional.

Gartner & Riessman (1979) have published a brief piece entitled "Professional Involvement in Self-Help Groups," which begins:

> Continuing our interest in the nature and extent of professional involvement in self-help groups, in this issue we deal with the referral function that professionals can fill. Although we are treating this role as if it exists as a separate entity, it is important to remember that the different roles played by professionals often may (and most often do) overlap (p. 4).

Although not categorized as such, this is manifestly a modest attempt to instruct or "train" mental health professionals.

Since helplessness, isolation, and loneliness are common motivations for the formation of mutual-aid groups, it is not without significance to note a recent article by Kureshi and Dutt (1979) from Japan, entitled "Dimensions of Alienation—A Factor-Analytic Study," which notes: "Alienation is among the foremost problems of our age. . . . alienation was found not to be a unitary phenomenon. However, it carries a negative affect, designated as the 'alienation syndrome'" (p. 99).

Here is another contribution serving to link academic psychology with the small-group movement.

In *Community Mental Health Journal* (Summer 1979), there appears an article entitled "Social Support and Social Adjustment Implications for Mental Health," by Froland, Brodsky, Olson, and Stewart. Two sentences of the article's Abstract amplify the meaning of the title:

> The general importance of an individual's support network has been recognized in the field of community mental health; yet a more detailed understanding of how a client's available social ties may contribute to his or her adjustment is presently lacking. This study used network analysis to examine differences in the social networks of mental health clients to identify factors associated with positive social adjustment (p. 82).

Here again is an indication that conceptual frameworks and research are developing in academic circles that can provide a bridge to the operation and effects of mutual-aid groups.

Since most of the studies cited, while important, have nevertheless been chiefly dialectic, programmatic, admonitory, or empirical to only a very limited extent, it is something of a landmark to discover a more systematic investigation in the area here under scrutiny. The *Journal of Clinical Child Psychology,* (Summer 1979), carries an article entitled: "Enhancing Primary Prevention: The Marriage of Self-Help and Formal Health Care Delivery Systems," by Hermalin, Melendez, Kamarck, Klevans, Fallen, and Gordon (1979). The authors report, in part:

This is the first known study to have examined responses from clinical staff workers regarding participation with self-help groups. The survey results present a comprehensive portrait of the current role of such groups in a community-based mental health system. The results can be useful in mapping out a strategy of increased interaction between these two major sources of community support.

Of particular importance are two findings: (1) that 88 percent of the clinicians surveyed endorsed the involvement of the CMH/MR center with self-help groups; and (2) 61 percent indicated an interest in working with self-help groups (7 percent of the sample did not respond to this question). These figures represent much higher percentages than the study team had expected. The implication is that (a) clinicians recognize the valuable contribution to be made by self-help groups; and (b) they are desirous of participating in such joint programs (p. 129).

Additional references and discussion which are less current but still relevant to this paper can be found in Mowrer (1976), Mowrer(1979), and Mowrer and Vattano (1976).

The following brief statement, made by Jack R. Beebe as testimony at the Illinois/White House Conference, held December 4, 1979, in Champaign, Illinois, provides an appropriate note for the ending of this paper. Speaking both as a Department of Mental Health administrator and as the sponsor of a local mutual-help group, he said:

To those people who do planning for future services, and to those who decide where to use money, I ask you to keep community support groups in mind, and create ways that small amounts of funds can be channeled to these groups now, where you get a high return for the dollar. To the rest of you, I encourage you to ask yourself how you can start such a group now, in your church, school, apartment complex, or club, and begin making a difference today.

SUMMARY

For several decades after the beginning of the small-groups movement early in this century, there was relatively little interaction between them and the mental-health professions. But now that mutual-help groups have markedly increased in both membership and diversity, and because of changing circumstances in the professions, the two approaches to "problems of living" have become increasingly aware of each other and more interactive. However, as yet, there is not a complete concensus concerning the optimal nature of this interaction.

In the foregoing pages various facets of this situation are considered; and, despite some tendency toward control or even co-optation of mutual help groups by one or more of the professions, there are many signs of growing cooperation, even synthesis. This is occuring on the premise that a certain amount of reciprocal education or "training" is often helpful, without, however, any impairment of the specialized functions which professionals and indigenous workers are, respectively, able to render. In some instances, this mutual education and collaboration is reaching the point that the capabilities of both types of participants are becoming so similar that an alloy, or new type of specialist, in the field of the "human services" seems to be emerging.

Part III

EVALUATION AND ASSESSMENT

Chapter 12

ISSUES IN RESEARCH
AND EVALUATION

Leon H. Levy

The psychologists who elects to do research on self-help groups may find a disconcerting juxtaposition of the familiar with the uncharted, even the alien. This opening observation is not offered so much out of concern for the psychologist's mental health as it is to highlight many of the important issues presented by research with self-help groups. How psychologists come to terms with these issues may well determine the value of their study for our understanding of self-help groups and the role that they might play in mental-health delivery.

Viewing self-help groups as modalities for the alleviation of human distress, we immediately recognize the applicability of the process-outcome distinction, generally proven serviceable in structuring psychotherapy research. And with this distinction, we find ourselves on familiar ground in recognizing the methodological issues with which we shall have to be concerned—the reliability of our coding and measurement schemes in process research; the internal validity of the treatments that define the experimental groups; and all the other threats to the validity and generalizability of our findings that have dogged the efforts of psychotherapy researchers. All these issues are as important in the study of self-help groups as they are in psychotherapy research. If they have not yet been satisfactorily resolved by psychotherapy researchers, at least they have generated an extensive literature to which the self-help group researcher may turn for precedents and guidance—and this will be found reassuring, at least in the short run. For, as I shall elaborate, the complexity of each of these issues increases by several orders of magnitude in the study of self-help groups, and it is urgent that this be appreciated by investigators in this area.

But then there is also the unfamiliar with which the self-help group researcher must deal. Self-help group members serve as both providers of help and recipients of help, and in many instances they may be functioning in both roles at the same time. The context within which research on self-help groups takes place is, in most cases, quite different from the organized, professional-care settings in which psychotherapy research is conducted: instead of the clinic or hospital setting, self-help group researchers find themselves in living rooms, church basements, school classrooms, and lodge halls, as well as, occasionally, rooms provided by mental health and other community agencies. Unlike professional psychotherapists, self-help group members rarely share the researcher's commitment to the value of research or the evaluation of their effectiveness.

And, lastly, research findings, especially those permitting some evaluation of the effectiveness of self-help groups, are as likely to be valued for their social and political implications as for their scientific and clinical contributions. In addition to their therapeutic role, self-help groups have also been taken by many writers as evidence of attempts to remedy one or another defect in modern society (Gartner and Riessman, 1977; Killilea, 1976). In short, the world into which the psychologist enters in deciding to study self-help groups is the hurly-burly of modern society, unconstrained by either a common purpose, a shared agenda, or a consensual value system. Thus, the demands placed upon the psychologist's adventuresomeness, flexibility, ingenuity, and integrity are probably among the most challenging that one might encounter in psychological research. But the potential rewards, in personal intellectual growth, contributions to scientific knowledge, and the welfare of society, are no less great.

In this chapter, I should like to discuss a number of research issues confronting workers in this area. I shall be drawing largely upon the experience of my associates and myself in our investigation of over 20 different self-help groups (Knight, Wollert, Levy, Frame, and Padgett, 1980; Levy, 1976; Levy, 1978; Levy, 1979; Wollert, Knight, and Levy, 1980), as well as that of others (Lieberman and Bond, 1976; 1978) who have also conducted empirical studies of self-help groups. My purpose is not prescriptive; that would be both a presumption and a disservice at this early stage of research on self-help groups. Rather, it is to alert prospective researchers to the range of research issues involved in the study of self-help groups, and to share a perspective that I believe will be helpful in dealing with them.

Before proceeding with a discussion of these issues, however, I believe that it is essential that we discuss certain political considerations which both the literature and the research on self-help groups make particularly salient, for they serve as an appropriate backdrop against which to view the research issues raised by self-help groups and the consequences of alternative approaches to their resolution.

POLITICAL CONSIDERATIONS

The myth of a value-free behavioral science has been pretty much dissipated. The implications of our deprivation of this myth are, however, still unclear, and undoubtedly will vary in effect depending upon the problem under study. But it certainly seems obvious that researchers whose findings are likely to exert an impact upon social policy and fiscal decision making must become as politically astute as they are scientifically sophisticated. For they are not only vulnerable to charges of personal bias—charges as impossible to disprove as the null hypothesis is to prove—but they also bear some responsibility for the political consequences of their research. Thus, evaluation researchers have grown increasingly aware of the political dimensions of their research (Anderson and Ball, 1978; Weiss, 1975), and I would argue that self-help group research must similarly be seen as falling toward the politically sensitive end of the behavioral science research spectrum.

Three different, but interrelated, foci of the potential political impact of self-help group research may be readily identified. Each of these foci, in turn, may be seen as a potential source of bias, either on the part of researchers themselves, or in the interpretation of their findings by others.

1. *The established helping professions.* Research on both the effectiveness of self-help groups and on the processes by which they achieve their effects has the potential for altering our conceptions of the nature of psychopathology and human distress, and the means by which they are best treated. Consequently, such research has the potential for altering the status of the helping professions, their role in the mental-health delivery system, and, perhaps most importantly, their economic well-being. Self-help groups tend not to be overawed by the claims of professionals to special expertise. If research findings could be interpreted as justifying these views, the consequences could be revolutionary.

2. *The mental health delivery system—its structure and funding.* Self-help groups are not a formal part of our mental health delivery system, although isolated instances can be found in which care-giving agencies sponsor self-help groups or otherwise cooperate with them. Moreover, in their totality, the intervention goals of self-help groups tend to be more comprehensive than those of our current mental health delivery

system. The efforts of the current system are directed almost entirely toward secondary and tertiary prevention (Caplan, 1964), while many self-help groups, such as Parents Without Partners and Compassionate Friends, serve a primary prevention function as well. Thus, should research support self-help groups as an effective modality of mental health delivery this would call for a restructuring of the mental health delivery system so as to maximize the role of self-help. And assuming a steady state in the level of funding for mental health—probably a most optimistic assumption —such restructuring could pose a drastic financial threat to existing human services agencies, both tax supported and eleemosynary.

3. *The public at large.* We live in an era of greater questioning of traditions and credentials as grounds for entitlement and access to power and status. This spirit is well represented in the self-help literature by such authors as Gartner and Riessman (1977), Hurvitz (1974), and Vattano (1972). Although much of this literature lacks sound empirical undergirding, should research on self-help groups yield findings compatible with this ethos, its impact is likely to extend far beyond the mental health arena in challenging many of the fundamental assumptions upon which the structure of all professions rests in our society.

Lest readers consider these idle speculations, I would suggest that they be considered in the light of a recent review of 42 studies comparing the clinical effectiveness of professional and paraprofessional helpers, dealing with a fairly wide variety of problems (Durlak, 1979). Among these studies, only one could be found in which professionals were significantly superior, no significant differences between professionals and paraprofessionals were found in 28 studies, and in 12 studies paraprofessionals were significantly more effective than professionals. Not surprisingly, these findings led the author to conclude that "professional mental health education, training, and experience are not necessary prerequisites for an effective helping person " (p. 89). Although studies are yet to be conducted comparing self-help groups and professionals, it would be surprising if their results turned out very differently, and I would propose that no matter how carefully they are labeled with the appropriate scientific caveats, they cannot help but have some impact upon the areas identified. Thus, those who would conduct this research bear a heavy burden: how they conduct and report their research could have profound social and political consequences.

Two Objectives of Research on Self-Help Groups

Research on self-help groups may contribute to either of two objectives:

1. The production of scientific knowledge about the nature of therapeutic processes, social support systems, and small groups, and
2. Program development and evaluation.

Conceivably, the same program of research might contribute to both
objectives (Anderson and Ball, 1978), although, in most instances, the
primary aim of the research (including its funding) will focus on one or the
other of these objectives. Thus, although the pursuit of both objectives involves many research issues in common, we will discuss those that are
specific to each objective first, and then consider those issues common to
both objectives.

The Production of Scientific Knowledge

Self-help groups have much to recommend them as sources of information about the nature of therapeutic processes, social support
systems, and small groups. Although many are governed by quite strict
policies and procedures—e.g., Recovery, Inc., and Alcoholics Anonymous—all groups are characterized by a pragmatic attitude toward their
operation. What we observe in these groups therefore is more likely to reflect what they have found to be effective than is the case with professionals
whose identities and credentials often are as much testimony to their
mastery of the conventional wisdom of their professions as to their effectiveness as service providers. Thus, by observing the operation of self-help
groups, we have a unique opportunity to gain insight into the natural
psychotherapeutic processes of everyday life (Bergin and Lambert, 1978),
which, in turn, holds the promise of increasing the effectiveness of all therapeutic modalities; as well as for our understanding of how humans attempt
to help each other cope with the stresses of everyday life.

Two distinctions have proven helpful in pursuing this objective. The
first is between *procedures and processes,* recently elaborated by Bandura
(1977) and by Mahoney and Kazden (1979). Processes are the inferred
mechanisms by which change is brought about; procedures are the observ-
able activities engaged in by groups which are assumed to subserve the
operation of one or more process. In the groups we studied (Levy, 1979),
we were able to identify four behaviorally oriented processes and seven
cognitively oriented processes and a total of 28 procedures. The procedures
were identified on the basis of our observations of a number of groups and
our review of the self-help group literature, while the processes were inferred from our observations, guided by the question of how we could account for the changes, either observed or claimed, in self-help group
members on the basis of what we had observed.

Although we did not approach our task as naive observers, we took the
attitude that if we were to discover anything new our best chance was to

begin our study of these groups as unfettered as possible by preconceptions as to appropriate categories of observation, procedures we expected to observe, or processes that must be operating if the groups were at all effective. In this approach, we found little guidance from conventional texts on methodology in psychological research, and found ourselves relying on the methods of qualitative sociology as expounded by Glaser and Strauss (1967). At this stage of our research we were operating within the *context of discovery* (Reichenbach, 1938): one which fosters an openness to experience and speculation, which I believe is essential if researchers are to do more than tinker with and solidify the conventional wisdom, whether in connection with self-help groups or other phenomena. For my colleagues and myself, this was a most liberating and exhilarating experience.

The second distinction that we have found of value, is one proposed by Argyris (1976) between *espoused theories* and *theories-in-use*. Although Argyris proposed this distinction in the context of adult learning and leadership training, we believe that it has much wider applicability. The Twelve Steps of A.A., and Recovery, Inc.'s *Mental Health Through Will Training* (Low, 1952), as well as what group members tell us they believe about their afflictions and the means by which their groups help them, are all instances of espoused theories. The correspondence between these groups' espoused theories and their theories-in-use, which we infer from our observations, may vary considerably and is worthy of study in its own right. Espoused theories undoubtedly play an important role in the functioning of self-help groups. These theories may be gleaned from their literature as well as from interviews with their members; they represent the group's ideology (Antze, 1979). But it would be a mistake to use them as the sole basis for inferring the processes that actually operate in these groups or the procedures used by them. Without direct observations of self-help groups, we may learn only what they believe, but not what they do or what processes account for their effectiveness.

Data acquisition poses the major problem in pursuing this objective. In our experience, self-help groups would not allow either tape recordings or note-taking at their meetings—not due to concerns about confidentiality, but because they felt that these activities would make their members self-conscious and interfere with their spontaneity. Our solution, in most instances, was to have two observers present at each meeting and to have them prepare narrative reports of the meeting immediately after leaving it—preparing the reports separately and then reconciling discrepancies. These reports were in two sections: the first (and longer) part was pure narrative description, while the second contained each observer's interpretations and speculations about what was happening at the meeting.

In this way, we attempted to reduce observational error to a minimum, stay as close as possible to the phenomena themselves, and maintain a clear distinction between observations and inferences.

Nothing precluded our observers completing rating scales after they had left the group meetings. We believed, however, that the time for developing such scales and other measuring instruments came after our qualitative analyses. It is my hope that our initial formulations of the procedures and processes found in self-help groups may now provide the necessary basis for such scales. To have developed rating scales and checklists at the start would only have served to confirm or disconfirm our hypotheses; it would have done little to foster the generation of new insights and hypotheses, one of our prime reasons for studying self-help groups.

Many of the phenomena of self-help groups are of interest to social psychologists as well as to mental-health professionals. These groups vary in their structure, manner of conducting meetings, the quality of their social interaction, and their longevity. Thus, they also lend themselves to studies of group development and leadership. However, the problems involved in testing hypotheses concerned with these and other phenomena, including factors involved in the differential effectiveness of groups as change agents are complex. Given the fact that we are only able to study these groups at their sufferance, and that any attempt to manipulate them experimentally might well destroy the very qualities of the phenomena in which we are interested, it would appear that well controlled, rigorous, experimental studies are virtually impossible.

The idea of sponsoring groups ourselves was considered, on the assumption that in this way we could build in stipulations concerning their participation in our research. But, again, the question would always be present as to whether these groups were comparable to those that arise "naturally." And while this question cannot be answered at present, it does suggest a much-needed line of research: studies of the natural history of the development of self-help groups. Methodologically, such studies would borrow much from enthnography, would obviously be longitudinal, and would be costly. But their informational yield can be expected to repay their cost: they would provide us with general social psychological knowledge of group and leadership development, and they would provide knowledge that would have direct applicability for programs attempting to foster the development of self-help groups.

It is also possible to test specific hypotheses generated through the study of self-help groups in the laboratory. For example, in one case, we investigated the role of self-disclosure in fostering group cohesiveness by settng up a number of *ad hoc* small groups in our lab and attempted to vary the amount of self-disclosure engaged in by the different groups. In another case, we attempted to investigate some of the elements thought to be involved in Riessman's "helper therapy principle" (1965). More specifically, we were interested in the relative contributions to enhanced self-esteem of having played the helper role as compared with having been effective in helping another person. This was investigated with a dyadic situation in which the feedback "helpers" received from the experimenter about how well they had learned to act as helpers, and from their "clients" about how well they had actually helped them, were both manipulated.

Although the experiment was inadvertently flawed in certain respects, thus requiring that it be replicated before submission for publication, its results suggested that role performance was more significant in enhancing self-esteem than having actually been helpful. I cite these two examples in order to whet the reader's enthusiasm for the research possibilities in this area, ánd to illustrate the feasibility of a mixed research strategy, combining the virtues of field observation and qualitative analysis with those of experimental manipulation and rigorous, quantitative analysis.

Our discussion of the problems of data acquisition would not be complete without warning potential investigators of the lure of questionnaires and survey-research methodology. Self-help groups are frequently small in size, the number of groups concerned with a particular problem in any given community is likely to be limited, and the time consumed in individual interviews and attendance at meetings is enormous. Thùs data on a sample of any respectable size will not be easily accumulated unless one turns to a survey approach. We did so at one stage in our own research (Knight, Wollert, Levy, Frome, and Padgett, 1980; Levy, 1978; 1979); Lieberman and Bond (1976) did so in their study of consciousness-raising groups. In addition to its efficiency in data collection and increasing sample size, the use of questionnaires is important in facilitating standardization and susceptibility to sophisticated data analysis. Questionnaires are certainly a valuable research tool, but in investigations intended to generate new knowledge, researchers must beware of introducing them too early in their studies lest they limit this knowledge to [only] that which their *a priori* assumptions and concepts allow to filter through.

There are a number of factors of which researchers must beware which threaten the generalizability, or external validity, of research findings with self-help groups. Because of the seriousness of these threats and because they must be taken into consideration, regardless of the given research objective, they will be discussed in a separate section, following our consideration of research issues associated with program development and evaluation.

Program Development and Evaluation

Evaluation of the effectiveness of self-help groups is as important to the pursuit of scientific knowledge about their functioning as it is for assessing their contribution to mental health delivery. Testimonials to their effectiveness range all the way from their role in mitigating the effects of circumscribed crises such as widowhood (Silverman, MacKenzie, Pettipas, and Wilson, 1975) to their serving as the vanguard of the revitalization of human and spiritual values, possibly representing the "emerging 'church' of the 21st Century" (Mowrer, 1971). But scientific evidence of their effectiveness is largely lacking—and for a number of very good reasons:

1. Few self-help groups have had any doubts about their effectiveness or find any need either to conduct, or to collaborate in, an evaluation of their effectiveness. When self-help group members are asked about dropouts and apparent "failures," their replies are not unlike those one might get when the same question is put to professionals: persons who drop out or do not seem to benefit from the group simply are not ready for what the group has to offer.

2. Until very recently, self-help groups have operated completely outside the established system of care delivery and have, therefore, not had to deal with the issue of accountability.

3. Self-help groups have only recently become recognized as a challenging and fruitful area for research.

4. The problems of doing outcome research with self-help groups are considerably more severe and complex than those involved in psychotherapy outcome research, so that under the best of circumstances few researchers are likely to have the resources to conduct rigorous, empirically grounded evaluations of their effectiveness. But even to make this statement is to oversimplify the question of evaluation of self-help groups since it implies that it is no *different* from outcome research in the case of psychotherapy, only more *difficult*. I believe that the validity of this view is questionable, for reasons shortly to be presented.

5. The difficulty in defining the criteria by which to evaluate self-help groups is again more formidable than in the case of psychotherapy. Lieberman and Bond (1978) have recently presented a thoughtful discussion of this, as well as other problems in measuring outcomes with self-help groups. Drawing upon a tripartite model of outcome measurement in psychotherapy proposed by Strupp and Hadley (1977), they argue for a multiple-criteria approach, reflecting the perspectives

of self-help group members, the self-help group itself—whose goals may only partially coincide with those of its members—and the researcher, whose values and criteria for effectiveness are more likely to reflect the perspective of his/her professional affiliation and/or the organization sponsoring the research, and may only partially overlap with either of the two perspectives. While Lieberman and Bond's discussion of criterion selection and the problems of outcome measurement is cogent, it still appears to regard evaluation of self-help groups as analogous to that of psychotherapy. And it fails to appreciate the systemic character of self-help groups, and the many other functions that evaluation might perform when these groups are viewed from a general systems theory perspective.

The adoption of a general systems perspective (Auerswald, 1969; Miller, 1955; von Bertalanffy, 1968) leads naturally to regarding self-help groups as component systems functioning within a larger system—either the mental health system or the social system, depending upon how broad a view one wishes to take. Two of the important characteristics of systems is that their components are interdependent—alterations in the functioning of one component affects the functioning of other components—and their functioning is governed by feedback loops through which information about the state of the system vis-a-vis the achievement of some goal or desired state leads to modifications of its functioning. Translated into terms applicable to our concerns about self-help groups, this would seem to argue that we think of *program* evaluation, in its broadest sense, rather than simply outcome evaluation. Each self-help group may be viewed as following a particular program of intervention (process research may be seen, in part, as an attempt to articulate this program) while at the same time the functioning of this group may be regarded as a component within a broader program of intervention or mental-health delivery. From this point of view, the effectiveness of a particular self-help group cannot be meaningfully studied apart from a consideration of the social and institutional context within which it operates.

The Distinction Between Summative and Formative Evaluation

This distinction, introduced by Scriven (1967), has gained widespread acceptance among program evaluators, and seems particularly apt in considering evaluation issues involved with self-help groups. Summative evaluation provides an assessment of the overall effectiveness of a particular program at some set point in time. Most outcome studies of psychotherapy, and the assessment of outcomes of self-help groups as Lieberman and Bond discussed it, are instances of summative evaluation—as were assessments of Head Start and many other social programs. From a general-systems perspective, summative evaluations provide assessments of how well the system is functioning in achieving its purposes, whether measured by success rates, cost-effectiveness criteria, or any other accepted measurement of achievement. Summative evaluation can also provide the basis for choices between systems as a means of achieving a particular goal or set of goals. But the validity of such evaluations and choices is always recognized as potentially limited to the ecology of the particular group(s) being considered.

Formative evaluation is intended to provide assessment data which will aid in the development and improvement of programs, and represents a dynamic view of the assessment process. From a general systems perspective, formative evaluation may be conceived of as the feedback loop by which the system monitors and improves its functioning. This kind of evaluation can lead to modifications in the relationships between particular program components—for example, how resources are shared between two mental health agencies, or the role played by an agency in sponsoring a self-help group—or it could lead to modifications in how a particular self-help group operates. The latter is exemplified in our research team's consultation with a chapter of Make Today Count, which had been part of our study but which also asked us for help in improving the quality of their meetings and increasing their membership (Wollert, Knight, and Levy, 1980.

Drawing upon our observations of their meetings and the knowledge gained from study of other groups, we developed a brief handbook in collaboration with the chapter's leaders. This included suggestions intended to increase the involvement of all members in the conduct of their meetings, methods for avoiding quarrels between members, ways of facilitating self-disclosure, and a recommendation that they increase the frequency of their meetings. Although we did not conduct a formal evaluation of our intervention, several sources of evidence—reports by members of increased satisfaction with meetings, increased frequency of meetings, a feature story on the group in the local newspaper, and the chapter's reputation within the national Make Today Count organization as one of its more effective chapters—suggest that it was effective. I would argue that it may also be taken as an example of formative evaluation at its best: it led to a number of changes in how the group operated and it also allowed us to test, informally, several hypotheses we had developed about the elements necessary for effective self-help group functioning.

It is in program development and evaluation that the political considerations discussed earlier are most likely to be engaged. And for this reason, I believe that the more differentiated view of evaluation represented by the summative-formative distinction must be clearly articulated, both in our communication with self-help groups and with the readers (and sponsors) of our research. For it is summative evaluation that most people think of, and it is summative evaluation which is likely to be the most threatening, personally and politically. Yet, it is also summative evaluation which is the more difficult to carry off, both technically and socially. More importantly, I would argue that summative evaluation should not be undertaken until program development—either at the self-help group level or at a higher systems level—has had sufficient opportunity to benefit from formative evaluation. To do otherwise, seems certain to bias the outcome in favor of abortion of the system.

Specific Research Issues

Without doubt, the development of appropriate criteria is the most fundamental issue, whether the concern is with summative or formative evaluation. What is "appropriate" will, of course, vary with the kind of evaluation undertaken, but it must also, always, take into consideration the goals and values of the participants if they are to accept and act upon its outcome. Here, I would refer the reader to Lieberman and Bond's (1978) discussion of the criterion problem, but wish also to suggest a methodology which allows for the systematic application of the multiperspective approach to criterion definition that they advocated. This is the use of goal-attainment scaling (GAS), developed by Kiresuk and Sherman (1968) and more recently elaborated by Kiresuk and Lund (1978).

Originally developed in order to provide a systematic approach to program evaluation within a community mental health center, GAS consists, in essence, of defining for each patient several treatment goals based upon the patient's needs; constructing five-point rating scales for each of these goals as a means of determining the extent to which each was realized at some specified future point in time; differentially weighting the scales in terms of the values attached to the achievement of each of the goals by the patient; and, then, at the specified time, determining the extent to which each goal was attained, multiplying each scale score by its appropriate weight, and computing a single index based upon these weighted scale scores. The points on each of the scales are defined by concrete behavioral outcomes, with the midpoint representing the most probable outcome, one end point the probable outcome under the most favorable circumstances, and other the probable outcome under the least favorable circumstance.

The GAS method has a number of virtues: it is flexible and allows for a combination of both ideographic and nomothetic perspectives—the various scales can just as easily represent program goals from several different perspectives, such as those of the individual, the self-help group, and a sponsoring agency. It encourages collaboration and negotiation between all parties having an interest in the evaluation, requiring them to make explicit the goals they seek and the values they place upon their attainment. And it fosters a more differentiated analysis of the functioning of a program, allowing one to identify those goals for which it is most effective and those for which further program development or modification is necessary. Thus, a GAS approach to criterion development lends itself equally well to both summative and formative evaluation.

Summative evaluation raises the issue of research design and confronts us immediately with the impossibility of the use of true experimental designs, except under circumstances so extraordinary that they would impost severe limits on the external validity of our findings. Random assignment of individuals to self-help and control groups would only be possible under circumstances in which the investigator was able to control entry into the groups, something which violates one of the most fundamental characteristics of self-help groups. Thus, if our interest is in summative evaluation, it is evident that we must choose a quasi-experimental approach, the most useful of which is likely to entail a long-term longitudinal study of one or more groups, possibly making use of an interrupted time series design (Cook and Campbell, 1979). To insure its acceptance by self-help groups, this approach requires that they be brought into the planning of the investigation as full participants, since it will require the continuing presence at group meetings of members of the research team and the periodic administration of assessment instruments.

Although expensive, longitudinal studies may be the only feasible approach to the assessment of self-help groups, whether for summative or formative evaluation, short of survey-research methods. This is because, as these groups normally operate, they do not keep records of their membership or their attendance. Thus only through longitudinal studies would investigators be able to estimate attrition rates or track changes in group functioning as a result of feedback or the occurrence of other events. A longitudinal approach would also allow investigators to identify dropouts and other "casualties" of these groups who would not otherwise be available for study. In short, self-help groups do not generate the archival data normally produced by professional caregivers. Therefore investigators requiring such data have no alternative but to produce it themselves through a longitudinal study.

Formative evaluation is likely to grow in importance for self-help groups. As the federal government, state, and local agencies begin to take cognizance of their potential as mental-health resources, and as various human services agencies and individual professional care givers begin to explore ways in which they can work with these groups, a whole raft of organizational and programmatic questions may be expected to emerge which can only be adequately answered by systematic research. These questions include how an agency can initiate a self-help group, referral arrangements between the agency and the group, how financial support and other resources can best be provided to self-help groups, and how professionals can best utilize them and be used by them. Questions of this kind came up quite frequently in a survey of mental health professionals' attitudes toward self-help groups (Levy, 1978). Self-help groups themselves in many instances have become interested in how they can improve their effectiveness, their recruitment, gain financial support and obtain professional back-up. At present, most of these questions are being answered on the basis of hunches and extrapolations from small-group research. But the time is ripe to go beyond this, calling for systematic formative evaluation research.

Before we are ready for this, however, we need a rough body of data and experience from which insights and generalizations can be derived. We must have as thorough documentation as possible of existing programmatic arrangements, relationships between self-help groups dealing with particular problems, and so on, from which we can develop the rational bases for the first-order approximations of programs, which can then be investigated and improved through formative evaluation. Providing this kind of documentation requires a research method in which few psychologists today are trained—the case study method. This method makes use of systematic, detailed observation, reporting, and speculation, well-illustrated in Wechsler's (1960) study of Recovery, Inc., and Kleiman, Mantell, and Alexander's (1976) description of an attempted collaboration between the American Cancer Society and a group of cancer patients who wished to form a visitor program making use of self-help principles.

Since formative evaluation by definition entails programmatic changes, a final research issue with which the investigator must be concerned is internal validity—the extent to which the called-for program modifications are correctly implemented and produce the intended effect. Whether it be the development of a chapter handbook, a client-referral system for the utilization of self-help groups, or an understanding of the degree of autonomy to be accorded a self-help group sponsored by a community mental-health clinic, the investigator must make provision for accurately monitoring its implementation and effect. This calls as much for good consulting skills as it does for ingenuity in research design, since in the final analysis both the institution of programmatic recommendations by agencies and self-help groups and the opportunity to monitor them depend upon the relationship the investigator has established with the program participants.

GENERALIZATION ISSUES

The generalization of findings in self-help group research—whether process-oriented or concerned with program development and evaluation— requires special consideration by investigators because of their possible political impact, as well as because of their potential scientific significance. Although the factors affecting the generalizability or external validity of these findings are, in principle, no different from those involved in the design and interpretation of all psychological research (Campbell and Stanley, 1963; Cook and Campbell, 1979), three factors merit special consideration in the case of self-help groups.

Heterogeneity of Groups

Apart from their sharing a self-help, mutual aid orientation, it would be impossible to come up with any other characteristic holding true for all self-help groups. Therefore, it would be futile to ask questions (or to make any assertions) about their effectiveness in general as a mental-health service modality. Their heterogeneity of operation alone would seem to make any such generalizations suspect. Among eight different groups included in our research, for example, we found correlations ranging between .38 and .88 in their reported frequencies of engaging in 28 different help-giving activities (Levy, 1979).

Perhaps less apparent, but considerably more frustrating, is the substantial variation also found among groups that are part of the same national organization. Some groups, such as Recovery, Inc., tightly controlled by their parent organization, show little variability from one chapter to another. Others, however, with greater autonomy, may be quite variable. Thus, for example, we found discussions in one chapter of Parents Anonymous following fairly traditional, insight-oriented lines, while those of another chapter, in the same city, were closely adhering to a transactional-analysis paradigm. Therefore, although there is some degree of similarity between self-help groups in their methods, the differences are so great that any generalization about their effectiveness, or the reasons for their effectiveness, must be drawn with the greatest caution. Knowing the identity of a group provides little assurance about the nature of its functioning, except in broadest outline. Thus aggregating the data from a large number of identically named self-help groups may obscure important differences among them, both in how they function and in their effectiveness.

This does not mean that outcome studies are fruitless or that investigators should abandon self-help groups as potential sources of insight into the helping process. Rather, it counsels patience and a meticulous respect for the limitations of one's data, and it suggests that, in the short run, program evaluation and development is probably best conducted on a group-by-group, situation-by-situation basis. But this should not be grounds for despair. For if one accepts the search for "unity in variety" as the overriding mission of science (Bronowski, 1956), then the heterogeneity of self-help groups poses a tantalizing challenge: finding those structural and functional parameters of self-help groups which will allow us to make meaningful generalizations about them. And here, again, I would argue for the intensive immersion in the phenomena of these groups, sampled as widely as possible, by investigators trained in ethnographic analysis, as the first step in this search.

Self-Selection of Members

In virtually no other mental health service modality is there less control over who receives what kind of treatment than is the case with self-help groups. Although all members of the same self-help group usually share the same afflication, its severity may vary; and they may also be quite heterogeneous both demographically and clinically. In two chapters of Take Off Pounds Sensibly (TOPS), for example, we found some members who would be considered obese by any standards, and a few who might be described as svelte; the mothers in the Parents Anonymous chapters in our study included a very few who had physically abused their children, many more who engaged in verbal or emotional abuse (at least, what they considered to be abuse), and still others who, in our view, were primarily confused and anxious over distinguishing between discipline, punishment, and abuse. Similar examples could be cited involving other groups.

Open access and self-definition by individuals as sufferers of the distress which is the group's concern are the rule among self-help groups, and these may be two of their more valuable characteristics. These are also fundamental ways in which they differ from other components of the mental health delivery system. For research purposes, however, they wreak havoc with attempts either to assess or to control for sampling biases and hence with the possibility of drawing any general conclusions about self-help groups' effectiveness in achieving their goals. This problem has been discussed in detail in the case of studies of A.A. (Baekland, Lundwall, and Kissin, 1975), but it is inherent in all voluntary groups whose members essentially decide on their own qualifications for membership.

Self-selection poses a problem in evaluation not only because it makes it difficult to state for whom a group is effective and to what degree, but also because it is likely to contribute to error variance—how a particular group operates as well as its general atmosphere—and hence its effectiveness—are also dependent upon its composition. And occasionally coincidences of composition may even conspire to defeat a group's best efforts, as was the case in one women's support group with which we worked. One member was struggling with what to do about her husband's infidelity, while another was trying to work through the problems attendant to her affair with a married man. Not surprisingly, neither woman could empathize with the problems of the other, and the other members felt impotent in dealing with both of them. Thus, as compared with psychotherapy outcome research, the extent to which we can control either the treatment population or the method of intervention is considerably limited; consequently, we must also be more cautious in our assertions, both positive and negative, about the effectiveness of self-help groups.

But, again, this does not brand as futile any attempt to assess self-help groups' effectiveness. Rather, it suggests that knowledge about their effectiveness will be hard won, most likely the product of numerous intensive studies—many of single groups over extended periods of time—each adding incrementally to our growing understanding of which individuals, problems, and circumstances, self-help groups offer an effective adjunct or alternative to other modes of psychological intervention.

Also, and very importantly, to the extent that investigators develop good collaborative relationships with the groups they are studying, it may be possible in many instances to introduce procedures which would allow data-gathering about group members utilizable to compensate statistically for lack of control over group composition. Finally, while self-selection does pose a major threat to the external validity of all self-help group research, it is important to recognize that it is also a potential source of knowledge about self-help groups, once we turn our attention to the questions of who joins them, why, and under what circumstances.

The Ecology of Self-Help Groups

No data of which I am aware bear upon this issue, but I believe that it must be considered by any investigator concerned with self-help groups. As miniature social systems, we should expect that self-help groups' characteristics will vary as a function of the larger social systems of which they are a component. Thus, the degree of support that a self-help group receives from professionals within the community, the nature of its institutional affiliations, if any, and characteristics of the community in which it is located may all be expected to affect both how a self-help group functions and its effectiveness.

For example, we found the meetings of an A.A. chapter in one community to be always well attended by the members and their spouses, and usually to evolve into social affairs lasting well into the night. Those of another chapter, in a community approximately 25 miles away, were smaller in size and always quite businesslike affairs. We can only speculate on why these two chapters were so different. But, in the former case, this was the only chapter in the community, while in the latter, the chapter was one of two; the town itself was somewhat smaller in the former case than in the latter; and, overall, it seemed to us that one reason for the "successful" meetings of the first chapter was that "it was the only game in town." The AA chapter appeared to serve as a major center for the social life of the community, while the other community was much more richly endowed culturally and recreationally, so that its AA chapter's functions were more narrowly limited to achieving AA's espoused goals. Whether our speculations are correct or not, it seems reasonable to expect that the experiences of members of these two chapters would differ considerably, especially in the needs met by A.A. membership.

As community institutions and agencies become increasingly involved in sponsoring self-help groups, knowledge of the characteristics of those sponsor-group relationships that foster the growth and effectiveness of these groups and those that do not will become increasingly needful. In gaining this knowledge, it would seem that a natural history approach to individual cases of sponsor-group relationships would be the most useful initially, leading inductively to the postulation of those parameters that should systematically be studied as a basis for proposals of the most effective forms of sponsor-group relationships. These points were discussed earlier in this chapter in the context of program evaluation. They warrant reiteration here because they bear crucially on the generalization of research findings, and because they point to a prime area of research in self-help groups. They argue for the inclusion of ecological variables in all self-help group research, and they caution against the too hasty aggregation of research data from such groups which obscure important interactions between self-help groups and ecological variables.

Cook and Campbell (1979) present a thoughtful discussion of strategies for increasing the external validity of research in field settings, and conclude with the following statement, which I believe strikes a particularly appropriate note on which to end this discussion: "Our pessimism about external validity should not be overgeneralized. An awareness of targets of generalization, of the kinds of settings in which a target class of behaviors most frequently occurs, and of the kinds of persons who most often experience particular kinds of natural treatments will, at the very least, prevent the designing of experiments that many persons shrug off willy-nilly as 'irrelevant'" (p. 79).

Chapter 13

ACTION RESEARCH
A New Model of Interaction Between
The Professional and Self-help Groups

Francine Lavoie

Natural helping networks are a valuable resource in the mental-health field. Various types have emerged, some less structured, others highly structured: communications among neighbors and relatives, information from an influential member of the community with no specialized role in mental health, voluntary and mutual-aid groups (Gershon and Biller, 1977). Very often at the base of the medical (Ozonoff and Ozonoff, 1977) and social (Levine and Levine, 1970) programs at the turn of the century, these networks were gradually set aside at the institutional level following the professionalization of the helpers and the specialization of the modes of treatment (Levine, Tulkin, Intagliata, Perry and Whitson, 1978). Intervention then became the exclusive prerogative of professional associations which aimed to offer services meeting the needs of the population and to protect access to the professional act. But natural networks kept on functioning, and gradually entered a new course of action such as the formation of psychotherapeutic self-help groups, though for a few decades the institutional and the natural helping networks were two distinct and irreconcilable entities.

In the 1970s professionals evinced a new interest in these community resources. Since all professionals cannot establish a constructive relationship with the natural networks, those who are interested must revise their expectations and their notion of involvement. If they choose to work with these natural-support systems, specialists must refrain from jeopardizing

the systems' originality by dictating their own pattern of analysis and intervention, which would then result in the professionalization of lay helpers
(Gartner and Riessman, 1977). It also would lead to the loss of their natural
abilities (Gottlieb, 1979) and very often to the loss of their self-confidence
(Richan, 1977). Therefore, these professionals must share values and
abilities different from those of their colleagues working at the institutional
level (Collins and Pancoast, 1976).

They must also adopt a new style of intervention (Patterson, 1978) and
adapt themselves to the groups with which they work. Where friends and
kinship networks are concerned, professionals must take the first steps in
establishing a contact, since people involved in these support systems
seldom realize they are offering a helping relationship and therefore do not
seek advice from professionals. The situation is different with mutual-aid
groups, since they are more conscious of the helping role they offer; they
question their intervention and may choose to share their queries with professionals. The establishment of relations between self-help groups and
professionals can therefore originate from either party.

Apart from their specific objectives, self-help groups share the same
philosophy of action. Their principles are the constancy of their support,
the offer of services to populations neglected by institutions, the offer of
assistance based on mutual aid between old and new members and the
autonomy of the individual. Yet a brief analysis of the functioning of self-
help groups reveals that in the pursuit of their aims, obstacles are unavoidable. First, alongside stable groups, we find groups which are declining or
facing great difficulties (Kleiman, Mantell and Alexander, 1976). Second,
certain classes of the population (such as the underpriviliged) do not seem
to fit in the self-help groups. Third, in a few self-help groups, the maintenance of long-standing membership is skewed by the fact that meetings are
geared chiefly to the benefit of the new members. And finally, the para-
mount problem is the lack of participation and the passivity of the
members. Self-help groups must therefore contemplate new solutions to all
these problems if they hope to meet their objectives. In the search to solve
these problems, the recourse to a consultant could be one strategy. It
therefore is important to analyze current contributions of professionals who
have chosen to interact with self-help groups, if we are to evaluate the
impact of such intervention.

PRESENT ROLES OF THE PROFESSIONALS

Relations between professionals and self-help groups vary somewhat
from those of other types of networks. As a matter of fact, while some professionals were involved in the formation of the oldest and most widely

spread self-help groups as as Alcoholics Anonymous and Recovery, contacts were usually minimal or nil between professionals and other natural networks. Even today, when professionals participate in establishing self-help groups, their most frequent role seems to be that of consultant. In this capacity, they are generally called upon to solve the immediate needs of the group such as physical and financial resources, referral of members with special problems, supervision of volunteers, and the lending of moral support to the leaders. Professionals are less likely to be involved in the organization of activities.

To meet these demands, professionals may proceed in various ways: they may have recourse to professional experience or to that of other self-help groups, they may proceed by trial and error, or they may suggest problem-solving with the group or its leaders. But considering the limited time they can offer the group, professionals will often choose the most expeditious recourse, that is, to their professional knowledge. This may be adequate in specific cases (referrals, organizational problems), but not when it is the only source of inspiration. At other times, they may draw on knowledge acquired through working with similar self-help groups. Unfortunately, the available documentation supplies few analyses of practical problems in context. This second solution could also lead to unsuitable approaches, especially if they are not in rapport with the cultural and social characteristics of the members. On the other hand, proceeding by trial and error restricts one's action, typically to a crisis situation, and does not lead to a global philosophy of action.

All these interventions hold the danger of professionalizing the practice of self-help groups because the professional is then considered the source of knowledge. This tendency to resort to the knowledge of the professional may be fed into by the members themselves, and not be due to the professional's takeover. Indeed, the sustenance of groups having complex needs beyond the exchanges of neighbors and friends may prompt resort to techniques usually known only by the professional.

The recourse to problem-solving methods enhances the ideas originating from members of the group. They can participate in formulating strategies on an equal basis with the professional. And while they resolve a problem, they can acquire skills enabling them to carry on by themselves and learn to integrate a similar style of reflection in their regular practice. But, a step in the right direction, the problem-solving method could result in difficulties. When it entails questioning the merits of the solutions contemplated, as is often the case, members could choose the solution according to their values rather than to rational criteria. Facing such a situation, the consultant should propose the recourse to a research on the pertinence or on the effect of the contemplated solution before making a choice.

No studies, so far as I know, of self-help groups in a problem-solving context are extant. But, other types of studies with self-help groups are of value in providing an opportunity to analyze the attitude of members toward this research which is not of *prima facie* design to answer group problems. The impact of such research must also be taken into consideration.

In the present context, the role of researcher is not accepted in self-help groups. These groups identify themselves primarily through their service function and question the limited relation betweeen research and action, thus replicating the concept held by professionals in institutions that a service function excludes a research function.

An investigation of some of the studies of self-help groups may reveal the reason for the mistrust on the part of the groups. These studies relate to one or the other of the following aspects: the efficiency, the processes and sometimes the demographic characteristics of the groups. We shall discuss the first two types of research.

The efficiency of groups is most often gauged by evaluation studies. Researchers undertake a comprehensive analysis of the impact of the group activities on members. According to Weiss (1975) human-service program evaluations most often reach negative conclusions. Since self-help groups are already convinced of the positive results experienced by their members, the are unimpressed by these global studies. Shown negative findings members may question the outcome measures used by the research workers or conclude that their judgement is better than the research.

Thus for practical purposes, an environment where evaluation could be put to use does not exist (Rossi, 1978). Lieberman and Bond (1978) suggest an evaluation strategy. In their opinion, first to be determined are the objectives of the members, those of the group, and those of researchers together with the group. Determination of the outcome measures is geared to these objectives. This approach could facilitate the acceptance of the results of the evaluation, the members having participated in the choice of its criteria and dimensions. Nevertheless, an evaluation program should help a group to choose activities best suited to the needs of its members. Toward this end the research should compare styles of activities offered (e.g., structured human-relations courses as against unstructured discussion session) . An evaluative approach which stresses the global impact and ignores comparisons of the group's activities appears of little use to the self-help group.

Research on the process aspect of self-help groups analyzes therapeutic factors within a group in a global manner (Knight, Wollert, Levy, Frome, and Padgett, 1980) or in interactions at the comunication-skills level (Lavoie, 1982; Levy, 1976). These studies of processes do not include outcome measures, except for a few subjective ones (Knight *et al.*, 1980). Therefore they cannot be of value to the group in retaining processes recognized as the most efficient. On the other hand, process research could be of dramatic use to the group in clarifying the important dimensions of interpersonal relations in the group. An analysis of the frequency and duration of specific interpersonal behaviors or an analysis of opinions by members on the the presence of these behaviors could help establish the importance of various processes. Hill (1977) and Moos (1973) consider that such feedback could be useful to the group itself or to the leaders as a means to expand knowledge. However, studies of the process apparently have not been used to this end.

It would seem that these two types of research, evaluation studies and process analyses, do not aim to meet the problems nor the preoccupations of the group. Fry (1977) adds that the studies proved more profitable to the researchers than to the groups studied. The explicit objectives of the researchers are the development of knowledge and the analysis of self-help groups as a potential alternative to traditional services. Perhaps such studies have been designed to improve the functioning of the groups and have served this end but the authors do not mention it. It would be preferable to write research reports in such a way that they not only satisfy the preoccupations of the scientific community but also meet the practical requirements of the groups themselves.

PROPOSITION OF THE ROLE OF CONSULTANT IN ACTION-RESEARCH

Self-help groups are interested in establishing relations with a consultant who can fulfill their needs. Thus far they have not perceived research as a means of meeting these needs. Before submitting any research project, the professional should consider two essential preliminary steps: to convince the group of the pertinence of such an approach and to create a climate favorable to research.

In the first step, the consultant who considers research useful must persuade the groups of its advantages. Two strategies are possible in that case. One strategy derives from the role of consultant. It is in fact in this function that the professional becomes acquainted with problems brought forward by the group. It is also in this function that the professional has the opportunity to suggest that research could generate solutions to some of these problems. Since certain discrete problems do not demand urgent solution, they could form the object of research.

A second strategy which could prompt the group to accept a research project would be a proposition from the consultant to describe from experiences of the members either the group's philosophy or an explanatory model of the causes of the problem and of the curative factors. Very often self-help groups, especially new ones, still have to define their approach or to verify their intuitions and they would appreciate these conceptual means developed from their points of view (Vattano, 1972).

After convincing the group of the pertinence of research work, there remains a second preliminary step in the elaboration of research. This is the cultivation of a climate favorable to research in which both the problems group objectives may be defined and problem-solving techniques applied. This entails on the part of the group a capacity for self criticism and a certain tolerance for ambiguity. It is also necessary to develop a sense of trust and openness of mind. The research worker must obtain the approval of various authorities: the board of directors, leader, members, etc. Finally, the expectations of the group must remain realistic.

Once the group is conscious of the pertinence of research and a favorable climate has been established, the consultant can proceed with the research. There are two possible approaches to formulating a plan of study: research on definite problems and the development of explanatory models.

The first approach consists of developing research relating to problems identified by the group. In most groups, the besetting problems are lack of participation by members, and the role of the volunteers. Participation is defined on the one hand by engagement in activities of the group, and on the other hand by the assumption of one's own problems.

As far as involvement in activities is concerned, various ecological, organizational, and behavioral factors could account for the passive behavior. In a review of studies on participation in voluntary groups, Tomeh (1973) suggests that the homogeneity of the group, the type of leadership, the style of interaction, and the level of consensus should be scrutinized. In the context of research it is possible to modify these factors and to analyze the consequences of the participation of members on various activities. Certain groups will hold different hypotheses on the responsible factors and in this case research could also clarify their importance. Participation refers also to the assumption of responsibility for their needs by the consumers. Green, Werlin, Schauffer and Avery (1977) emphasize the fact that in the field of physical health, the assumption of problems by individuals depends on a knowledge of health, on the importance placed on self-care, and on the individual's conception of internal control on health (locus of control: ability to control external forces or to be controlled by them).

In the field of mental health, it would be interesting to analyze the influence of such factors. In self-help groups the "helper therapy" principle seems moreover to play an important role in the autonomy of the one helped. Content analysis of mutual-aid interactions and interviews are the most appropriate methods of research to verify the individual's autonomy and involvement as a helper. The attitudes of the members toward professional services could also be considered as an indication of *prise en charge*.

At the formation of a group the problems submitted to research are primarily concerned with the action of volunteers. This includes the selection criteria of volunteers involved in a self-help relationship and their training as well as that of the volunteers doing office work and those elected to the board of directors.

The problem of the selection of volunteers offering a helping relationship takes on greater magnitude in groups which offer tutoring services (e.g., widows' and widowers' groups). Actually these groups use two criteria: the volunteer must share the problem and be able to cope with it. But, criteria in themselves do not warrant the capacity for a helping relationship. Social adaptation and adaptation to the role of helper must also be considered. Even if it is recognized that lay helpers possess natural gifts essential to helping, nevertheless certain complications such as subserving their own needs can arise (Richan, 1977).

The problem of training volunteers as helpers is crucial; it could give rise to the professionalization of the groups' practice, especially when the group does not assume this training, but utilizes the services offered at low cost by numerous agencies. Even when the formation is given by a member of the group, it is too often inspired by professional techniques. These problems are inherent particularly in self-help groups with loose structure, that is to say where the agendas of the meetings vary according to the members' needs. However that may be, many authors (Collins and Pancoast, 1976; Gottlieb, 1979; Patterson, 1978) state that any program of formation of lay helpers working in natural helping networks jeopardizes the natural abilities of helpers. Even if this training period is used as a selection procedure for volunteers, its inherent risk is too high. Therefore a more comprehensive mode of selection could avoid the necessity for a helping-relationship training period. The formation of volunteers working in offices is less often questioned. It is interesting to consider volunteers' participation as a step leading many to greater socialization. It is also necessary to encourage the turnover of the personnel and to include in their training preparation for their return to the job market (Signell, 1978). At the board of directors' level, essential information for a true participation must be provided in order not to give the users a factitious role.

In the case of programs using paraprofessionals or nonprofessionals a verification of the modes of selection and formation must be undertaken, not only at the level of the helping relationship (D'Augelli and Danish, 1976) but at other levels of participation as well (Signell, 1978). The elaboration of adequate formation programs of volunteers in helping-relationship presupposes a thorough knowledge of the style of intervention particular to members of the group.

In addition to an approach which consists of developing research relating to problems identified by the group, there is another approach suggested in the framework of action-research which could be useful to the acquisition of this knowledge.

This approach proposes the development of an explanatory model including the causes and the evolution of the problems, the therapeutic factors, and the phases of change elaborated from members' experiences. Levin (1976) reports that the contribution of people involved is essential to the development of an adequate pattern of self-care. Since self-care and mutual-aid movements have been developed outside the professional's field, the latter must endeavor to understand the point of view of these new service-producers with regard to the identification of variables affecting self-care and mutual-aid practice.

Various strategies permit the study of groups' explanatory models. The ethnographic evaluation of a group appears to hold high potential in the development of such a model. Knapp (1979) thus describes the essential principles of ethnographic research: 1) an initial exploratory approach; 2) an intensive involvement in the social setting being studied; 3) the use of multiple-research techniques with emphasis on participant observation and key-informant interviewing; 4) an explicit attempt to understand events in terms of the meaning held by those in the social settings; 5) an interpretative framework which emphasizes the role of context in determining behavior; 6) a research product which describes the setting in vivid detail.

According to the same author, ethnographic research is the appropriate method when results are presented to the group itself. Collins (1978) is the only research worker on self-help groups to have adopted it. Studying groups of Parents Anonymous over a long period of time, she was concerned with obtaining the point of view of members on the functioning of the group and on the processes of identification within the group. She tries to identify the evolution of the identification with the abusive parent to that with the competent parent, as well as the therapeutic factors involved. She resorts to participant observation and to the interview; in the course of her study she had to share the life of the group and to play the role of helper in the group's style. All the principles of ethnographical research thus are mobilized by Collins, who provides one of the few developmental analyses of self-help groups. Antze (1976) inspires himself with the ethnographical approach by drawing our attention to the ideology of three types of groups as formulated in writings and slogans. He also considers that the essential therapeutic factors reside in this ideology which each group adapts to the characteristics of its clientele.

Another strategy of explanatory model development is the approach of Freire (1974). People involved in this group process define their environment and the causes of their problems. This codification leads to a community involvement in problem-solving process. Such education encourages people to talk about their conception of the problem by offering them ways to animate the discussion without influencing its content. The radical political context favored by Freire does not facilitate the adaptation of this method to all self-help groups. Researcher-consultants may, however, instill in themselves a fundamental attitude in this new type of education: respect for the knowledge of the nonprofessional.

Particularly used in conjunction with the natural networks of family, friends, and neighbors a third strategy limits itself to the study of the therapeutic factors as perceived by the helper and the helped, and does not attempt to integrate an analysis of causes and problems. It supplies precise data on the type of help offered by a lay worker and on the perception the helper and the helped share on the relative efficacy of various types of help. Gottlieb (1979) develops a classification of the types of help offered to single mothers. It derives from these mothers' own assessments of supportive experiences as relevant to their problems. Patterson (1978) directly interviews lay helpers identified as offering help in their neighborhood. She analyzes what sets apart the style of help of the lay helper from that of the professional. In comparison with ethnographical research and with the type of education promulgated by Freire, this strategy limits itself to a curtailed definition of problems and focuses on the identification of the abilities comprising helping skills. Weiss (1975) proposes that specialists in human services stop analyzing the impact of variations in psychosocial interventions heretofore inefficient, and instead work to define a new explanatory model. The study of self-help groups allows an analysis of an innovative type of intervention, but this must not preclude the simultaneous research of new explanatory models.

The most promising development strategies of explanatory models appear to be those which integrate the analysis of the causes of the problem with those of the modes of change in mutual-aid groups.

Following the description of the type of relations existing at present between self-help groups and professionals, I have submitted as a new model of relation, the model of action-research which could be useful not only to groups but also to the scientific community in search of a new approach to psychosocial problems.

After the preliminary steps which are the presentation of the pertinence of research for the group and the creation of a favorable climate, the professional may have recourse to two approaches in research. This may be to elaborate research on discrete problems formulated by the group or to develop an explanatory model from the experience of its members.

According to Gregg (1979), it would seem that pressure from organized groups of people sharing a problem must be brought to bear so that research with regard to this problem can be amplified by the scientific community in social sciences. The proposed action-research model describes the aspects and the advantages of a collaboration between professionals and self-help groups.

ACKNOWLEDGEMENT

The comments of François Dore and the editorial assistance of Berthe Lavoie are acknowledged.

Chapter 14

SOME HEALTH RELATED OUTCOMES OF SELF-HELP PARTICIPATION
Recovery, Inc. as a Case Example of a Self-help Organization in Mental Health

Norma Radol Raiff

Recovery, Inc., The Association of Nervous and Former Mental Patients, is one of the nation's oldest and most distinguished self-help "ex-mental patient" organizations. Founded in 1937 by Dr. Abraham A. Low as an adjunct to hospital treatment and as a means of aftercare, Recovery has operated as a free-standing lay-run alternative mental-health resource since 1952. According to Gartner and Riessman (1977), Recovery Inc. bears the distinction of being the "most cited" self-help organization in the now proliferating case literature. Besides its survival in an arena marked by organizational failure (Steinman and Traunstein, 1976), Recovery Inc. is remarkable in another respect: it has established clear routines and policy guidelines for recruiting, training, and socializing its lay self-help group leaders. As a result of these institutionalization processes, Recovery self-help group leaders—all of whom are typified as either "nervous persons" or former mental patients—apparently display a high degree of homogeneity in leading self-help groups (Lee, 1976; Levy, 1976) and in conforming to Recovery group-policy guidelines (Recovery, 1971).

In 1975, Recovery Inc. agreed to cooperate with the present author, an academic "outsider," in conducting a self-study of its leadership characteristics and internal training procedures. Questions were asked relating to long-term participation as either group leader or Recovery administrator. The measured outcomes incorporated a variety of health indicators including utlization of mental-health services and mental status self-reports. This paper summarizes certain of these findings and links them to aspects of the self-help career ladder. It thus provides major new information on longitudinal effects associated with specified contingencies in self-helping behavior.

THEORETICAL FRAMEWORK

The theoretical model guiding the research conceptualization and subsequent questionnaire was that self-help groups were to be primarily understood as alternative mental-heath providers, and that tested outcomes should reflect a "well role" model rather than the perspective of individual pathology or deviant subculture behavior. Two sociological traditions influenced our choice of outcome measures. First, self-help group leadership was defined as a subset of voluntary association behavior and, in a conceptual lineage that included de Tocqueville (1959) and Wirth (1938); also Wechsler, 1960), was therefore to be studied as a possible source of social integration and enhanced feelings of self. This theoretical orientation translated into a number of questionnaire items relating to quality of life judgments and self-reports of happiness and satisfaction.

The second theoretical perspective was that self-helpers as alternative mental-health providers experience "careers" (Goffman, 1961) or changes in self-other relationships that are in turn related to social structural and socialization variables. This led to the decision to organize the study's outcome measures in such a fashion that diachronic variation associated with sustained self-help performances and career contingencies could be separately analyzed. Thus, we asked not only "What are self-help outcomes?" but also, "How are these outcomes related to how *long* a person has been a *member* of Recovery?" "A *group leader* or *administrator*?" and "What is the effect of *promotion* within Recovery's organization structure?"

CHARACTERISTICS OF RECOVERY, INC.

Recovery's central frame of reference is derived from Low's initial perspective that mental-health patients possess numerous untapped healing resources—referred to as "the Will"—which can be used to modify behavior, ameliorate distressing symptoms, and combat social stigma (Low, 1950). On the personal level of meanings, this philosophy translates into prescriptions for behavior which emphasize freedom of the will and self-control. Similarly, on the collective level of meanings, Low's philosophy translates into normative expectations that meetings will be orderly, follow a prescribed schedule of events, and be formally structured according to group meeting guidelines (Recovery, 1971; 1969).

At the time of the study, Recovery Inc. had branches in the United States, Canada, Puerto Rico, and Ireland. There were over 1,000 Recovery self-help groups and 7,000 dues-paying members at that date. In common with other self-help organizations, a person did not have to pay dues nor come into the organization through professional referral in order to participate in meeting routines.

THE SAMPLE AND METHOD OF DATA COLLECTION

An anonymous pretested 23-page questionnaire was mailed to a sampling of Recovery leaders who had been stratified according to their degree of self-help experience and/or administrative responsibility: (a) group leaders who staffed Recovery's administrative structure (the "leader-administrators"); (b) "regular" group leaders (persons whose official functions were confined to leading self-help groups); and (c) apprentice group leaders (persons identified by group leaders and leader-administrators as their "helpers"). The first section of the questionnaire concerned pathways into self-helping and medical histories; the second was designed to understand group leadership as a social role; a third section requested demographic information; and a last section requested judgments relating to quality of life.

The sample was developed using a combination of randomization procedures and information chaining. Of 520 questionnaires distributed, 260 were initially mailed to a randomly selected sample of group leaders as well as the entire universe of leader-administrators. These randomly sampled subsets accounted for 63 percent of all questionnaires returned. In addition, group leaders and leader-administrators were asked to give a second copy of the questionnaire to their "helpers" who were then counted as an opportunity-sampled comparison group. Since many group leaders and leader-administrators were without identified "helpers," we cannot estimate the latter group's rate of response.

In our sample of 393 Recovery leader-administrators, group leaders and "helpers," there was considerable variability in years of membership and office. Of the respondents, 6 percent had been Recovery members for less than 2 years, 16 percent between 2 and 4 years, 22 percent between 4 and 6 years, 22 percent between 6 and 10 years, 25 percent between 10 and 18 years, and 9 percent for 18 years or more. The fact that almost one-quarter of the sample had been members for less than 4 years suggests the speed with which self-help groups recruit individuals into the organization structure. Among the subsets of leaders and leader-administrators, 24 percent had been leaders for less than 2 years, 27 percent between 2 and 4 years, 28 percent between 4 and 10 years, and 21 percent for more than 10 years. Again, the large number of comparatively "young" leaders may be treated as an indicator of personnel "flow through."

The sexual composition of the sample was markedly female (72 percent). Most of the respondents were from the United States (89.3 percent), white (99.7 percent), and middle-aged (62.5 percent were between forty and sixty). Three quarters (74.5 percent) were married, 9 percent were single, and 16.5 percent were either divorced, separated, or widowed. The great majority (83 percent) had at least one child.

The Recovery sample was well-educated as compared to "ordinary" American volunteers (Action, 1975). Forty-seven percent had at least some college education. Among occupational categories the distribution was as follows: professionals (15 percent), managers, administrators and proprietors (9 percent), clerical and sales (20 percent), skilled, semiskilled or unskilled (9 percent), part-time employed (6 percent), and unemployed, housemakers, and students (42 percent).

Almost all of the sample had been involved with professional health-care systems: 52.5 percent had been previously hospitalized for mental illness and of these, 76 persons (19 percent of the sample) had been hospitalized three or more times. One-third (n = 125) had been treated with electric convulsive therapy (ECT). Almost nine in ten (n = 352) had been treated with drugs or medicines for a nervous problem, and over eight in ten (n = 321) had been under a physician's care for a nervous or mental problem.

SOME SURVEY OUTCOMES

Although many self-help researchers have attempted to explicate the nature of self-help processes (Gartner and Riessman, 1977; Frank, 1961; Antze, 1976), the state of the art remains remarkably primitive in terms of specific research documenting behavioral outcomes. The absence of comparison-group data and the need to rely on self-reports are two major research difficulties (Smith and Reddy, 1973). This study sought to address these operational needs through two strategies. First, we employed several different medical-history and self-referenced statements as a means of "triangulating" (Webb et al., 1966) measured outcomes. Secondly, we stratified the sample on several dimensions as a means of distinguishing between short and long-term effects associated with differences in self-help careers.

MEDICAL UTILIZATION RATES

Six indicators of medical-system utilization patterns were taken as sur-
rogate measures of mental health status: (1) whether the self-helper had
ever been hospitalized for a nervous or mental condition; (2) whether the
self-helper had ever received electric convulsive therapy (ECT); (3) whether the self-helper had ever been treated by a physician for a nervous or
mental condition; (4) pre- and post-Recovery comparisons on quality of
patients-physician relationship; (5) whether the individual had ever taken
medicines (pills, drugs, injections) for a nervous or mental condition;
(6) whether those now taking medicines either were treated routinely or
exercised personal judgment ("My doctor leaves it up to me").

As Table 1 indicates, the Recovery sample consistently displayed
"improvement" on all six medical utilization measures. The most striking
comparisons related to the measures of hospital recidivism and experience
with ECT. Although 199 Recovery members had at some time been hospitalized, only 35 (17.6 percent) of this group had been hospitalized after
joining the organization. In addition, although 125 persons (32.3 percent)
within the sample had experience with ECT, only 3.3 percent had experienced ECT after affiliation. In addition, internal analysis of the data
indicated that those with post-Recovery ECT were also those who reported
multiple hospitalization prior to affiliating. Thus it would seem that
previous number of hospitalizations were more related to both post-
Recovery rehospitalization and post-Recovery ECT than any Recovery-
specific variables.

The entire sample also reported gains on the indicators describing
physician-patient relationships and medication regimens. Analysis of the
two related items describing physician utilization patterns indicated that of
the 338 persons who were *ever* under a physician's care, 39.1 percent
(n = 132) left a physician's care after affiliating with Recovery, 17.5 percent
(n = 59) remained under a physician's care but on a more "limited" basis,
35.8 percent (n = 121) remained under a physician's care without change in
status, and a 3 percent minority (n = 10) traveled from a "limited" to a
more involved relationship.

Analysis of the two items describing medication regimens indicated
that almost nine in ten had taken medication. Of the 352 who were *ever* on
medication, 33.2 percent (n = 117) stopped medication after joining
Recovery, 15.9 percent (n = 56) continued medication for some time but
are no longer taking medication now, 26.1 percent (n = 92) remain on med-

TABLE 1.   BEFORE-AFTER COMPARISONS OF RECOVERY, INC. SAMPLE ON SELECTED INDICATORS OF MEDICAL SYSTEM UTILIZATION PATTERNS (PARTIAL TABLE)[a]

INDICATOR	Per cent Sample (n)	Per cent Before (n)	Per cent After (n)	Per cent Both Before & After (n)
Ever Hospitalized?	52.5 (199)	43.4 (167)	** (5)	7.8 (30)
ECT Ever?	32.3 (125)	28.9 (112)	** (2)	2.8 (11)
Ever Treated by a Physician for a Nervous or Mental Problem?	87.3 (338)	34.1 (132)	4.4 (17)	48.8 (189)

If Yes: Was the relationship limited or ongoing?

	Per cent	(n)
Ongoing-before & after	46.3	(88)
Limited-before & after	17.4	(33)
Ongoing before-Limited after	31.0	(59)
Limited before-Ongoing after	5.3	(10)
	100.0	(190)

INDICATOR	Per cent Sample (n)	Per cent Before (n)	Per cent After (n)	Per cent Both Before & After (n)
Ever Taken Medicines (Drugs, Pills, Injections)?	89.6 (352)	29.8 (117)	3.1 (12)	56.7 (223)

If Yes: Are you taking medicines (drugs, pills, injections) right now?

	Per cent	(n)
Yes- ongoing	22.2	(77)
Yes-my doctor leaves it up to me	26.4	(92)
No	51.4	(179)
	100.0	(348)

a   Per cent of those responding

ication although they describe it as involving some degree of personal judgment ("My doctor leaves it up to me"), and 21.9 percent (n = 77) take medication routinely.

Internal analysis of these six medical utilization pattern outcomes reveals that self-help benefits are widely distributed among all of the respondents, and that the variables of years of leadership, years of membership, and career promotion do not discriminate the pattern of benefits. This is largely due to the piling of responses in the positive direction, leaving little room for systematic variation in the residual categories to appear. This suggests that Recovery's ability to "preserve" individuals in well-role status occurs shortly upon entry into the self-help system—at least for this group of organizationally involved self-help consumers. The findings also seem to negate the suggestion sometimes made in self-help literature that sustained self-helping promotes sick-role identity and/or leads to deteriorated health status over time.

SELF-JUDGMENTS OF HEALTH AND MENTAL HEALTH STATUS

Two measures of the self-helpers' engrossment with "health" and two global estimates of mental health well-being were included as subjective outcomes of self-help participation. The choice of these measures was predicated on their wide currency as indicators of mental-health status (Mechanic, 1978). In addition, the availability of comparable data on "normal" Americans made these measures desirable as sources of ready-made or "found" contrast populations (Webb et al., 1966).

INDICATORS OF ENGROSSMENT WITH HEALTH

Two questions designed to tap the self-helpers' involvement with illness identities were (a) the degree to which respondents claimed they were "satisfied" with their health and (b) the extent of their "worry" about health. In the former indicator, it is presumed that "satisfaction" employs a cognitive yardstick that is potentially open-ended and unanchored. "Worry" involves self-judgments about use of time and perception vis-a-vis daily routines.

As on the previous findings, the Recovery sample appeared to rank high on self-assessments in the domain of health. This was true both for items relating to health "satisfaction" and "worry." The Gamma correlation between the two indicators was 75.8 percent, indicating that the items were tapping related (but not identical) aspects of the same state of mind.

In general, the Recovery population was satisfied with their health. Of Recovery respondents, 89.4 percent as compared with 85.5 percent of "normal" Americans (Campbell, 1976) give positive replies to the question, "Of course most people get sick now and then, but overall, how satisfied are you with your own health?" This strongly implies that Recovery leaders, administrators, and "helpers" are indistinguishable from the general American public on this factor.

The specific breakdown of responses to the question relating health "satisfaction" was' "very satisfied" (36 percent), "fairly satisfied" (53.4 percent), "fairly dissatisfied" (7.8 percent) and "very dissatisfied" (2.6 percent. The distribution of responses to the question "About how often would you say that you worry about your health?" was "just now and then" (49 percent), "some of the time" (41.4 percent), "most of the time" (8.3 percent), and "all of the time" (1.8 percent).

As in the previous findings, the overwhelming number of positive responses among all Recovery strata tended to wash out any differences between leaders of various experiences and responsibilities. Nevertheless, certain trends, while not statistically significant, were noticeable. For example, both years of membership and leadership promotion appeared to provide self-helpers with marginally additive benefits. Thus, within the entire sample, persons with less than 2 years of Recovery membership were most likely to respond negatively to the health "worry" and "satisfaction" items. In addition, there was a slight positive correlation between promotion and attitudes toward health. Thus 94.6 percent of leader-administrators, but only 88.9 percent of group leaders and 85.6 percent of "helpers" responded positively to the question of "satisfaction." Similarly 96.8 percent of leader-administrators, but only 88.8 percent of group leaders and 87.5 percent of "helpers" stated that they worried only rarely or some of the time.

GLOBAL ESTIMATES OF QUALITY OF LIFE

The survey replicated questions relating to self-estimates of global satisfaction and happiness as a means of gaining access to feelings of personal and social integration (Gurin et al., 1960; Campbell, 1976).

As Table 2 indicates, 92 percent of the Recovery respondents replied positively to the question of relative happiness with the way "things are these days." The chief difference between Recovery leader-administrators, leaders, and helpers, and large samples of "normal" Americans would appear to be that the former are not as likely to voice extreme self-ratings. Two possible explanations can account for this effect. First, the apparent difference between the Recovery sample and the two previous samples is an

TABLE 2

COMPARATIVE "HAPPINESS" REPORTS [a]

		Very Happy	Pretty Happy	Not too Happy
1957	Gurin[b]	35%	54%	11%
1971	Campbell[c]	29%	61%	10%
1977	Ralff[d]	26%	66%	8%

a Per cent responses to question, "Taking all things together, how would you say things are these days --would you say you're very happy, pretty happy, or not too happy these days".
b Gurin et al., 1960
c Campbell et al., 1976
d Present Study

artifact of the trend in a declining happiness rating reported for Americans in general (Campbell, 1976), that is: that Recoveryites are indistinguishable from the general American public as it would appear if the latter were to be retested at this date. The alternative is that the differences are real and reflect the effect of Recovery subculture which consciously teaches self-help members to seek a middle path.

Similarities also obtain between Recovery group leaders, leader-administrators, and "helpers," and members of the general American public on the dimension of life "satisfaction." In the total Recovery sample, 89.3 percent describe themselves on the positive pole of the question, "In general, how satisfied are you with your own life?" while only 82 percent of the Campbell study felt that way. The Recovery statistics were 26.0 percent "very satisfied," 63.3 percent "fairly satisfied," 8.9 percent "fairly dissatisfied," and 1.8 percent "very dissatisfied."

As the percentage distribtions indicate, the happiness and satisfaction self-ratings are widely distributed among the Recovery echelons and no leadership or membership subset is modally represented. Nevertheless certain statistical trends, while not significant mathematically, are discernible. These are as follows: first, that years of membership is a salient factor, especially for those with under 2 years of Recovery affiliation. Secondly, persons with less than 2 years of leadership experience were most likely to check the minority response of being either "not too happy" or "dissatisfied" with life. Finally, leadership promotion is marginally additive to the self-help experience. Thus 33.7 percent of the leader administrators, but only 22.3 percent of the "helpers" described themselves as "very happy." Conversely 9.7 percent of the "helpers" but only 3.3 percent of leader-administrators designated themselves as "not too happy."

OTHER FINDINGS

A review of the study's larger findings indicates that Recovery experience enhances the participants' involvement and satisfaction with many other domains of social behavior. However, regardless of the indicator, a minority subset of Recovery members appears to have been deprived of the full benefits of participation reported by the majority. These individuals are often persons who have been members of Recovery for less than 2 years, are still on medication, below the poverty level, and who lack other social-network involvements such as being employed and/or married.

CONCLUSIONS

Although health professionals have become increasingly sensitive to the potential benefits of sustained participation in self-help groups, there have been few empirical studies of specific outcomes associated with this phenomena.

In this study, 393 of the most highly "involved" participants of Recovery, Inc.—group leaders, administrators, and "helpers"—supplied questionnaire information on their medical backgrounds, current utilization of professionally organized health-care systems, and self attitudes regarding mental health. The overall conclusion is that the entire Recovery leadership cohort ranks high on all these health-related indicators. The evidence is made especially compelling insofar as all indicators were in the same positive direction. Further, they gained meaning through being compared with similar statistics on populations of "normal" Americans.

The study also attempted to analyze the separate effects of features in self-help careers as additive to the general self-help experience. Our general conclusion was that for those who are recruited into the Recovery leadership cohort, the benefits associated with self-help participation appear to have come early and upon entrance into self-helping. Nevertheless, acquiring leadership roles and functions would appear to "preserve" these earlier gains and seems to have marginal additive value to the long-term leaders and those who are promoted in the organizational structure.

Finally, we would articulate the need for mroe research in this area. Although Recovery Inc. has been often historically described as phenotypical of organized self-helping, its unique administrative mechanisms—such as sustained group leadership training—distinguish it from other self-help collectives. It is obvious that comparative information is needed on those self-help settings where the administrative and managerial supports for self-help participation are either lacking or take some other collective form.

Chapter 15

THE COMMUNITY NETWORK DEVELOPMENT PROJECT

Bridging the Gap Between Professional Aftercare and Self-Help

Eileen D. Edmunson
Jeffrey R. Bedell
Richard E. Gordon

"To be connected to others, to belong, to receive social support when it is needed and to be able to give it in return is an important part of mental health. . . . social and community support systems can help to contribute to a sense of well-being and of competent functioning (and thus, to be preventive). They can aid in reducing the negative consequences of stressful life-events and thus bridge the treatment and rehabilitative levels of prevention (p. 144)."

This quote from the Report of the President's Commission on Mental Health (President's Commission on Mental Health, 1978) emphasizes the long-neglected role of natural helping processes in the prevention and treatment of mental illness. Furthermore, the Commission calls for the development of models of articulation between professional systems of care and natural systems (p. 145). The Community Network Development (CND) Project, an after-care project developed at the Florida Mental Health Institute, represents one model of partnership between professional and natural helping systems. This chapter will briefly describe the CND Project, especially in terms of its unique use of psychiatric clients as leaders of mutual-aid networks. The effectiveness of this program, which provides a "bridge" between professional and self-help approaches, will be examined, both in terms of its impact on member recidivism and its effect on the client-peer leader.

Research evidence suggests that the natural helping provided by an individual's social network is protection against a wide range of physical and emotional problems (Gore, 1978; Nuckolls, Cassell and Caplan, 1972; Miller and Ingham, 1976; Brown, Bhrolchain and Harris, 1975; Medalie and Goldbourt, 1973; Goldstein, 1978). A growing body of literature also has begun to document the inadequacy of the typical mental-health client's support system (Pattison, 1977, 1979; Tolsdorf, 1976; Garrison, 1978; Sokolovsky, COhen, Berger and Geiger, 1978; Hammer, Makiesky-Barrow and Gutwirth, 1978). The natural, social network of mental-health clients is frequently small, dominated by family members, and is often not perceived by the client as a viable source of support or help in times of life stress. Thus, assisting mental-health clients to develop a support system that can approximate the type of natural helping that occurs in the lives of "normals" is a potentially powerful clinical intervention. In recent years, a variety of experimental approaches have been piloted which attempt to promote or create natural help. As part of a grant from NIMH, the Natural Helping Networks Project at the Regional Research Institute of Portland State University has begun to study various programs across the nation which attempt to foster natural helping and to develop a typology for categorizing them. As a result of their preliminary studies, Froland, Pancoast, Chapman, and Kimboko (1979) have identified five emerging forms of collaboration between natural and professional helping systems. Three of these models have potential applications with after-care clients: the Personal Network model, the Volunteer Linking model, and the Nutual Aid Network model.

In the Personal Network approach, the professional attempts to strengthen or modify the existing personal-support network of an individual client. However, this model has limited application within deinstitutionalization programs. Frequently the mental-health client's network is small. Even family members may have abandoned the client, or, if they remain an active part of their relative's support system, that interactions may be pathological. Working to change this impoverished and detrimental system is too difficult and time-consuming to be practical within a public after-care system.

The Volunteer Linking model has similar practical limitations. In this approach, the professional staff takes a directive role, attempting to create a supportive network for an individual client by the linking to volunteer helpers or other individuals in the client's natural environment. Again, there are serious logistical problems since the volunteers recruited for integration into a client's network may not remain overtime unless there is substantial professional support and monitoring.

The most efficient model for use with after-care clients would appear to be what Froland *et al.* (1979) have termed the Mutual Aid Network. Within this model, the professional focuses on a client population experiencing common problems and either collaborates with an existing self-help group or alternatively creates a network among a group of clients. The Community Network Development Project which has been in operation at the Florida Mental Health Institute for over 2 years illustrates how the creation of a mutual-aid network can be an effective method for reducing hospital recidivism among mental health clients.

The programmatic structure of CND reflects the rehabilitation philosophy of its founders in several essential ways. The CND program developed from a recognition of the fundamental role that social support and social networks play in determining the adjustment of "normals" and mental health clients. Thus, the individual's social network was seen as the primary target of CND treatment rather than specific intrapsychic or behavioral dysfunctions attributed to the individual alone. The goal of the CND program therefore became the creation of a large mutual-aid network in which peers exchange emotional and instrumental support.

The CND program structure also reflects the belief that rehabilitation can best be accomplished as the result of a partnership between formal, professional helping systems and informal, natural helping systems. CND affirms that mental-health clients have strengths and abilities that enable them to take an active part not only in their own rehabilitation, but in the rehabilitation of their peers as well. The type of help provided by a peer is more personal, spontaneous, flexible, and enduring than the help that can be provided by a professional. However, self-help or mutual-aid activities that exist outside the realm of professional influence have proven susceptible to a variety of ills. They may lack sufficient structure and organization, they may fail to link with professional systems of care, they may even assume an anti-professional stance, or they may develop over time undesirable dogma and norms (e.g., Synanon).

Therefore, CND's development was guided by the belief that a self-help or mutual-aid program for after-care clients would be most effective if it were structured and supervised by professionals. Ideally, this partnership should allow both professionals and natural helpers to complement each other's efforts. Natural helpers would be allowed to function within the network, maintaining their special characteristics and unique helping roles. Professional staff would be responsible for tasks that require high levels of training, knowledge, or professional expertise. The following description of CND's staffing pattern and role assignments will illustrate the programmatic structure that evolved in an attempt to implement these goals.

PROGRAM DESCRIPTION

The CND network is composed of nearly 100 mental health clients who reside in two adjacent counties following their discharge from residential treatment. To facilitate interaction and communication between members, and to ensure the effective operation of the program, this broad geographical area was subdivided into four smaller areas, each containing between 20 and 40 CND members.

Professional staff in the CND network are referred to as Staff Area Managers (SAM's). One SAM is assigned to work with each geographical area and has four major job responsibilities: (1) to coordinate and supervise the activities of the informal helpers; (2) to intervene directly with members in situations which require greater experience and expertise than the clients can provide each other (e.g., crisis intervention, advocacy for members to obtain needed services); (3) to coordinate CND activities in each area; and (4) to link CND with the relevant community and professional resources. SAM's are trained to work through the informal helpers, intervening personally only when members need help beyond the knowledge or expertise of the informal helpers.

Within each geographical area, one member is selected to serve as a bridge person between the professional staff and the members. This Community Area Manager (CAM) is paid a modest, part-time salary to act as a community leader, organizer of activities, professional-staff liaison, and to maintain contact with all CND members within the area. On a weekly basis, the CAM actively reaches out to members in the area, contacting them in person or by phone. Members are encouraged to attend CND activities and to socialize and make supportive contact between meetings. Also, they are encouraged to contact the CAM if they need support or assistance at any time. Since most individuals who need social support are unlikely to seek it actively, the pro-active stance of the informal helper causes many clients to use their new social-support network when it is needed as a buffer against stress.

The CAM's are also responsible for planning, organizing, and presiding over a weekly meeting in their area. Although these area meetings are predominantly social, a member of the group may request help with a personal problem. When these requests are made, the CAM facilitates "goal planning"—a structured, problem-solving process whereby all members attending the area meeting help the individual develop an appropriate action plan to deal with the problem.

Member Leaders and Member Volunteers are also identified within each geographical area of CND. These individuals assume leadership and organizational roles on an "as needed" basis. For example, a Member Leader may help with transporting other members to a meeting or social activity, may visit CND members, or may help organize a special fundraising activity. The Member Leaders work with the CAM and often function more directly as informal helpers than the CAM's, who have some role functions of a paraprofessional nature. Member Leaders are called on by the SAM or CAM when they possess some special knowledge, relationship, or expertise that can be of help to the network (e.g., leading a group on raising plants, organizing a potluck supper, transporting other members). By identifying Member Leaders and giving them this formal label, members are encouraged to share in the operation of the network and thereby receive recognition for their abilities and contributions. Designating this type of position has proven an effective means of encouraging natural helpers to use their talents in the CND program.

Obviously, the role relationships between the SAM, CAM, and Members Leaders are a complex and critical component of the CND program. Within the conceptualization suggested by Froland *et al.* (1979), the CND Project builds heavily upon a directive form of relationship since the staff is responsible for training the CAM's and supervising their activities. There are, however, strong coordinative aspects to the relationship as well, since the CAMs are encouraged to function autonomously in many areas and to use the unique qualities and skills that stem from their natural-helper status. Because of the directive and coordinative aspects of the role relationships established by CND, it has been observed that there is a "dynamic tension" in the program. This tension results from the attempt to keep separate, but at the same time utilize, both the expertise and training of the staff and the natural abilities of the helper to share experiences, establish personal relationships, and facilitate social support.

The services and activities provided within the CND network illustrate how the partnership between professional and natural helper may be structured to promote helping and social support. The basic structure of CND is maintained through weekly personal contacts between the CAM and each member, weekly social meetings in each area, and monthly meetings involving the entire two-county network. The regular occurrence of these activities is mandated by the professional staff who have primary responsibility for the networking of members. However, each CAM, along with the members in each area, are given almost complete latitude in determining the location, purpose, and content of any given activity.

Furthermore, ideas for program modification or program development are solicited from members and CAM's, and professional staff have often acted in the role of "consultant" to help either an area or the entire network meet an identified need. Professionals become involved with members in helping them to obtain community resources and developing new aspects of the CND program to improve its effectiveness. This involvement is always handled in such a way that members can assume responsibility for the new activity once the professional staff have helped in its establishment. Program additions which have occurred as a result of this type of cooperative process include the maintenance of a membership directory, the offering of educational and growth-oriented activities, the publishing of a monthly newsletter, the maintenance of a community-resource file, the establishment of an emergency-loan fund for members, and the creation of a cooperative living facility.

EVALUATION

Theoretically, the creation of a mutual-aid network should influence the lives and daily adjustment of mental-health clients in several ways. The actual structure and size of the client's social network should change in a positive direction as a result of membership in the CND network. Furthermore, members should be receiving more social and instrumental support in their daily lives as a result of their participation in CND. Finally, to the extent that these changes in clients' networks are effective in helping them to cope effectively with stress, CND members should have less need for rehospitalization or other forms of mental treatment.

Evaluation efforts to test all of these outcomes have been initiated and are at varying stages of completion. Data on changes in clients' networks and the exchange of support between network members is not yet available, but anecdotal reports indicate that members are establishing supportive relationships within the network. Many CND members contact each other socially between organized meetings and several have become roommates. Members have provided each other with such direct assistance as emergency housing, transportation, and assistance in moving. Most importantly, CAM's report numerous instances when members have informally contacted other members to "talk about how they feel" or "get their minds off their problems." This personal exchange of instrumental and emotional support suggests that CND has become a source of "mutual aid" for many members.

A preliminary follow-up of rehospitalization and outpatient treatment suggests that CND helps reduce its members' need for traditional mental-health services (Edmunson, Bedell, Archer and Gordon, 1980). Eighty clients who were being discharged from a 9-week intensive treatment unit were randomly assigned either to CND or to a control group. Both groups received equivalent discharge planning, including appropriate referrals to a local mental-health center for follow-up treatment. There were also no significant differences between groups in age, sex, race, marital status, diagnosis, previous hospitalization or length of follow-up time. At an average follow-up interval of 10 months, one-half as many patients in the CND group had required rehospitalization as compared with the control group (17.5 percent to 35 percent) and CND members' average total days of hospitalization was lower (7.0 days vs. 24.6 days). Finally, a significantly greater percentage of CND members were able to function without any mental-health system contact (52.5 percent vs. 26 percent).

These results suggest that a mutual-aid network like CND can have a significant impact on the community adjustment of its members. However, although CND had a positive impact on the average member, it seemed essential to evaluate the effect of CND on the CAM's and Member Leaders because they were singled out to perform roles involving leadership and increased responsibility. As was noted earlier in this discussion, the CAM and Member Leader function as a bridge between the client and the professional service-delivery system. While this role offers these individuals a chance for growth and increased self-esteem, it potentially places them in a role conflict and may subject them to increased stress. An evaluation of CND and the wisdom of this type of organization would, therefore, not be complete without an examination of the effect that this experience had on the network members who function in this unique mental-health role.

A structured interview was conducted with all former and present CAM's and Member Leaders (N = 20). The interview combined both objective-rating scales and open-ended questions, tapping a variety of attitudes and opinions about the peer leaders' experience. Confidentiality of all responses was assured and the interviewer was specifically instructed to probe for negative feelings and experiences that the peer leaders might express.

Likert scale items (see Table 1) were used to determine the level of job stress, job reward, significance of the job to the peer leader's life, and self-perception of job performance. The results suggest that the peer managers

Table 1

Means and Standard Deviations of Peer Managers Responses to

Likert Ratings of Job Stress, Job Reward, Job Significance and Job Performance

Question	Anchor Points		Mean	Standard Deviation
	1	5		
How stressful was your job as a peer manager?	Not at all	Extremely Stressful	1.85	1.42
How rewarding was your job as a peer manager?	Not at all	Extremely Rewarding	4.43	.75
How did the job affect you?	Incidental	Extremely Important to My Life	4.17	.84
How do you perceive your performance as a peer manager?	Poor	Outstanding	4.05	.86

did not perceive their roles as significantly stressful. In fact, functioning in the peer leader's role seems to have had the opposite effect; peer leaders described their job experience as extremely rewarding and important to their lives. Additionally, the peer managers rated their own job performance at high levels, indicating that the role of peer leader was conducive to a successful experience for the client.

A series of open-ended questions probed for the major stresses and rewards of the peer leader's role. Three unbiased raters were trained in the assignment of each individual response to rationally derived response categories. Responses which sustained agreement between two of the three raters were accepted as reliably classified. Positive comments about the peer leadership experience seemed to be related to the increased self-esteem and growth that occurred from the assumption of a responsible, helping role. Most negative responses to the peer leaders' experience occurred as a result of tension between the professional staff and the peer leaders, or as a result of programmatic changes that peer leaders felt were out of their control. Two program refinements seemed to be indicated: (1) there is a need for greater clarity about the professional staff/peer leaders' task boundaries; and (2) inevitable program changes need to include more input from peer leaders so that they will feel some investment in these changes and have an understanding of their necessity.

DISCUSSION

The experience of CND in developing social-support networks among mental health clients provides information in three important areas: (1) professionals and natural helpers can successfully combine talents to create a mutual-aid network; (2) participation in a mutual-aid network helps client members to be less dependent on traditional mental-health services; and (3) client leaders can successfully manage the stresses of the CAM role, often indicating personal benefits from the experience. The tension that was reported between the client leaders and the professionals remains an issue of concern and continued evaluation of this aspect of the program is warranted. On balance, however, the present report suggests that the implementation of a mutual-aid network may be a vital mechanism for bridging the gap between the professional and self-help approaches to mental-health aftercare.

Chapter 16

MUTUAL SELF-HELP GROUPS

Strengthening The Selectively Unsupportive Personal And Community Networks Of Their Members

Thomasina Borkman

Introduction

The social supportiveness of families, friends, and other personal community networks in relation to the prevention, treatment, and recovery from illness is receiving increased attention not only in the mental-health field but across the spectrum of health fields. Social support and social networks are often used interchangeably as if the existence of a certain network constitutes social support; the President's Commission on Mental Health (1978), for example, lists families, friends, work, and religious relationships, and mutual self-help groups as "community support systems." The assumption that having a personal network provides positive social support is challenged by evidence about mutual self-help health groups in this paper.

Mutual aid self-help groups are voluntary associations of persons with a common problem who band together to resolve their difficulties by mutual efforts; they are primarily developed and controlled by the persons sharing the common problem. Mutual self-help groups of interest are those that are primarily oriented to directly aiding their members and who will be referred to here as self-helpers. The self-help groups excluded are those primarily oriented to social advocacy and political action (e.g., psychiatric inmates' liberation movement groups, Latz 1979 and Hurvitz 1977) since they operate very differently from the direct support groups (Gussow and Tracy 1976; Katz and Bender 1976).

The professional literature about mutual self-help groups concentrates on their development and operation as naturally occurring social-support groups in response to inadequacies in professional knowledge and services (Katz and Bender 1976; Lieberman and Borman 1976; Gartner and Riessman 1977; Robinson and Henry 1977; Tracy and Gussow 1976). Little attention has been paid to interrelationships between these groups and their members' personal and community networks (Walker, MacBride and Vachon 1977 is an exception).

This conceptual paper introduces a neglected part of the story with a two-part thesis: 1) The self-helpers' families, friends, and other members of their personal networks are selectively unsupportive with respect to the focal problem of the self-help group, and 2) mutual self-help groups are as oriented to offsetting the unsupportiveness of their member's personal networks as they are to compensating for deficiencies in professional services.

The two-part thesis of this paper is developed in three sections. First, a distinctive theoretical framework (Borkman 1979) is presented to show how these groups view their personal and community networks as integral parts of their problem. This framework views mutual self-help groups as experiential learning units that have developed specialized experiential knowledge of their problem. Unlike most of the literature, experiential knowledge is distinguished from the folk or lay knowledge which is used by the self-helpers' personal and community networks. Second, four general ways in which mutual self-help groups regard their personal networks as unsupportive are described. Third, three means that self-help groups use to strengthen the supportiveness of their members networks are described. These points are illustrated from research on three local units of mutual self-help groups: Alcoholics Anonymous, Council of Adult Stutterers, and the various associations of ostomates.[1]

---

[1] Ostomates are persons who have had colostomies or ileostomies, surgical operations to create an artificial means of elimination of bodily wastes through an opening in the abdomen.

METHODS AND MATERIALS

The ideas developed here represent an extension of the author's theoretical work on self-help groups (Borkman 1979) which uses the "grounded theory" approach of Glaser and Strauss (1967); this theory is developed "from the ground up" based on observations and interviews with the subjects of the research on their perceptions of their situation.

The author conducted several studies on stutterers' self-help groups over an 8-year period (Borkman 1973, 1974, 1976b). A comparative study of local units of self-help groups of stutterers (one group), recovering alcoholics (four groups) and ostomates (two groups) in one metropolitan area in the eastern United States provided major data for this paper. Observations of meetings and other group activities, an examination of written materials and in-depth focused interviews with experienced members of each group were included (See Borkman 1977 for more detailed description of the research methods.)

The language and written materials of self-helpers and their groups are couched in specific lay terminology. The individuals and the groups do not describe their actions in generalized, abstract, or theoretical terminology. The ideas developed here are inferences based on what the self-helpers do and how they behave even though they would not describe themselves in these abstract and generalized terms.

THE THEORETICAL FRAMEWORK:
EXPERIENTIAL PROBLEM SOLVING IN MUTUAL SELF-HELP GROUPS

My experiential-knowledge framework (Borkman 1976a; 1979) is distinctive in the professional literature about these groups. Experiential knowledge is specialized information on a problem based on a first-hand experience of it (Borkman 1976a). Experiential knowledge is developed within self-help groups through a process of individuals reflecting upon and trusting as valid their experiences in a context of other people with similar experiences. Experiential knowledge is contrasted with folk or lay information (Berger and Luckmann 1967) which refers to ideas handed down from generation to generation or adopted from science and mass media by the general public and laypersons without experience or training.

Unfortunately, most of the professional literature about self-help groups (e.g., Alibrandi 1977) fails to distinguish between the specialized experiential knowledge developed by self-helpers and the folk information used by their families, friends, and the general public. The literature refers to both types of information as folk or lay knowledge. Because of this conceptual confusion, it is not surprising that the issues raised in this paper have been neglected in the literature. Although the literature recognizes that self-helpers have found, through experience, that professional solutions are often inadequate to resolve their problem, the literature has missed the fact that members of self-help groups also tried available folk ideas without satisfaction.

Each self-help group constructs its own experiential paradigm of their problem and the means to resolve it (Borkman 1979). The focus of each paradigm is specialized in that a given group concentrates on the delimited shared problem whether it be alcoholism, stuttering, or adapting to an ostomy. The experiential approach to problem solving, however, is broad, diffuse, and holistic. It is from the point of view of the experiencing individual as a whole person whose life space is total. It is holistic in the sense that all aspects of the problem in the life space of the individual are regarded as indivisible and inseparable.[2]

The experiential problem-solving orientation is largely "acausal"[3] (c.f. Ablon, 1976; Beels, 1978; Pattison, 1973; Steinglass, 1978; Speck and Attneave, 1973). The search for "causes" is minimized in part because of the problem-solving attitude; emphasis is on finding something that works to the satisfaction of the individual. Looking for "causes" is seen as a way of avoiding problem solving, or of exempting the individual from personal responsibility to do whatever is possible to ameliorate the personal problem.

The acausal approach in self-help groups is illustrated by the fact that any and all situations, interactions, influences, or persons in the life space of self-helpers which they view as meaningful or problematic are addressed by them as relevant. Therefore, the major reason that some network and community relationships are regarded as selectively unsupportive by self-helpers stems from their holistic concern with how the focal problem is manifested in uneasy, unsatisfying, and problematic interactions within their networks.

The manner and style in which self-helpers discuss their networks as part of their problem is critically important to describe. The selective unsupportiveness of network members is seldom made an explicit issue *per se* by devices of labeling, faultfinding, blaming, or separating themselves from their relationships by treating the other person as an object. Instead,

---

[2]Professional models of social ecological systems are similar in that multidimensional factors are viewed as existing independently. However, they are developed from the viewpoint of an objective independent observer, distantly looking at the whole system.

[3]Many self-helpers also become skeptical and distrusting of speculative, theoretical professional knowledge that is not grounded in experience. Many self-helpers become adept at identifying whether or not professionals have any personal practical clinical experience with their problem or only "book knowledge" of it.

their discussions often sound like mundane small talk. Incidents with family members, friends, etc. which are troubling are described in every-day language and sound like ordinary conversation. This deceptively simple dialogue may be one reason observers have overlooked its import.

As newcomers to self-help groups learn the experiential paradigm of their group, they develop trust in their own experiences, a process which simultaneously calls into question the validity and workability of folk infor-mation (and also of professional ideas). They frequently conclude that the folk ideas about their problems are not only stigmatizing but they are also simplistic, incomplete, and invalid, for they do not work.

The questioning of folk ideas applies more to stutterers and alcoholics than to ostomates since there is not a general body of folk information about ostomies except that provided by imaginative speculation.

Illustrations of the unworkability of folk ideas about stuttering and alcoholism follow. A thirty-year-old stutterer who was interviewed said:

If "lay" ideas of how to stop stuttering such as "relax and talk slowly" worked, I would have stopped stuttering years ago.

Alcoholics recovering in Alcoholics Anonymous report having tried folk ideas about controlling their drinking: they have changed their type of drink from hard liquor to beer or wine, or used "will power" to stop drink-ing for periods of time, or changed the situations in which they drank; but these "folk" ideas did not work in the long run.

When their family, friends, or network members express these folk ideas or behave on such basis, the experientially knowledgeable self-helpers come to view their network members as incorrectly informed and unedu-cated about their constructive experiential approach.

THE SELECTIVE UNSUPPORTIVENESS
OF PERSONAL AND COMMUNITY NETWORKS

Four ways in which the unsupportiveness of network members is manifested in the focal problem from the self-helper's point of view are summarized as: 1) stigmatization, 2) the emotionscape, 3) direct impinge-ments on role relationships, and 4) the problem as trouble for network members.

1. Stigmatization

Many problems for which mutual self-help groups are formed are stig-matized (alcoholism and stuttering, or potentially stigmatized (ostomies) and network members know the stigmas as part of folk knowledge (c.f. Borkman 1979). Network members who have to deal with the self-helper's persistent unresolved difficulties find this a problem for themselves, and often handle it by stigmatizing the person with the problem (Robinson and Henry 1977: p. 53).

Many network members exhibit stigmatizing reactions to the self-helper in some situations even though they may generally be nonstigmatizing. Common stigmatizing reactions reported by the self-helper's are: a) ignore, deny, or minimize the self-helper's problem; b) manipulate situations to protect the self-helper and avoid stigmatization; c) directly and actively treat the self-helper as the embodiment of the stigmatizing stereotypes (e.g., the wife of the alcoholic accuses him of having no will power to stop drinking) and d) react to interactions and situations with unease, embarrassment, or discomfort.

These stigmatizing situations are troublesome *per se* to self-helpers. In addition, such stigmatizing interactions create distance in the relationships. The self-helper feels more or less alienated from family, friends, or stigmatizers. Such stigmatization also reinforces the self-helper's self-stigma or the feelings of being inadequate, worthless, or undesirably different (less than an ordinary competent adult) (c.f. Goffman, 1963; Robinson and Henry, 1977).

2. The Emotionscape

Emotionscape is a concept I have coined as analogous with "landscape" which is defined as "a picture representing a section of natural, inland scenery." (c.f. O'Briant and Lennard, 1973). Emotionscape refers to the meanings and feelings about the troublesome features in living with a given focal problem.

Each problem around which a self-help group is formed has its own emotionscape or emotional picture of the difficult situations, places, interactions, and persons. What places, persons, and situations potentially or actually arouse what kind of meanings and feelings to the possessor of a specific problem? Although there are commonalities to similar problems, each finds its own distinctive set of troublesome issues in everyday life.

Activities and situations taken for granted by an ordinary adult may be threatening to self-helpers. This point will be illustrated by showing how the same situation has different meanings for several self-helpers. Ordering food from a waiter in a restaurant presents quite different issues to the ostomate, the stutterer, and the sober alcoholic. The stutterer may be concerned with avoiding stuttering and end up selecting food he does not want because it was easier to be fluent on those menu items. The ostomate may be concerned with ingredients in dishes or types of food that are problematic for digestion. The sober alcoholic may be concerned about appearing natural and off-hand in refusing a drink or the wine list.

New self-helpers consistently express feeling alone, not understood, and being the only person with the problem. They usually are not socially isolated, but the members of their personal networks do not understand the emotionscape of their problem. They feel alone in part because their network operates in the code of simplistic folk information, and few understand at all the complexities of their emotionscape. Well-meaning sympathetic network members who try imaginatively and logically to pinpoint besetting elements of the problem are frequently off the mark.

Many network members of self-helpers thus do not know or understand the emotionscape of the problem and are accordingly limited in their capacity to provide social support.

3. Direct Impingements on Role Relationships

The third category in which network members are selectively unsupportive is demands in role relationships. Each problem interferes in some respects with fulfilling obligations of role relationships. An alcoholic's problematic family, friends, and work relationships are well known. Stutterers often restrict their activities and limit their relationships to avoid stuttering, and their fear of talking. Frustrations, disappointments, demands, or other lack of fulfillment in role relationships by the self-helper's role partner is thus the third more direct type of unsupportiveness of network members.

4. The Problem as Trouble for Network Members

The existence of a focal problem affects network members. The extreme case is the self-help groups in which the focal problem is that of a network member. For example, there are many self-help groups composed of parents whose children have a chronic or problematic disease (e.g., Hatfield 1978).

Family members often take on a "courtesy stigma" (Birenbaum 1970), a sort of guilt by association with a stigmatized person. Many family members, friends, co-workers, and other network members express anxiety, concern, frustration, and other preoccupations because of the self-helper's probelm and its consequences for their lives. Self-helpers are frequently aware of and upset over the trouble and anguish through which they put their friends and kin.

These difficulties of network members decreases their social support of the self-helper. For, to the extent that network members are bothered by the self-helper's problem, their capacity to support the self-helper is reduced, and they thus may be selectively unsupportive.

INTERVENTIONS TO STRENGTHEN THE SUPPORTIVENESS
OF THE SELF-HELPER'S NETWORKS

How do the self-help groups intervene to strengthen the supportiveness of the self-helper's personal network? Three general means will be described: 1) provide complementary social support through participation in the mutual self-help group, 2) transform the self-helper's perspective on the network, and 3) reconstruction of the network.

1. The Social Supportiveness of the Mutual Self-help Group

Participation in the mutual self-help group is strongly socially supportive in itself (Levy 1977, Robinson and Henry 1977, Borkman 1979). Self-helpers feel cared about as a person, feel that their peer self-helpers do understand their difficulties and emotionscape, and believe that the experiential paradigm of the group provides a constructive means of resolving their focal problem. The complementary social support of the mutual self-help group within the context of the self-helper's daily life probably decreases the amount and kind of support the self-helper needs from his personal network.

The groups vary in the amount, kind, and expected length of support from peers and participation in the group. Ostomates whose problem is adapting to a new physical condition, obviating stigma, and learning that they can maintain most or all of their previous way of life often are active from 1 to 2 years in the ostomy association. Afterwards, many maintain loose ties or communicate with the association irregularly for special problems as the need arises. A special helping relationship in the ostomy association is the "ostomy visitor" who visits the new ostomate in the hospital and continues an "on call" helping relationship for several months as needed.

Stutterers who arrive with a long-term intractable stuttering handicap may spend 3 to 6 years of active participation in the group and then gradually decrease participation. Borkman (1976b) found that several years of participation in the group were necessary for the self-helper to feel significant gains toward resolving their problem. Stutterers expect participation to lessen as the individual constructs a larger more satisfying personal network.

Recovering alcoholics perceive that their alcoholism is a lifelong problem that requires life-long participation in A.A. to maintain their sobriety. Unlike stutterers and ostomates whose meetings are monthly, many recovering alcholics attend meetings weekly or several times a week. Sober alcoholics, like stutterers, report that several years' participation in the self-help group were necessary before they made significant gains for themselves. Sponsors are specialized helping relationships in Alcoholics Anonymous somewhat analogous to "ostomy visitors."

2. Transforming the Self-Helper's Perspective of His/Her Network

Gaining experiential knowledge of their problem and destigmatizing themselves (e.g., Trice and Roman 1970) changes the perspective of self-helpers toward lay persons and their network members. Self-helpers are aware that they know about their problem experientially. Concurrently, they recognize the unworkability of folk information about it. Thus, persons who express folk ideas are indicating that they are misinformed and lack personal experience. Lay people cannot be expected to know their emotionscape.

Self-helpers appear to lower their expectations of how supportive their network members can or should be, given their lack of personal experience and experiential knowledge.

Folk ideas previously stigmatizing because the self-helper took them seriously and enacted them are now regarded as indications of misinformation. For example, before the self-help group experience, if a friend, co-worker, or stranger told a stutterer to "relax and talk slowly," the stutterer would likely be embarrassed to receive unsolicited advice but would take it seriously. With experiential knowledge, the same remark elicits the reaction from the stutterer that the advisor is misinformed and is revealing ignorance about stuttering. The changed perspective helps to neutralize previously stigmatizing and negative reactions from members of their network, thereby reducing its unsupportiveness.

Another area of perspectival change is with respect to decreased concern at the trouble the self-helper's problem causes other people. The emphasis on taking responsibility for resolving one's own problem is accompanied by the corollary that it is not then the self-helper's responsibility to resolve the other's troubles. This idea will be referred to as the "sphere of limited responsibility."

Of the three groups, A.A. members are most explicit about the "sphere of limited responsibility." Recovering alcoholics are told that only they themselves can be responsible for dealing with their drinking problem. Similarly, family members are responsible for their individual troubles. If each individual takes personal responsibility for the self alone, then together they can work out mutual problems in the relationships.

If old relationships become unsupportive, as in the case of ostomates, or continue to be unsupportive, as is more likely the situation with alcoholics or stutterers, the sphere of limited responsibility denotes that the unsupportive reaction of the network member is that member's problem in the long run, not that of the self-helpers.

3. Reconstruction of Personal Networks

Self-helpers reconstruct their personal networks to be supportive and congruent with their personal transformations. This reconstruction is an integral part of the experiential learning process. First, continuing relationships are modified; network members are re-educated. Second, relationships that continue to be problematic may be minimized or dropped. Third, new supportive relationships are added to the network.

As self-helpers try out new ideas learned in the group in their natural ongoing life space, they simultaneously affect these relationships. With more positive self-images, they interact differently, setting in motion chain reactions in their relationships. Furthermore, continuing relationships are specifically and directly reeducated about the self-helper's experiential perspective of the problem. Each group has some special social activities (e.g., parties, lectures, picnics) for families and friends during which they can see and learn from the group. Troublesome situations are also explicitly discussed among self-helpers. For example, "Do I tell the people at work about my ostomy surgery?" or "My mother (or father or friend) does not want to believe that I am an alcoholic. What do I do?" Ideas for handling these situations are suggested by sharing experiences among self-helpers.

As mentioned before, if unsupportive family, friends, or others continue to trouble the self-helper over time, the necessity may be to reduce contacts or drop the relationship. A number of instances were observed in which stutterers or alcoholics divorced spouses, dropped friends, or limited other familial contacts because the network member did not change with the transformation of the self-helper.

Some unsupportive relationships are viewed as detriments to the self-helper resolving a problem. Recovering alcoholics view old drinking friends as dangerous to sobriety unless the relationship can be reconstituted in nondrinking terms.

Third, a more supportive network is created by adding new members to it. Peer self-helpers from the group often become friends and intimates. Recovering alcoholics and stutterers especially are likely to try new activities and develop new relationships.

CONCLUSIONS

This paper presents a novel challenge to the assumption in the literature that the existence of personal networks constitutes potential or actual social support. It raises the issue that lay network members who possess folk ideas without personal experience with specialized health problems may be inherently incapable of providing the necessary social support to the sufferer of the problem. Walker, MacBride and Vachon (1977) developed similar ideas with respect to the crisis of bereavement.

The importance of the mutual self-help group's use of experientially based information and support has been underscored. The specialized social support provided by mutual self-help groups may be unavailable from other sources.

Furthermore, the paper suggests that as a by-product the mutual self-help group's learning processes provide opportunities to educate or re-educate the self-helper's personal network. In addition, the groups provide direct educational and re-educational opportunities for network members especially about the emotionscape. The hypothesis is suggested that family and other personal network members of self-helpers will be more knowledgeable about a given health problem than network members of persons with the same health problem who resolve it without support from a mutual self-help group.

This research was conducted from the self-helper's point of view on personal networks. Similar research should be conducted from the perspective of the families and friends of self-helpers. What is the impact on families and friends of the self-helper's experiences? How do families and friends change their perspective toward self-helpers and their problems? Does the destigmatization of the self-helper reduce the "courtesy stigma" of the network member? These and other specific questions could be addressed by such research.

The ideas introduced here also relate to the issue of which persons with a given problem will consider joining a mutual self-help group. Research indicates that only some persons with the same problem, as defined in some "objective" way by a bystander, are attracted to mutual self-help groups. Self-helpers tend to be persons who perceive their problem to be persistently troublesome to themselves. Perhaps self-helpers are so troubled because they have particularly unsupportive and stigmatizing personal networks. Those who are not self-helpers may find their problem less troublesome because their personal networks are comparatively supportive and nonstigmatizing.

This conceptual paper has presented a number of new ideas linking social support to experiential knowledge in three self-help groups. Such formulation appears promising to consider in relation to other health problems and other mutual self-help groups. These ideas can also serve as a guide to additional research on social support among mutual self-help groups, self-helpers, and their personal and community networks.

Chapter 17

FROM PROFESSIONAL HELP TO SELF-HELP

An Evaluation of
Therapeutic Groups for the Elderly

Nancy Gourash Bliwise
Morton A. Lieberman

Since the early 1960s radical changes have occurred in mental-health services; people no longer believe that those who seek help for emotional distress require therapeutic intervention from highly-trained specialists. Help for psychological problems is now available and legitimatized from a wide range of professional and nonprofessional sources. Helpers take a more active, directing role in therapeutic interactions and use a vast array of healing techniques. The recent growth of self-help groups offering help for problems traditionally in the domain of professional therapists is perhaps the most diverse and widely documented example of changes in both the source and strategy of assistance. The study to be reported examines the effectiveness of one system as it moves from a professional to a self-help orientation. Our purpose is to focus on the implications of the findings for the development of viable and effective self-help organizations.

SAGE (Senior Actualization and Growth Explorations) is a group program developed in 1974 by lay and professional people who wanted to create a growth setting for the elderly. It derives much of its philosophy and technology from the human potential movement and sets as a primary goal continued development in the latter half of life. SAGE proposes that old age is a time for self-development and spiritual growth as well as a time for transition and preparation for death.

Central to the ideology of SAGE is the premise that much of what is commonly believed about aging is a myth. SAGE "teaches" that peoples' thoughts and attitudes create their feelings and shape both their bodies and lives. Implied in this view is that acceptance of the myths of aging lead to their ultimate fulfillment. Many of the chronic symptoms associated with age are held to be the result of long-term stress as well as a sedentary life style and poor diet. By actively working to change attitudes, however, people can increase their control over their lives, relieve much of their stress, and reverse the ailments of old age. SAGE's ultimate goal is "holistic health"—freedom from pain, disability, emotional hang-ups, and mental confusion—achieved through harmony between mind, body, and spirit. SAGE believes that the growth needed to attain this harmony, however, can only be accomplished under special conditions in which there is guidance, support, challenge, and deep emotional nourishment.

SAGE attempts to provide the special setting necessary for growth in its program of weekly meetings. Groups are composed of 10 to 15 members aged sixty or over who meet with two or occasionally three leaders weekly for 3- to 4-hour sessions over a 9-month period. The leaders take a facilitative role of guiding exercises and clarifying group processes. Members are encouraged to be supportive of one another, to maintain contacts beyond the formal group setting and to practice outside what was learned within the group. The group meetings are relatively structured and center around meditation, guided discussions in group or dyadic contexts, yoga, massage, dream analyses and exercises designed to enhance physical well-being and reverse the chronic symptoms of aging.

At its inception SAGE was one of only a few programs specifically created with the needs of the elderly in mind. It was a professional system; all groups were led by professionals trained in mental health. By 1976, however, the demand for groups far exceeded the supply of professionally-trained leaders. In response to this shortage SAGE group graduates were invited to become group leaders. Concurrently the founders of SAGE greatly reduced or ended their involvement in the program, turning over responsibility for both governance and policy to group members as well as to other professionals who had joined the SAGE staff. In addition, the founder wrote a book (Luce, 1979) carefully describing the philosophy and techniques and providing for the "codification" of SAGE. Thus, by 1979, SAGE had moved toward a self-help orientation: administration was more democratic with governance shared by professionals and group members; peers served as group leaders; a SAGE "community" evolved so that group members who had completed the formal group experience could remain active in the organization; and new groups inspired by SAGE were started in other cities and states.

In our study, we were guided by the question, "Can a professionally conceived and implemented help system successfully adopt a self-help orientation?" To answer this question, we examined the effectiveness of SAGE groups led by both professionals and peers, contrasting outcomes under both types of leadership with a control sample of applicants who had not yet begun their group experience.

DESIGN

Our findings are based on data from 108 SAGE group members who were part of an evaluation of the effectiveness of SAGE conducted by the authors over a 3-year period from late 1976 through 1979. After screening by the SAGE staff, applicants considered psychologically or physically vulnerable were excluded from the program and referred to alternate help sources (less than 5 percent of applicants were excluded for this reason). Those accepted agreed to participate in the research as part of their commitment to SAGE and were randomly assigned to an available group led by either a professional or peer leader.

The first study year used a different strategy for assignment; the demand for groups exceeded the available supply of group leaders. Consequently only the first 30 applicants accepted into the program were assigned to groups. The remaining 30 applicants were placed on a waiting list and asked to participate in the study as controls.

Identical interviews were conducted with all participants before the start of each SAGE group (T1) and immediately following its termination (T2). Interviews lasted from 3 to 4 hours and developed information about present life circumstances as well as personal goals (see Figure 1).

FRAMEWORK FOR ASSESSING OUTCOMES

Recognizing that the evaluation of psychotherapeutic outcomes often involves competing values (particularly in nontraditional therapeutic systems), Strupp and Hadley (1974) propose that assessment should include the potentially divergent viewpoints of the client, the mental-health professional, and the society. In a related manner, the tripartite model we developed to evaluate SAGE reflected the goals of the client, the organization, and our "external" point of view as researchers (for further elaboration of the model see Lieberman and Bond, 1979).

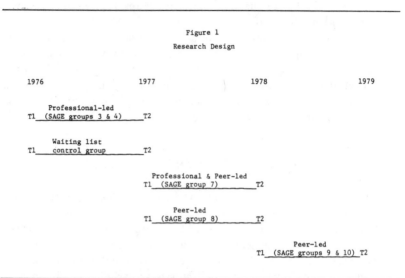

Figure 1

Research Design

1976 · 1977 · 1978 · 1979

Professional-led
T1 (SAGE groups 3 & 4)   T2

Waiting list
T1   control group   T2

Professional & Peer-led
T1   (SAGE group 7)   T2

Peer-led
T1   (SAGE group 8)   T2

Peer-led
T1   (SAGE groups 9 & 10) T2

An ideographic technique was used to assess the value of the group experience from the perspective of the client. Individuals were asked in the first interview to describe their major goals and objectives (Battle *et al.,* 1966). At the end of the group program they were asked to rate on a 9-point scale the degree to which they had accomplished these goals. This method not only permitted evaluation based on individualized outcome criteria, it also provided information on the issues that brought people to SAGE.

System-level goals guided the selection of measures reflecting the organization's perspective. Although reduction of psychological distress is a central aspect of the goal of holistic health, SAGE offers its clients not psychotherapy but experiential learning designed to foster harmony between mind, body and spirit. The primary emphasis of group and individual exercises is on physical exercises, meditation, and yoga through which SAGE encourages participants to exorcise self-images of fragile, deteriorating old people; to improve physical condition; to reduce reliance on health props (particularly psychotropic medications) and to discover the full range of their physical and spiritual potential. Because the required health-screening physical examination insured a healthy sample and made it unlikely that major improvements in physical well-being would occur, we felt that self-perceived health status and medical behavior would more accurately reflect group goals. Indices included self-ratings of health status compared to peers, and the extent to which health interfered with activities. Health behavior was evaluated on the basis of the number of physician visits in the last year due to illness and on the number and kinds of medications taken in the previous week.

In the present study, the researcher's external point of view is closely akin to the more traditional outcome goals of mental-health practitioners: symptom reduction and positive changes in self-image. Researchers report that most individuals who seek out growth experiences resemble psycho-therapy patients in their degree of psychological distress and their desire for symptom-relief (Lieberman and Gardner, 1975; Noll and Watkins, 1974). Since many of the SAGE clientele were similarly troubled and seeking psychological help, they could be appropriately studied from a traditional psychotherapeutic outcome perspective. Symptom-reduction was measured with the Hopkins Symptom Checklist. This self-report measure asks for ratings of the extent to which psychiatric symptoms such as feeling fearful, crying easily, headaches, sweating, blaming one's self, were experienced in the past month. Although the checklist provides assessment of specific symptom groupings (i.e. interpersonal, obsessive, somatic, depression, and anxiety), a principal-components analysis of the items with varimax rotations failed even to approximate in our sample the symptom subscales outlined by Derogatis, Lipman, Rickels, Uhlenhuth, and Covi (1974). Instead, a unidimensional factor was found which limited analyses to the total symptom score. A self-report self-esteem index (Rosenberg, 1966) comprised of such items as "I feel I have a number of good qualities," "I certainly feel useless at times," was used to assess changes in self-image. Hensley and Roberts (1976) recently contested the validity of using this measure with samples of the elderly because it did not produce the unidimensionality Rosenberg reported with his initial, adolescent sample. A principle-components analysis of scale items, however, sug-gested the scale was a valid, unidimensional measure of self-esteem in the present sample.

SAMPLE

The 86 women and 22 men interviewed formed an unusually well-educated sample of the elderly; over 75 percent had continued beyond high school. Their marital status and sex, however, were typical of populations over age sixty (See Table 1). Motivations for joining SAGE were diverse: to implement personal changes, to begin new activities, or to establish new interpersonal relationships. Many participants wanted assistance in coping with physical, emotional, and marital problems. Still others hoped that the SAGE experience would help them overcome negative personal and societal attitudes about growing old.

Their overall evaluation of health was generally positive; over three-fourths reported good health and 66 percent judged they were healthier than their peers. Some experienced health problems; 34 percent made five or more physician visits due to illness in the last year and 75 percent re-

Table 1

Demographic Characteristics of the Sample

	%	N*
SEX		
Male	20	22
Female	80	86
AGE		
– 60	1	1
60–64	40	43
65–69	36	38
70–74	12	13
75–79	8	9
80 +	3	3
EDUCATION		
Some high school	4	4
High school graduate	18	19
Some college	23	25
College graduate	32	34
Professional status	23	25
MARITAL STATUS		
Married	49	50
Widowed	22	23
Separated/Divorced	23	24
Single	6	6

* Some missing cases

ported using some form of medication in the last week. But, most participants spent little time thinking about health matters and claimed that physical problems had not significantly affected their lives. These same clients, however, reported experiencing psychological distress. The mean symptom level on the Hopkins Symptoms Checklist was higher than that found in a random sample of people over age sixty living in the Greater Chicago Metropolitan Area (SAGE $\bar{x} = 1.56$, GCMA $\bar{x} = 1.11$; $t = 2.29$, $p < .05$).[1] In addition, 37 percent of the sample reported seeking professional help within the last year for a nervous or emotional problem.

GROUP LEADERS

The formal education and amount of professional psychotherapeutic experience varied greatly among the ten group leaders with the clearest distinctions occurring, of course, between professional and peer leaders (See Table 2). All professionals possessed at least an M.A. degree in counseling psychology or a related field; four of the five professionals had previous experience in individual and group therapy; however, only one had previous professional experience with elderly clients.

The SAGE staff selected six interested SAGE group graduates to be trained as peer leaders. Five of the leaders were indeed nonprofessional peers; the sixth, however, was a retired psychiatrist with more clinical training and experience than any other leader. Although SAGE considered him to be a peer leader, his 30 years of work in the mental health field could not be discounted. Hence, he was included in classifications with other professionally-trained leaders.

Training in specific SAGE Techniques was through direct participation in the 9-month program. Professional leaders, except for the founders of SAGE, served in SAGE groups as interns before leading their own groups. Peer leaders supplemented their group membership with four all-day workshops focused on the setting of group goals, principles of group psychotherapy and a review of SAGE techniques. Supervision was provided to all leaders by the founders of SAGE and centered around group-process issues. The peer leaders met with the founders in weekly group sessions where professionals met once a month. In addition, the leaders of each group met weekly on their own to plan future sessions and discuss the needs and progress of group members.

Table 2

Leaders: Formal Training and Previous Professional Experience

Professional Leaders

G.L. - Group #3	K.D. - Group #3	E.G. - Group #4
Ph.D. Psychology 5+ years - leader of relaxation and biofeedback workshops	Ph.D. Psychology 4+ years - leader of Esalen groups	M.A. Family and Child Counseling 5+ years - individual and family therapy
D.C. - Group #4	H.A. - Group #7	
M.A. Creative Arts 2 years - director of counseling and recreation program for the elderly	M.D. Pediatrics Resident Fellow Psychiatry 30+ years - individual and group therapy	

Peer Leaders

A.B. - Groups #7, 10	M.M. - Group #7	C.S. - Group #8
B.A. Education No previous experience	High School Diploma No previous experience	Liberal Arts - 2 years No previous experience
V.S. - Group #8	B.L. - Groups #9, 10	M.G. - Group #9
Liberal Arts - 2 years No previous experience	B.S. Business Administration No previous experience	B.A. Letters & Sciences No previous experience

---

FINDINGS

Of the original 108 participants, 11 either dropped out of the groups ($N = 9$) or were unavailable ($N = 2$) for interview leaving a total sample of 97 for these analyses. Compared with those who completed the program, the dropouts were younger ($t = 2.80$, $p < .01$), had less education ($t = 2.83$, $p < .01$), and reported less likelihood of health problems to interfering with day-to-day activities ($t = 2.40$, $p < .05$).

In professional-led groups 36 participated, 32 were in peer-led groups, and 29 were wait-listed and comprised our control group. The SAGE group led by both a professional and peer leader was considered a professional-led group. Since group differences in baseline scores can bias later estimates of change, one-way ANOVAs and the Chi-square statistic for categorical variables were used to examine the comparability of T1 scores between people in each condition (professional, peer, control). Despite the similarity in recruitment procedures over time and the demographic equivalence of the groups, this analysis yielded two significant differences: 1) members of peer-led groups, compared with those in professional-led or control groups reported that health matters rarely or never interfered with activities; and 2) members of peer-led groups had lower scores on the measure of self-esteem (See Table 3).

Analysis of covariance was used to evaluate differences in outcomes between members of professional-led and peer-led groups relative to change over an identical time span by those on the waiting list. Covariance statistics were calculated on T2 scores for members of each condition, using T1 scores as a covariate in order to control for bias due to observed base line group differences. A one-way analysis of variance was used to compare differences in goal achievement since no base-line measures were possible. When significant group effects were found, the Scheffe (1959) post-hoc procedure determined which comparisons between conditions accounted for significance.

The evaluation of the target goals indicated that members of both professional-led and peer-led SAGE groups felt they had accomplished their desired goals to a greater extent than those in the wait-control group (See Table 3 for all outcome findings). No significant changes were found on any of the measures of physical status or health behavior. Analyses of mental-health variables, however, yielded significant differences betwen conditions in symptom-reduction and changes in self-esteem. Psychiatric symptoms diminished from T1 to T2 among members of professional-led groups where mean-symptom levels increased for both members of peer-led SAGE groups and those placed on the waiting list. Overall positive shifts in self-esteem were observed for members in all three conditions. Post-hoc comparisons, however, revealed that the increase in self-esteem was significantly greater than that experienced by controls only for members of professional-led groups.

Discussion

We approached our study of SAGE's impact utilizing a framework that included traditional psychotherapeutic perspectives and ones more closely tied to individual and system-level goals. SAGE had a considerable impact when assessed from the participants' own perspective; after 9 months of group meetings, SAGE group members felt they had substantially met their initial goals. From the organizational perspective, no systematic changes in health status of health behavior were reported by study participants. Some definite psychotherapeutic benefits, however, accrued to members of professional-led groups. They experienced fewer psychiatric

TABLE 3

COMPARISONS OF T1 AND T2 SCORES BY LEADERSHIP CONDITION

	Scores						Significance Test	
	Professional led		Peer-led		Control		T1 Comparisons	Covariance
Outcome Measures	T1	T2	T1	T2	T1	T2		
Individual Perspective								
x̄ - Goal Achievement (HI=9)	--	5.62	--	5.68	--	4.24	--	6.25*
System-level Perspectives								
x̄ - General Health (HI=4)	3.07	2.94	2.79	2.66	3.07	3.10	2.78	1.08
x̄ - Health Comparison (HI=3)	2.70	2.51	2.71	2.71	2.60	2.56	0.26	0.84
x̄ - Health Interferes IHI=5)	2.56	2.47	1.97	1.84	2.67	2.55	5.60*	0.21
% - 5+ Physician Visits (yes)	28%	32%	35%	30%	38%	28%	1.02	0.64
% - Medication Use (yes)	72%	73%	75%	75%	83%	79%	1.17	0.82
Mental Health Perspective								
x̄ - Symptoms (HI=4)	1.54	1.48	1.55	1.59	1.61	1.64	0.78	5.90*
x̄ - Self-Esteem (HI=6)	4.06	4.81	3.07	3.53	3.90	4.07	4.20*	4.97*

* p ≤ .05

symptoms and a marked increase in self-esteem after participation in the SAGE program relative to those in peer-led groups and wait-control groups. Since the implications of these findings for the efficacy of the SAGE approach to therapeutic change in the elderly has been discussed in detail elsewhere (Lieberman and Gourash, 1979) our discussion will focus on their meaning for self-help.

When we began the present evaluation of SAGE we were guided by the question: "Can a professionally conceived and implemented help system successfully adopt a self-help orientation?" We knew from our earlier work (Lieberman and Gourash, 1979) that as a professional system, SAGE had a positive effect on its members. Would the organizational shift toward self-help have any consequences for the program's effectiveness? Clearly, it did. Although members of peer-led groups were equivalent to members of professional-led groups in the extent to which they felt they had achieved personal goals, they did not experience the symptom-relief and increases in self-esteem reported by those in professional-led groups. In order to understand the general implications of our findings for the development of viable and effective self-help organizations, we must first examine SAGE in the context of other help systems.

As indicated at the outset of this chapter, self-help is just one aspect of a growing deprofessionalization of mental-health services. Radical changes in service delivery have legitimated increasing numbers of treatment approaches implemented by a wide range of therapeutic agents. Traditional distinctions between professional and nonprofessional helpers and helping methods have become blurred, making classification of new therapeutic systems difficult. Because of the wide range of options available to new or changing help systems, perhaps the clearest understanding of SAGE's transition from professional help to self-help can be gained by focusing on characteristics that cross-cut all mental-health systems. We shall therefore attempt to place SAGE in the context of other professional, nonprofessional and self-help systems along the dimensions of: 1) client control, 2) the psycholgical distance between helper and client, 3) the assumptions underlying the selection and training of helping agents and 4) treatment methods.

Contrary to existent myths about self-help, many self-help organizations were developed or were heavily influenced by mental-health professionals (Lieberman and Borman, 1979). Thus a more important variable for differentiating help systems becomes the control rather than the origin of the help system. Regardless of whether services are offered by professionals or nonprofessionals, service delivery is rarely controlled by the client. Self-help organizations are unique among help systems in that the client rather than the professional or an external agency has primary responsibility for service delivery both at the organizational and the individual helper/client level. SAGE has evolved toward client control, and is, in this respect, most similar to self-help therapy systems.

One of the major criticisms directed toward professional helping systems is the social and psychological distance between the helper and the client. Classical psychotherapy models rely on maximizing psychological boundaries between client and therapist. In reaction to this characteristic of professional help, many help systems have turned to "alternative" therapeutic models and nonprofessional helpers in order to reduce social and psychological distance and improve access and communication between helper and client. Frequently the nonprofessional helper is drawn from the same community and social strata as the client. Self-help systems extend the selection of such indigenous helpers one step further; help is provided by individuals who are in the system for their own therapeutic needs thereby eliminating traditional distinctions between helper and client.

SAGE resembles self-help organizations in that peer leaders entered SAGE seeking help for problems similar to those of their group members. And yet boundaries still exist between helpers and group members. SAGE's peer leaders work in the same setting as professional leaders and receive special training and supervision by these professionals. While other self-help groups have leaders who receive training and supervision (Recovery, Inc.), they operate outside a professional setting. SAGE peer leaders, through their close alliance with professionals, have special access to information and technical resources not readily available to but perhaps coveted by group members. By remaining in the professional setting and preserving a professional system of supervision, SAGE also preserved much of the psychological distance between helper and client that is characteristic of professional relationships. The use of peer leaders to deliver services may have made boundaries between SAGE peer-group leaders and members less impenetrable, but it certainly did not result in the parity between helper and client that is central in most self-help organizations.

Another important aspect of all help systems is the set of assumptions underlying the selection and training of therapeutic agents. Professional systems assume that high-level skills are essential for providing effective therapy: hence the requirements for scholastic ability and years of increasingly specialized education. With the development of new labor resources in the mental-health field, traditional educational criteria were abandoned. This expanded the range of individuals serving as therapeutic agents and increased variability in the assumptions guiding the selection and training of helpers. For some help systems, the nonprofessional helper was seen as a mechanism for creating larger numbers of skilled individuals able to provide services similar to those offered by professionals. The Rioch experiment in which mature homemakers were intensively trained for 2 years to become psychotherapists (Rioch, Elkes & Flint, 1963) represents one extreme of this viewpoint. Rioch assumed that therapeutic techniques used by professionals are critical in helping others and attempted to teach professional skills to nonprofessionals. A contrasting viewpoint is provided by Goodman (1972) who selected college students to provide "companionship therapy" to emotionally disturbed youngsters. He assumed that people possess natural helping abilities and that, without special training, psychologically healthy individuals can provide help to those experiencing emotional distress.

A somewhat different strategy involves choosing therapeutic agents who share the affliction of those seeking aid. Here the nonprofessional is viewed as having unique skills not readily available among professional therapists. Direct experience with or resolution of the problem is assumed to be necessary and sufficient for acquiring the therapeutic skills important for providing effective help. This perspective, while sometimes evident in agencies offering individual counseling, is most prevalent among self-help groups. SAGE, with its peer leadership and specialized training, falls somewhere in between these differing viewpoints. SAGE assumes that for the nonprofessional helper effective intervention requires both the insight gained from personally experiencing the problems of old age, and special skills that can be learned through training in SAGE techniques.

Perhaps the most salient distinctions among help systems lie in the assumptions made about the nature of the problem and how it is to be addressed. Professional treatment methods, while extremely varied, tend to rely on highly abstract notions about the nature of emotional distress, and technologically complex cures. The curative mechanisms most frequently stressed in professional systems are heavily dependent on the influence of the therapist and require high degrees of training for effective implementation. In contrast, therapeutic interventions based on factors inherent in any warm, confiding relationship utilize common sense notions of effective help-giving rather than specific technical operations derived from an abstract theoretical framework. Helpers are encouraged to be supportive and to act as they would with a friend who was seeking help. The therapeutic agents employed in settings using this approach are frequently nonprofessionals since the treatment mode requires little, if any, special training.

Treatment methods derived from the common experiences of the afflicted are most typical of help systems (particularly self-help groups) in which the helper shares a problem with the client. Although help strategies in such systems often change over time and reflect a variety of influences (professional, societal norms about helping, methods borrowed from other systems, common experiences of the afflicted), they tend to be problem-specific and to respond to basic features of the condition shared by both the helper and the client (Antze, 1979).

Again, SAGE cannot be easily characterized by any one approach. SAGE responds to the specific needs of the elderly by focusing on both the physical ailments of old age and the psychological issues relevant to late life. Common problems emerge within the group setting and individual and group exercises are created to counteract basic elements of these problems. But, the treatment methods of SAGE also incorporate central aspects of professional models. SAGE's ideology rests on abstract notions of growth borrowed from the human potential movement. Healing techniques require a leader/teacher and specific training. Group leaders structure the weekly sessions. By building these characteristics of professional treatment models into their help strategy, SAGE has remained more closely allied with professional rather than with self-help treatment approaches.

In an attempt to place SAGE in the context of other professional, non-professional and self-help organizations, SAGE has been examined in the light of four dimensions common to all mental health systems: 1) client control, 2) the psychological distance between helper and client, 3) the assumptions underlying the selection and training of helpers and 4) treatment methods. SAGE resembles most self-help organizations with regard to client control of the system, the selection of nonprofessional helpers sharing an affliction with the client, and the use of healing techniques specifically designed to meet the needs of their group members. But in terms of the psychological distance between leader and member, leader training, and the additional use of highly complex treatment methods, SAGE remains more closely allied with professional mental health approaches. Having located SAGE in the larger realm of help systems, we are still faced with the task of explaining the observed differences in outcome under peer and professional leadership. We will now turn to the literature on therapeutic outcome and attempt to determine the relative influence of these dimensions of SAGE's effectiveness.

Gartner and Riessman (1974) argue that increased client control of human services encourages greater effectiveness since the client has a fuller, more self-determining role in the help process, which is more likely be self-benefiting. To our knowledge, no research has been published to date comparing self-help psychotherapy groups (in which there is client control as well as client participation in service delivery) with other mental health services. Our findings suggest that client control may not be a significant determinant of outcome since fewer psychotherapeutic benefits were reported by those in peer-led groups. But without comparative data it is impossible to assess whether SAGE is the exception or the rule.

Reductions in the psychological distance between helper and client are thought to promote rapport and identification, which in turn lead to greater role modeling and openness to change on the part of the client (Durlak, 1979; Karlsruher, 1974; Sobey, 1970). Indeed, comparative research on indigenous helpers has shown that therapeutic agents who share similar backgrounds, life styles and social characteristics with their clients are at least as effective, and often more effective than their professional counterparts (Brown & Myers, 1975; Hall, 1972; Lamb and Clack, 1974; Russell and Wise, 1976; Zunker & Brown, 1966).

In self-help groups where traditional distinctions between helper and client are nonexistent, further benefits are gained from the opportunity to provide help to others in distress (Lieberman, 1979). In the SAGE context, peer leaders share common experiences as old people with their group members. But, as argued earlier, psychological boundaries between helper and client still exist within the system. These boundaries may inhibit identification, generate psychological disengagement from the group process and interfere with the peer leaders' ability to serve as effective role models: factors which could account for fewer psychotherapeutic gains under SAGE peer leadership. Designated leadership may also have reduced opportunities for mutual aid among SAGE group members and the increases in self-esteem that can result from seeing oneself as a positive, helpful member of a group (Fremous and Harmatz, 1975; Gruver, 1971; Riessman, 1965).

SAGE's use of a therapeutic model and treatment methods borrowed from the human potential movement may also be important for understanding the different outcomes observed under professional and peer leadership. Studies that have examined the type of help offered by nonprofessionals all agree that lay helpers are most effective when they provide friendship and support, give practical advice and teach daily-living skills (see review by Anthony and Carkhuff, 1977). Most self-help groups capitalize on the special skills of their helpers and encourage them to share problems and give practical advice (Levy, 1979).

SAGE, however, more closely resembles growth groups in that they focus on positive experiences and discourage members from bringing personal problems and negative feelings into the group. Thus, SAGE peer leaders may have been unable to provide the support and advice that seems contributive to effective intervention by nonprofessional helpers. SAGE also relies on specific treatment methods commonly used in growth and encounter groups. Given that yoga, autogenic healing, dream analysis, etc., involve more than the pragmatics of daily living, there is no reason to assume that novices will be able to teach these methods as successfully as those with years of training and practice with the techniques. Indeed, research suggests that when the treatment approach requires more than just friendship and support, nonprofessionals can function effectively only when provided with systematic, in-depth training (Anthony and Carkhuff, 1977; Carkhuff and Truax, 1965; Weinman, Sanders, Kleiners & Wilson, 1970). Perhaps the SAGE peer leaders needed more than four training sessions and their own group experience to be able successfully to implement the diverse and often complex methods at the heart of SAGE's help strategy.

SAGE's transition from a professional to a self-help system involved adopting the client control and peer leadership characteristic of most self-help organizations. But, SAGE also retained key aspects of the professional system which appear to have negatively affected outcome under peer leadership. By remaining in a professional setting, preserving a professional system of supervision and retaining ideological constraints on group behavior that were closely tied to the professional-treatment model, SAGE may only have succeeded in converting peers into less well-trained professionals. Perhaps if the SAGE members were left to pursue goals of personal growth and development under some structure based on their own devices, outcome results for the peer leaders would have matched those of the professionals.

The implications of our findings for the development of effective self-help organizations are clear. Before professionals can successfully create a self-help setting, they must recognize the importance of an ideology that grows out of and responds to the needs of the afflicted. In a similar vein, if a professional help system is to be successfully converted into a procedure delivered by nonprofessionals, then the teaching, support, and advice skills of the nonprofessional helper should provide the focus for the helping interaction.

This study was supported in part by a National Institute of Mental Health Research Grant, No. PHS #-K01-MH 20342.

[1]Comparison data were drawn from the Life Events and Adaptation in Adulthood study. This study was supported by a National Institute of Aging Research Grant, No. NIA #-P01-AG00123.

Part IV

POSTSCRIPT

Chapter 18

SELF-HELP GROUPS:
An International Perspective

Alfred Katz

As might be anticipated from other sections of this volume the international self-help scene is a very active one. Even though the mental-health "industry" in the United States is much larger than in any other country, the array of social and psychological forces that have sparked interest in alternative mental-health approaches, and in self-help forms in particular, is similar throughout the western world of industrialized countries, and also influences third world and socialist countries.

The familiar model of health services, including mental-health services, in these countries is one that establishes specialized agencies of help, with professional providers who are believed to possess unique knowledge and technology. Consumers are viewed as possessors of the problem, who it is hoped will seek a solution from, or with the aid of, professionals. If consumers do not conform to professional expectations, or follow the requirements laid down by the service agency they are thought to be resistant or refractory. Clients' views on the kinds of services they need and desire are rarely elicited or attended to.

The last decade has brought forth a powerful popular critique of the limitations of this professional model of health, including mental-health, care (Levin, Katz, and Holst, 1979). This critique has been given concrete expression by the formation of hundreds of self-help groups in many diverse fields, ranging from physical and mental illness or disability, to addictions, to problems arising from a deviant or stigmatzied social position (ex-mental patients, ex-prisoners, homosexuals) to situational crises (widowhood, single-parenthood, child-abuse, parenting "runaway" children).

The common denominators in groups, formed around such diverse problems and composed of such diverse populations, were the inadequacies found in the professional help-giving model, and the need to establish greater self-determination and control over personal and group destinies.

As an expression of a drive for growth and human dignity, the impulse for such self-reliance engenders self-help groups which become vehicles for social support and mutual aid, identity fulfillment, and constructive social achievement. These groups have the corollary benefit of reducing mono-polistic social controls by professionals (who are usually affiliated with the medical-care system) while enhancing the use of the community's natural care-giving resources of family, extended family, informal friendship and workplace networks, religious organizations and the like. (All these aspects parallel closely the recommendations under "Community Support Systems" of the President's Commission Report on Mental Health, 1978).

A WORLD-WIDE MOVEMENT

Given the social-political-professional forces and concepts that have dominated 20th century health and mental-health care, especially in the developed countries, it is not surprising that the lay-initiated critique and counter-movement for greater lay involvement through self-care and self-help groups has become worldwide.

Thus there is a rapid growth and a wide interest in self-help groups and self-care in many parts of the world. Some insights into the scope and significance of these phenomena are to be found by sketching recent developments in some specific countries.

- *In the United Kingdom* Robinson and Henry (1977) have reported on more than 200 different self-help groups, many concerned with mental-health issues. Some 50 of these groups discussed their programs at a conference in July 1977, sponsored by the Department of Urban Affairs, University of Bristol. Also in 1977, a Self-Help Clearing House was established in London by Share, Inc. A mutual aid center was also founded that year in London to promote self-help activities in third world countries.
- *Australia* shows a high level of activity in self-help. In September 1977 the Victorian Council for Social Services, a

social agency serving the whole state of Victoria, convened a conference of self-help groups in Melbourne. It was attended by more than 80 representatives of self-help groups; following the conference, two detailed descriptive and analytical brochures were published by the Victorian Council. As an indication of the liveliness of self-help interest in Australia, no fewer than five Australian lay groups raised monies so that their representatives could attend the 1979 Dubrovnik Self-Help Conference, which will be described at a later point.

• *In West Germany*, Alcoholics Anonymous is widespread, in almost every town, with a large number of local groups and so-called "intercity groups." Two chapters of Emotions Anonymous were founded in 1972 (Berlin, Dusseldorf); 14 groups in 1974 groups in 1974 after the organization established a central office. Today there are more than 70 groups called "Self-Help Groups for Mental Health." Since 1972, a professor of mental health at the Center for Psychosomatic Medicine of Giessen University (total 15,000 students) has helped to set up 30 self-help groups comprising:
15 students self-help groups (emotional problems)
5 self-help groups mainly for patients of an ambulatory clinic (emotional problems; psychosomatic diseases)
5 couple self-help groups
3 so-called "new parents self-help groups"
2 overeaters self-help groups.

There are also local self-help groups for elderly people, for patients with neurological diseases (stroke; traumatic lesion of the brain; multiple sclerosis) and for patients with cardiac infarction. The connection between professionals and self-help groups is a special coordinating monthly meeting of local groups called *Gesamttreffen* (a meeting of all) which is as important as the self-help sessions.

In 1975 a nation-wide German Association of Self-Help Groups (*Deutsche Arbeitsgemeinschaft Selbsthilfegruppen*) was founded which has the same objectives as the National Self-Help Clearinghouse in New York. It promotes regional or local associations of self-help groups (*Regionale Arbeitsgemeinschaften Selbsthilfegruppen*). There are existing local associations in 12 cities, including Berlin, Bielefeld, Hamburg, Essen, Dusseldoft, Giessen, Munchen, Kempten, etc. The German Association publishes a semiannual periodical *Self Help Groups News* (*Selbsthilfegruppen-Nachrichten*).

In September 1979, the First Conference of Regional Associations of Self-Help Groups was held in Germany with federal financial support. The

Federal Government Research Council has financed studies of self-help groups now underway in four urban localities: Hamburg, Regensburg, Konstanz, and Giessen. A psychiatrist at the University of Giessen, Dr. M.L. Moeller, who has conducted self-help therapy groups for the past several years and is now doing research on psychotherapeutic groups, has recently published an important theoretical and practical account in a book entitled "Selbst Hilfe Gruppen" (Moeller, 1978).

- In *Holland and Belgium*, similar studies of a variety of local and national self-help groups are being conducted by academics, who have been impressed by the dynamism and apparent success of many groups that have been initiated either through lay initiatives or by professionals.
- In *Poland*, the Union of Invalid Cooperatives, which has been in existence since shortly after World War II, continues to provide various services, particularly sheltered industrial workshops, for about one-third of the handicapped population in that country.
- The *Scandinavian countries have shown a particular interest in exploring the possibilities of medical self-care; they were active participants in the 1975 Copenhagen Symposium on the Role of the Individual in Primary Health Care, which led to an expansion of self-care programmatic activity and research; and there are several empirical studies in progress in Sweden, Denmark, and Norway.*

These separate developments all stemmed from the conviction of the importance of self-help approaches by initiating programs and research, and exchanging experiences. They helped prepare the way for the International Conference on the Role of Self Help and Mutual Aid in Contemporary Society, held in Dubrovnik, Yugoslavia, 1979.

INTERNATIONAL CONFERENCES

Fifty-eight participants, comprising self-help group activists, scholars and researchers and government officials attended the Dubrovnik conference, which had been organized by an international committee, and was jointly sponsored by the International Centre for Post-Graduate Studies in Dubrovnik, and the Self Help and Mutual Aid International, based in Los Angeles.

The 58 participants came from 16 countries and four continents:

Australia	5	New Zealand	1
Austria	1	Norway	1
Belgium	2	Phillipines	1
Canada	5	San Salvador	1
Denmark	4	Sweden	2
England	4	U.S.A.	11
Israel	1	West Germany	4
Holland	4	Yugoslavia	11

About 20 persons who had preregistered for the conference, including individuals from Poland, Italy, Senegal, Egypt, and Great Britain, were for one reason or another unable to attend.

The conference format was designed by the program committee to maximize the spirit of mutual aid; there was, throughout, an extraordinary amount of participation and sharing.

Each participant elected to join one of five interest groups which met for about 12 hours each during the conference. These were: (1) health and self-care, (2) family and mental health, (3) research, (4) social policy and administration, and (5) futures and future planning.

On each of the mornings the conference met as a whole; case histories were presented of the emergence of new groups and the expansion of existing groups and organizations. Also heard were presentations of theoretical, research, or policy nature. The scope was wide and varied and almost all participants gave papers or reported their own experiences in such groups. Two additional meetings were organized at the request of the participants. One was on women's issues, the other on the relationship of politics to self-help developments.

Among the highlights of the conference were round-table discussion of the extensive Yugoslavian self-help clubs for hypertension control, papers on self-help community movements organized by poor and physically handicapped people in Australia and New Zealand; accounts of national studies of self-help groups in West Germany, Belgium, Holland, and England; self-care groups for multiple-sclerosis patients in Denmark; programs for Indians and other ethnic minorities in Canada; self-help housing construction in El Salvador; self-care health programs for children in Connecticut.

OTHER MEETINGS

In addition to the Dubrovnik meeting, which had particular significance as the first international meeting solely focused on self-help issues, a number of recent international conferences have touched on self-help and medical self-care. At the International Sociological Association meeting in Uppsala, Sweden, in August 1978, in a section devoted to the study of voluntary action, several papers dealing with aspects of self-help were presented. Following that meeting, an International Association of Voluntary Action Scholars was organized including on its steering group prominent self-help students from the United States and the United Kingdom. Related topics and issues were discussed at two meetings in Holland: at the University of Maastricht, in June 1978, the role of the patient and the provider and self-care with the Dutch Patients' Association taking a prominent part were discussed, and in May 1979 the *Excerpta Medica* Conference on Patient Education was held at the Hague.

It should also be noted that a considerable number of international "disease-specific" organizations, which were originally created and still operate on a self-help basis, carry on worldwide programs of public and professional education, research, and patient care. Such groups as the International Federation of Societies for the Mentally Retarded, The World Hemophilia Foundation, Alcoholics Anonymous International, and so on, should be differentiated from purely professional or scientific bodies that meet solely for the exchange of scientific information. The former are true self-help organizations of patients, their families, interested professionals, and community leaders in a number of countries who find it profitable to convene every year or two to exchange ideas and experiences regarding solutions to the social living and rehabilitation problems faced by their constituents.

Of related interest, but not representing a self-help constituency or main focus, are some international professional bodies, such as the International Association for Social Psychiatry, which often has presentations on aspects of self-help related to mental health at its meetings. Mention should also be made of the 1978 addition to the prestigious Expert Committee on Alcoholism of the World Health Organization of two representatives from Alcoholics Anonymous International. This inclusion of representatives of a lay body on an important technical advisory group of the World Health Organization is a further indication that self-help is coming of age, and that its proponents are achieving wider recognition as important resources and contributors to professional understanding.

PUBLICATIONS

The heightened level of self-help activity throughout the world has been accompanied by a wide increase of both popular and professional publications. In the English language, at least six books dealing with self-help groups from descriptive, analytical, and theoretical viewpoints appeared between 1976 and 1979 in both the United States and the United Kingdom. (It is probable that the number is greater than this.) In Holland, 1978 saw the publication of a volume entitled *Zelfhulp* by Van Harberden and La Faille of Tilburg University, (1978), which contains both translations from well-known studies or papers in English, and a number of original descriptions and analsyses of Dutch self-help groups.

The German volume by Moeller has already been referred to; it will shortly be followed by the publication of his second book and a number of studies now under progress in Western Germany. The studies under way in Belgium and Holland will no doubt also see early publications. The international journal, *Social Science and Medicine,* has carried numerous articles in the past 3 years which specifically deal with self-help research or theory. No doubt this publication record could be duplicated in other internationally circulated journals in professional fields such as social work, nursing, psychiatry, and psychology. Paralleling the special self-help issues of *The Journal of Applied Behavioral Science,* and of *Social Policy* that appeared in the United States in late 1976, a Dutch social-work publication *(Welzi, Smaadblad, Haarlem)* brought out a whole issue devoted to self-help, in April 1979, and a special self-help issue of The Australian journal, *Social Alternatives,* appeared in February 1979.

SOME INTERNATIONAL DIFFERENCES

It seems worthwhile to attempt to identify differences of a conceptual, organizational, programmatic, or methodological character, which may exist among various countries with respect to self-help phenomena. For example, the differences in definitions that are employed, differences in conceptual approach, or of methodological approaches in research greatly influence how the phenomena are viewed and studied. In this connection, it is worth noting again that several European countries have instituted well-funded nationwide or national studies of self-help phenomena, a development which seems clearly beyond the resources of present United States researchers.

The major differences between U.S. self-help groups and those in other countries may be summarized under three heads: a) conceptual-ideological; b) programmatic and organizational; and c) financing.

The simplest difference is the last named. Financing of self-help groups and other citizen initiatives by public funds is a common occurrence in some European countries, such as Holland, Denmark, and the United Kingdom. In these countries, there is a conscious governmental policy of subsidizing lay groups that offer useful human services, even though they might not employ persons with professional training. This practice contrasts with the usual one in the United States of confining public grants to professionally-staffed agencies and institutions, (DeCocg, 1976).

Conceptually, the Dubrovnik Conference, through papers, debate and discussion, brought forward some important theoretical formulations.

In his major theoretical keynote address, John R. Seeley (1979) located the primal, archetypal self-help activity in the baby at its mother's breast:

> What the infant...does by way of self-help-and-mutual-aid—its first self-help being to begin to become a self—is to evoke, elicit, "accept" and "allow" the "help" or "demand," "drink in" and develop its capacity-to-receive. In so doing, patently, it constitutes the giver a giver, the carer a carer; it bestows the grace of unconditional receiving of the gift, and thus opens the rare way for the other to unconditional giving, a "help" to the giving self that is at once its fulfillment and expansion and the completion of the act crying for that from its own infancy of unconditional receiving. As development proceeds—as nurturer and nurtured by self-help-and-mutual-aid alter and enlarge— as the "family" grows larger, as interactions and interpenetrations multiply, enrich, and become more various—the polar-reciprocity-in-the-very-nature-of-the-aids diminishes, of course. Children and parents may begin to rejoice in each other's admiration or appreciation, or profit by reciprocal criticism, or gain strength from struggle against (as well as for) each other. But as long as there is that of the familiar—and, by extension, of the "friendly," the "neighborly," the comradely, indeed, the social as against the ecological—this form of self-help-and-mutual-aid will be sought, harked-back-to, and approximated when circumstances permit—which is almost, if not quite, to say, when structures to make it impossible, based on narrowed, if not erroneous, views of self and society, do not decisively countervail.

Seeley went on to trace the variety of ways in which the self-other-help principle grows in social life, but is brutally curtailed in the materially, commodity-oriented "developed" world, with the aid of bureaucratic professions. "In such a world, there springs up a variety of points, for a variety of reasons, a variety of entities or enterprises of self-help and mutual aid."

In her summary of discussions at Dubrovnik, Ilona Kickbusch distinguished between human services established on a monetary and a non-monetary basis (Kichbusch, 1979). The latter include all the traditional forms of self-help and mutual aid, which range from mothering and child-rearing, medical care through family or friends, neighborly help, informal systems encouraging self-care, and so on. "Monetary" services include those that embody the "insurance principle," state welfare programs, professionally-dominated services, even though some of these may have originated on a self-help basis. This analytical distinction, which emphasizes the "expressive" functions of self-help groups, may have profound effects on future concepts.

The political significance of self-help groups' is widely debated in Europe. Are they to be considered an organizational model for bringing about social change? Is there a preferred organizational pattern that will enable them most effectively so to function? What is their relationship to their marketplace, i.e., to the production of services and "goods," now almost monopolized by professional help-giving industries?

The European answers to these fundamental questions reflect a more radical view of the political significance of self-help groups than the most prevalent one in the United States. There is much less interest in developing or mediating a harmonious partnership and division of labor with established agencies and professionals. There is a feeling that the popular critique of professionalism, put forward most strongly by self-help groups, is so basic that nothing short of a fundamental restructuring of the whole professional system will suffice.

Even with respect to research into the self-help, self-care phenomena, differences of viewpoint are clearly apparent. The Dubrovnik discussions revealed a general international consensus on the need for research into self-help, and interest in its pursuit. The nature of self-help activities in all their varied forms, their origins, socio-cultural determinants, effects on participants, internal organizational patterns—all these and more aspects, were clearly thought important to study—locally, nationally and cross-culturally.

But differences arise around the posture and methodological approaches taken by researchers. Some social scientists feel that it is adequate to apply methodologies derived from previous work to this new field, with researchers essentially determining the goals, measurement instruments, outcome criteria, etc. Many European scholars take the contrasting view that the aspects important to study must be derived from self-help groups themselves. Thus, *effectiveness* or outcomes of participation in self-help activities should not be measured by criteria derived from professional sources alone, but should be framed in terms of self-help members,' rather than professionals, values and beliefs about what constitutes "success" or relevant behavioral change.

A strong conviction was widely expressed at Dubrovnik that self-help research will require investigators with ideological values that differ considerably from the orthodox perspectives that health, health care, and outcomes are synonymous with the values of conventional systems and their professionals. It was emphasized that both sensitization of researchers to their previous professional biases, and the involvement of self-help group members, are essential pre-conditions to identifying necessary innovations in methodology. Thus, the self-help, mutual-aid, lay resource was seen as the most important component and expression of care-giving in general, and attention to its further development, in all aspects including research, was seen as the chief task ahead.

AFTERWORD

The significance of the self-help strategy lies in the fact that it is responsive to major problems and criticisms of the human services today. What are these criticisms of the formal service structure?

1. The services are too big, bureaucratized, distant from the consumer, inaccessible, and overly dominated at the central core. They are seen as one more reflection of unresponsive big government;

2. The services are too costly, often ineffective, not accountable, and over-regulating. In essence, this is related to the argument of political overload and the critique of the welfare state;

3. Large numbers of human-service workers, professionals, and others are affected by a deep malaise—feeling burned out, cynical, and defeated by the rigidity of the bureaucratic forces that beset them;

4. Many of the services are overprofessionalized, producing a great deal of iatrogenic dependency in which consumers remain uninvolved, apathetic, acted upon, rather than energized;

5. Many of the service interventions are essentially patch ups, not directed toward basic cure or prevention. Frequently they stress pathology models and have not built on the strengths of the consumers or clients. Also, they appear to be less effective with problems such as the compulsions, drug abuse, gambling, as well as chronic illnesses—arthritis, hypertension, etc.

In essence, there is a need for a human-service reconstruction—a basic reorganization or reform in which there will be a shift of emphasis from the professional service giver to the consumer—consumers who are not simply receivers but doers, workers in their own behalf. This is accompanied by a need for decentralization, deinstitutionalization, moving people away from institutions that incarcerate them and restrict them, and moving them,

243

instead, to an environment which is less restrictive, more open, and community-based.

Finally, it is becoming recognized that the need for services is, in a way, a bottomless pit. There is no end to it and there is no way that expanding professional resources can possibly meet the need. There are at present 1 million arthritics, 18 million hypertensives, 5 million diabetics, over 20 million with emotional disorders. The list goes on and on.

It is in this context that the self-help strategy takes on enormous meaning because it attempts in various ways to deal with the above issues. Mutual-aid groups are inexpensive, highly responsive, and accessible to the consumers who themselves are service givers as well as receivers. Self-help services are not distant, bureaucratized, or over-regulating. They can expand infinitely to deal with the ever-expanding need—arthritics can serve arthritics, hypertensives likewise, emotionally troubled people similarly, and so on. In essence, as the need arises so does the response or potential for response.

Dependency is not encouraged as in the traditional model of professional service giving, for the consumers are themselves helpers, helping other people and thereby being helped. A pathology model is not emphasized; but rather, the strengths and potential power of people are called upon as they are empowered in providing the services. No problem is bypassed; self-help groups were among the first to deal with drug and alcohol abuse.

Moreover, the self-helpers themselves are typically infused with great energy and enthusiasm partly because the need or the problem is theirs, which perhaps powers their activity. Consequently, they are far from burned out, defeated, or cynical, and their energy is urgently needed in the human services system. Lastly, the research data indicate that one of the most important, curative powers is human support and this is provided in large doses by the self-help system.

TRENDS IN THE SELF-HELP MOVEMENT

A number of new trends characterize the self-help mutual and movement in the present period. One major trend is the involvement of professionals in the mental-health fields in various ways: in initiating and facilitating self-help groups; in providing consultation, training, and referrals to and from the groups; in convening conferences, conducting research, providing resources and publicity, etc.

Another major trend is the concern of many self-help groups with advocacy and social change in contrast to the traditional model of AA, which saw the individual as primarily responsible for personal change, with little or no concern for societal change.

The advocacy mood in many ways builds upon and captures some of the civil-rights spirit of the sixties as well as the participatory, empowering themes of the late sixties and seventies. Thus, the parents of handicapped children are not simply concerned with their own mutual aid, but their interest extends to affecting national legislation directed toward the fair treatment of handicapped children. The Center for Independent Living in California is not only concerned with mutual support of its own members but is directed toward electing people to legislative office and affecting legislative policy for disabled people. Disabled in Action is similarly concerned with effective legislation for the disabled.

The gay movement is not only concerned with the mutual support and positive identification of its members, but also is interested in civil rights issues and in affecting national, state, and local legislation.

The women's movement functions at one level through local consciousness-raising groups and on another level through national politically oriented organizations, such as the National Organization for Women. NOW, incidentally, is concerned both with the development of consciousness-raising at the local level and larger legislative matters. Other organizations such as the various rape counseling groups, like Abused Women's Aid in Crisis, and groups directed against wife battering also are interested not only in mutual support but in social and political legislation. The advocacy mood is seen also in the Sisterhood of Black Single Mothers and a great variety of lesser known groups.

Neighborhood self-help groups also direct their energy toward various local issues such as red-lining, crime, traffic, etc. while in a mutual support mode. It should be noted that there are some changes emerging in Alcoholics Anonymous, particularly as it moves into low-income minority neighborhoods and into prisons. A.A. chapters now direct some attention toward social-change issues in these local areas. All this is particularly significant because one of the dangers of the self-help mutual aid movement is an overconcern with individual and small-group change and insufficient attention to the need for structural reorganization in the larger society.

The main danger here is that social action on the broad scale may be deflected if people take responsibility for their own problems with shrinking awareness of the need for major changes in the society. At its extreme, blaming the victim could be the result. Thus, the advocacy orientation of self-help is an important contervailing component.

DANGERS OF THE PROFESSIONAL SELF-HELP INTERFACE

Professionals and their agencies need self-help groups to revitalize them, to infuse them with new energy and enthusiasm, to multiply and expand their resources, and to win a new constituency, namely the consumers. The latter may be particularly needed to blunt the political attack on the services and to prevent cutbacks. The question remains, however, whether the involvement of the self-help model will really "consumerize" the character and structure of the traditional professional services.

Will these services place the consumer at the center of their concern? Will emphasis shift internally so that more recognition is given to consumer needs and rights and less to professional credentials and monopolistic controls? Will the knowledge base of the agency include more of the experiential input of the self-help group and not be overly professionalized by the forms and trappings of professional service giving? Will the elitism of the professional structure be reduced as laypeople become intrinsically involved with giving service, as distinguished from sitting on the boards or advisory committees of agencies? Will the professionals and their agencies challenge the self-help mutual aid groups to develop different styles and approaches, to be less parochial, to reach out to the masses of people in need who are not now attracted to the particular self-help group and the mode it offers?

Positive answers to the above questions would indicate a superb ideal dialectical integration of the self-help and professional systems. The questions really suggest a set of useful goals—a vision. While recognizing, of course, that nothing like this has been accomplished in the present period, we feel nevertheless, the yardstick or vision is relevant in appraising current developments.

While there are some negative examples, there is a great range of positive illustrations of professional self-help cooperation; some are noted in the introduction: the Caplan and Silverman Widow-to-Widow project in Boston and its work throughout various parts of the United States; the various peer counseling approaches; Recovery Incorporated, started by a professional psychiatrist; SHARE, developed by a surgeon, Dr. Thiessen; the arthritis self-help project developed at Downstate Medical Center in Brooklyn; the relationship of Mended Hearts to various professional service givers; Reach to Recovery and Laryngectomy, Inc., sponsored by the American Cancer Society; the National Self-Help Clearinghouse of the Graduate School and University Center, City University of New York: the Florida Mental Health Institute program for deinstitutionalizing patients reported on in this book, and countless others. It is possible for professionals to initiate self-help groups and to work with them effectively.

There are, however, dangers which we should consider: professionals may co-opt self-help groups and attempt to dominate them; they may *obsess* endlessly in attempting to help develop a self-help program; they may simply encourage the self-help group to provide the same service that the professional provides, not recognizing the need for a different kind of service; they may be competitive with the self-help group, constantly pointing out its errors and weaknesses; they may fail to develop self-help groups among low-income populations; and, finally, as professionals and human service agencies become involved in developing and initiating self-help groups, there is the possibility that these groups will become an appendage to the agency—a parallel system existing alongside services traditionally provided by an agency—but in no way will they penetrate the character of service delivery of the agency or the practice of the professional.

In some ways we see this already in the operation of peer-counseling programs in the public schools. Many such programs exist and are worthwhile, but do not seem to affect the basic character of guidance and education provided by the school. One would think that as peer counseling, peer-caring, and peer-teaching, youth-teaching-youth, and children-teaching-children programs progress in the school system, that the schools might become more youth centered, both in their general curriculum, their culture, and in the respect given by teachers and administrators to young people. There is little evidence that this is the case, even in programs where peer-counseling and peer-support programs are well developed. If these peer-oriented programs were really to become the essence of the school, one would anticipte that young people would find the school much more meaningful and there would be less absenteeism, dropping out, apathy, violence, etc. One aim of the mutual aid self-help approach is to affect service delivery in its heartland—in the main way that the traditional professionals relate to the service population; and not simply to provide an added appendage, a special program off to the side.

Perhaps circumscribing these potential dangers, there are arrayed a number of countervailing forces, not the least of which is the development of new models of positive integration. But more fundamental than any specific models of cooperation is the fact that the professional structure badly needs self-help groups and the potential constituency that they represent. Under attack by the taxpayers' Proposition 13 mood, the professional service givers need a consumer constituency, not only to maintain their funding, but also the public's recognition of their worth. When a hospital is threatened with being closed down, for the most part it is the workers—doctors, nurses, etc.—who protest. This a self-serving constituency. These workers may maintain that the service is needed, but unless patient groups demand that service, the public and media reaction is dim.

Self-help groups working together with the professional agency in many cases formed by that agency—and utilizing some of its resources, such as space—provide a far more vital source of support. We anticipate that these self-help groups will form a major link to the consumer community in protesting any cutback of service. Not only can they themselves protest, but their links with other consumers provide a strong political arm, building a very different network of support. Moreover, since they are not paid workers of the agency, they are not under its control and thus their co-optation is much less likely than, let us say, that of an employed paraprofessional. Nevertheless, it is true that the self-help group may be dependent upon an agency for some of its resources and general support. What we are saying here, then, is that the new potential constituency and all that it represents is an important limiting factor to professional control, even though there are certain constraints in the other direction.

Finally, it should be noted that as their energy is unleashed, self-help groups generate an enormous power. They supply an infusion of inner strength, along with some competition and criticism of professional practice. This fortifies against co-optation.

As with any powerful development, the currents are strong and not all are surging in the exact same direction. But our view is that the self-help mutual aid phenomenon is too important to be allowed to grow in isolation from the professional care-giving system, and it is too strong to be endangered by such interfusion.

Alan Gartner
Frank Riessman

BIBLIOGRAPHY

A Brief Guide to Alcoholics Anonymous. New York: Alcoholics Anonymous World Services, 1975.

Adams, J.E. *Competent to Counsel.* Grand Rapids, Michigan: Baker Book House, 1970.

Alan Guttmacher Institute. *Eleven Million Teenagers.* New York: Planned Parenthood Foundation, 1976.

Albon, J. Family structure and behavior in alcoholism: A review of the literature, in B. Kissin and H. Begleiter (Eds.), *Social Aspects of Alcoholism.* New York: Plenum Press, 1976.

Alibrandi, L. *The Recovery Process in Alcoholics Anonymous: The Sponsor as Folk Therapist.* Unpublished Ph.D. dissertation in Psychology, University of California, 1977.

Alpert, L. Approaches to breast cancer: A pathologist's perspective. *Women and Health,* Fall 1979, 3: 269–287.

American Medical Association. And now the 'Liberated' woman patient. *American Medical News.* October 1974.

American Psychiatric Association. Resolution on relations of medicine and psychology. *American Psychiatric Association Mail Pouch.* October 1954, p. 50.

America's Volunteer. Washington, D.C.: Action, 1974.

Anderson, S.B., & Ball, S. *The Profession and Practice of Program Evaluation.* San Francisco: Jossey-Bass, 1978.

Anonymous. *Alcoholics Anonymous Comes of Age—A Brief History of A.A.* New York: Alcoholics Anonymous Publishing, Inc., 1957.

Anonymous. *Multi-Model Behavior Therapy: Use of Professional and Paraprofessional Resources.* Unpublished Manuscript, 1979.

Anthony, W.A. & Carkhuff, R.R. The functional professional therapeutic agent. In A.S. Gurman & A.M. Razin (Eds.), *Effective Psychotherapy: A Handbook of Research.* New York: Pergamon Press, 1977.

Antze, P. The role of ideologies in peer psychology organizations. Some theoretical considerations and three case studies. *Journal of Applied Behavioral Science*, 1976, 12: 323–346.

————. Role of ideologies in peer psychotherapy group, in M.A. Lieberman and L.D. Borman (Eds.), *Self-Help Groups for Coping With Crisis: Origins, Members, Processes, and Impact*. San Francisco, Jossey-Bass, 1979.

Argyris, C. Theories of action that inhibit individual learning. *American Psychologist*, 1976. 31: 638–654.

Auerwald, E.H. Interdisciplinary versus ecological approach. In W. Gray, F.J. Duhl, N.E. Rizzo (Eds.), *General Systems Theory and Psychiatry*. Boston: Little Brown, 1969.

Back, K.W., & Taylor, R.C. Self-help groups: Tool or symbol. *Journal of Applied Behavioral Science*, 12: 295–309.

Baekeland, F., Lundwall, L., & Kissin, B. Methods for the treatment of chronic alcoholism. A critical appraisal. In R.J. Gibbins et al. (Eds.), *Research Advances in Alcohol and Drug Problems, Vol. 2*. New York: Wiley and Sons, 1975.

Bandina, A. *Social Learning Theory*. Englewood Cliffs, New Jersey: Prentice-Hall, 1977.

————. Toward a unifying theory of behavioral change. *Psychological Review*, 1977, 84: 191–215.

Barish, H. Self-help groups. In *The Encyclopedia of Social Work, Vol. 2*. New York: National Association of Social Workers, Inc., 1961, pp. 1163–1169.

Bassin, A. Daytop Village. *Psychology Today*, 1968, 2: 48–52.

————. The rise and fall of Synanon. Fourth International Congress of Therapeutic Communities, New York, 1979.

Beebe, J.R. Testimony to Illinois/White House Conference on Families. Champaign, Illinois: Mimeographed, December 4, 1979.

Beels, C. Social networks, the family and the schizophrenic patient. *Schizophrenia Bulletin*, 1978, 4: 512–521.

Behavior Associates. *Parents Anonymous, Self-Help for Child Abusing Parents Project: Evaluation Report*. Tucson, Arizona, 1977.

Belgum, D. *Guilt: Where Psychology and Religion Meet*. Englewood Cliffs, New Jersey: Prentice-Hall, 1962.

Berger, P.L., & Luckmann, T. *The Social Construction of Reality: A Treatise in the Sociology of Knowledge*. Garden City, New York: Doubleday/Anchor Books, 1967.

Bergin, A.E., & Lambert, M.J. The evaluation of therapeutic outcomes. In S.L. Garfield & A.E. Bergin (Eds.), *Handbook of Psychotherapy and Behavior Change*. New York: Wiley and Sons, 1978.

Berkeley Planning Associates. *Evaluation of the Joint OCD/SRS National Demonstration Program on Child Abuse and Neglect*. December 1977.

Berstein, B. Sashatapes—Self-led automated series on helping alternatives. University of California at Los Angeles, Department of Psychology, Interpersonal Process Research Group, 1979.

Birenbaum, A. On managing a courtesy stigma. *Journal of Health and Social Behavior,* 1970, 2: 196–206.

Blake, J.B. Women and medicine in ante-bellum America. *Bulletin of the History of Medicine,* March-April 1965, 2: 99–123.

Borkman, T. A cross-national comparison of stutterers' self-help organization. *New Zealand Speech Therapists Journal,* 1974, 29: 6–16.

_____. Experiential Knowledge: A new concept for the analysis of self-help groups. *Social Service Review,* September 1976, 50: 445–456.

_____. *Experiential Knowledge in Self-Help Groups as the Basis of Selective Utilization of Professional Knowledge and Services.* Paper presented at Pennsylvania Sociological Society, Pittsburg, October 1977.

_____. *Ingredients for Survival: A Profile of Stutterers' Self-Help Organizations.* Mimeograph. December 1973.

_____. *Mutual Self-Help Groups: A Theory of Experiential Inquiry.* Services Analysis Branch, NIAA (Xeroxed), 1979.

_____. Participation patterns and benefits of membership in a self-help organization of stutterers. In A. Katz & E. Bender (Eds.), *The Strength in Us: Self-Help Groups in the Modern World.* New York: New Viewpoints, 1976, pp. 81–90.

Borman, L. Characteristics of development and growth. In M.A. Lieberman & L.D. Borman (Eds.), *Self-Help Groups for Coping with Crisis.* San Francisco: Jossey-Bass, 1979.

Bowley, J. Processes of Mourning. *The International Journal of Psychoanalysis,* 1961, 42: 317–340.

Bronowski, J. *Science and Human Values.* New York: Messner, 1956.

Brown, C.R. & Myers, R. Student vs. faculty curriculum advising. *Journal of College Student Personnel,* 1975, 16: 226–231.

Brown, G.W., Bhrolchain, M.N., & Harris, T. Social class and psychiatric disturbance among women in an urban population. *Sociology,* 1975, 9: 225–254.

Bryant, T.E. *Report of the President's Joint Commission on Mental Health.* Washington, D.C.: U.S. Government Printing Office, 1978.

Bumbalo, J.A. & Young, D.C. The self-help phenomenon. *American Journal of Nursing,* 1973, 73: 1588–1591.

Campbell, A., Converse, D.E., & Rodgers, W.L. *The Quality of American Life.* New York: Russell Sage Foundation, 1976.

Campbell, D.T., & Stanley, J.C. *Experimental and Quasi-Experimental Designs for Research.* Chicago: Rand-McNally, 1963.

Cantor, M. Life space and the support system of the inner city elderly of New York City. *Gerontologist,* 15: 23–27.

Caplan, G. *Principles of Preventive Psychiatry*. New York: Basic Books, 1964.

_____. *Support Systems and Community Mental Health*. New York: Behavioral Publications, 1974.

_____. *The Theory and Practice of Mental Health Consultation*. New York: Basic Books, 1970.

Carkhuff, R.R., & Truax, C.B. Lay mental health counseling: The effects of lay group counseling. *Journal of Consulting Psychology*, 1965, 29: 1–15.

Chase, N.F. *A Child is Being Beaten*. New York: Holt, Rinehart and Winston, 1975. *Child Protection Reports*. November 1, 1979.

Coak, T.D., & Cambell, D.T. *Quasi-Experimentation: Design and Analysis issues for Field Settings*. Chicago: Rand-McNally, 1979.

Cobb, S. Social support as a moderator of life stress. *Psychosomatic Medicine*, 1976, 38: 300–314.

Collins, A.H., & Pancoast, D.L. *Natural Helping Networks: A Strategy for Prevention*. Washington, D.C.: National Association of Social Workers, 1976.

Collins, M.C. *Child Abuser, A Study of Child Abuses in Self-Help Group Therapy*. Littleton, Mass.: PSG Publishing Company, 1978.

D'Angelli, A.R., & Danish, S.J. Evaluating training programs for paraprofessional and non-professionals. *Journal of Counseling Psychology*, 1976, 23: 247–253.

DeCocq, G. European and North American self-help movements: Some contrasts. In A. Katz and E. Bender (Eds.), *The Strength in Us: Self-Help Groups in the Modern World*. New York: New Viewpoints, 1976.

Deitsch, D. The rise and fall of Synanon, Part II. Fourth International Congress of Therapeutic Communities, New York, 1979.

Derogatis, L., et al. The Hopkins Syndrome checklist: A self-report symptom inventory. *Behavioral Science*, 1974, 19–15.

Dewane, M. Humor in therapy. *Social Work*, September 1979.

Dewar, T. Professionalized clients as self-helpers. *Self-Help and Health: A Report*. New York: National Self-Help Clearinghouse, Graduate School and University Center, City University of New York, 1976.

Dincin, J., Selleck, V., & Streicker, S. With parents of the adult mentally ill. *Schizophrenia Bulletin*, 1976, 4: 597–608.

Drakeford, J.W. *Integrity Groups: A Christian Evaluation of a New Approach to Mental Health*. Nashville: Broadman Press, 1967.

Dumont, M. Self-help treatment programs: An overview. *American Journal of Psychiatry*, 1974, 131: 631–635.

Durlak, J.A. Comparative effectiveness of paraprofessional and professional helpers. *Psychological Bulletin*, 1979. 86: 89–92.

Durman, E.C. The role of self-help in service provision. *Journal of Applied Behavioral Science*, 1976, 12: 433–448.

Edmunson, E.D., Bedell, J.R., Archer, R.P., & Gordon, R.E. Integrating skill building and peer support: The early intervention and community network development projects. In R. Slotnick & A. Jaeger (Eds.), *Community Mental Health: A Behavioral—Ecological Perspective.* New York: Plenum Press, 1980.

Ellis, H. *Studies in the Psychology of Sex.* New York: Random House, 1936.

Evans, G. *The Family Circle Guide to Self-help.* New York: Ballantine Books, 1979.

Fastinger, L. A theory of social comparison processes. *Human Relations,* 1954, 7: 117–140.

Findley, P. *Priests of Lucina: The Story of Obstetrics.* Boston: Little, Brown and Company, 1939.

Frank, J.D. *Persuasion and Healing.* Baltimore: Johns Hopkins University Press, 1973.

Freire, P. *Pedagogic des Opprimes.* Paris: Maspero, 1975.

Fremouw, W.J., & Harmatz, M.G. A helper model for behavioral treatment of speech anxiety. *Journal of Consulting and Clinical Psychology,* 1975, 43: 652–660.

Froland, C., Brodsky, G., Olson, M., & Stewart, L. Social support and social adjustment: Implications for mental health professionals. *Community Mental Health Journal,* 1979, 15: 82–93.

Froland, C., Pancoast, D.L., Chapman, N.J. & Kinibako, P.J. Professional partnerships with informal helpers: Emerging forms. Paper presented at the American Psychological Association. September 4, 1979.

Fry, L.J. Research grants and self-help programs: What price knowledge? *Journal of Health and Social Behaviors,* 1977, 19: 405–417.

Garrison, V. Support systems of schizophrenic and nonschizophrenic Puerto Rican migrant women in New York City. *Schizophrenia Bulletin,* 1978. 4: 561–596.

Gartner, A. & Riessman, F. *Help: A Working Guide to Self-Help Groups.* New York: Franklin Watts, 1979.

————. Professional Involvement in Self-Help Groups. *Self-Help Reporter,* 1979, 3: 4–5.

————. *Self-Help in the Human Services.* San Francisco: Jossey-Bass, 1977.

Gershon, M. & Biller, H.B. *The Other Helpers: Paraprofessionals and Non-professionals in Mental Health.* Lexington, Mass.: D.L. Heath, 1977.

Glaser, B., & Strauss, A. *The Discovery of Grounded Theory: Strategies for Qualitative Research.* Chicago: Aldine, 1967.

Goffman, E. *Asylums.* New York: Doubleday, 1961.

————. *Stigma.* Englewood Cliffs, New Jersey: Prentice-Hall, 1963.

Goldstein, M.B. *Stress, Support, and Coping Among First Year Dental Students: A Correlation Analysis.* Unpublished doctoral dissertation, University of Michigan, 1978.

Goodman, G. *Companionship Therapy.* San Francisco, Jossey-Bass, 1972.

Gore, S. The effect of social support in moderating the health consequences of unemployment. *Journal of Health and Social Behavior,* 1978, 19: 157–165.

Gottlieb, B.H. The development and application of a classification schema of informal helping behaviors. *Canadian Journal of Behavioral Science,* 1979.

_____. Lay influences of the utilization and provision of health services-A review. *Canadian Psychological Review,* April 1976, 17: 126–136.

Green, L.W., Werlin, S.H., Schauffer, H.H., & Avery, C.H. Research and demonstration issues in self-care: Measuring the decline of mediocentrism. *Health Education Monographs,* 1977, 5: 161–189.

Gregg, G., Preston, T., Geist, A., & Caplan, N. The caravan rolls on, Forty years of social problem research. *Knowledge: Creation, Diffusion, Utilization,* 1979, 1: 31–61.

Grosz, H. J. *Recovery, Inc.* Chicago: Recovery, Inc., 1972.

Gruver, G. G. College students as therapeutic agents. *Psychological Bulletin,* 1971, 76: 111–127.

Gurin, G., Veroff, J., & Feld, S. *Americans View Their Mental Health.* New York: Basic Books, 1960.

Gussow, Z., & Tracy, G.S. The role of self-help clubs in adaptation to chronic illness and disability. *Social Science and Medicine,* 1976, 10: 407–414.

Hall, S.M. Self-control and therapist control in the behavioral treatment of overweight women. *Behavior, Research and Therapy,* 1972, 10: 59–68.

Hamner, M., Makiesky-Barrow, S., & Gutwirth, L. Social networks and schizophrenia. *Schizophrenia Bulletin,* 1978, 4: 522–545.

Hatfield, A.B. Psychological costs of schizophrenia to the family. *Social Work,* September 1978, 23: 355–359.

Hensley, W.E., & Roberts, M.K. Dimensions of Rosenberg's self-esteem scale. *Psychological Reports,* 1976, 38: 583–584.

Hermalin, J., Melendez, L., Kamarck, T., F., Ballen, E., & Gordon, M. Enhancing primary prevention: The marriage of self-help groups and formal health are delivery systems. *Journal of Clinical Child Psychology,* Summer 1976, 125–129.

Hill, W.F. Hill interaction matrix (HIM): The conceptual framework, derived rating scales, and an updated bibliography. *Small Group Behavior,* 1977, 8: 251–268.

Hornstein, F. et al. Gynecological self-help. *Self-Help and Health: A Report.* Queens College, New Human Services Institute, September 1976.

Hurd-Mead, K.C. *A History of Women in Medicine from the Earliest Times to the Beginning of the Nineteenth Century.* Haddon Press, 1938.

Hurvitz, N. Peer self-help psychotherapy groups and their implications for psychotherapy. *Psychotherapy: Theory, Research and Practice,* 1970, 7: 41–49.

_____. Peer self-help psychotherapy groups: Psychotherapy without psychotherapists. In P.M. Roman and H.M. Truce (Eds.), *The Sociology of Psychotherapy.* New York: Jason Aronson, 1974.

_____. We'd rather do it ourselves!: A people's movement for mental health rejects professional assistance. *Journal of Voluntary Action Research* 6: 69–72 January-April 1977.

Kahn, R., et al. (In collaboration with R.A. Rosenthal). *Organizational Stress.* New York: Wiley and Company, 1964.

Kaiser, B.L. & Kaiser, I.H. The challenge of the women's movement gynecology. *American Journal of Obstetrics and Gynecology,* 1974, 120: 625–665.

Karlsruher, A.E. The nonprofessional as a psychotherapeutic agent: A review of the empirical evidence pertaining to his effeciveness. *American Journal of Community Psychology,* 1976, 4: 145–154.

Katz, A., & Bender, E. *The Strength In Us: Self-Help Groups in the Modern World.* New York: Franklin-Watts, 1976.

Katz, J. *Gay American History.* New York: Thomas Y. Crowell Company, 1976.

Kelly, J.G. *Toward a Psychology of Healthiness.* Presented in an address to the Western Psychological Association, April 27 and the Ichabod Spenser Lecture, Union College, Schenectady, New York, May 2, 1974.

Kelly, O. & Murray, K.C. *Make Today Count.* New York: Delacorte, 1975.

Kerr, D.H. *Competency Recognition, Credentialing Model.* Communication to the Directors of Therapeutic Communities of America. Newark, New Jersey: Integrity Incorporated, 1979.

Kichbusch, I. Summary of conference discussion. Proceedings of Conference on the Role of Self-Help Mutual Aid in Contemporary Society in Dubrovnik, Yugoslavia, September 1979.

Killilea, M. Mutual help organizations: Interpretations in the literature. In G. Caplan & M.Killilea (Eds.), *Support Systems and Mutual Help: Multidisciplinary Explorations.* New York: Grune and Stratton, 1976.

Kiresuk, T.J., & Lund, S.H. Goal attainment scaling. In C.C. Attkisson, W.A. Hargreaves, I.J. Horowitz, & J.E. Sorenson (Eds.), *Evaluation of Human Service Programs.* New York: Academic Press, 1978.

_____. & Sherman, R.E. Goal attainment scaling: A general method of evaluating comprehensive mental health programs. *Community Mental Health Journal,* 1968, 4: 443–453.

Kleiber, N. & Light, L. *Caring for Ourselves: An Alternative Structure for Health Care.* University of British Columbia, School of Nursing, Vancouver, B.C., Canada, April 1978.

Kleiman, M.A., Mantell, J.E., & Alexander, E.S. Collaboration and its discontents: The perils of partnership. *Journal of Applied Behavioral Science,* 1976, 12: 403–410.

Knapp, M.S. Ethnographic contributions to evaluation research: The experimental schools program evaluation and some alternatives. In T.D. Cook and L.S. Reichardt (Eds.), *Qualitative and Quantitative Methods in Evaluation Research.* Beverly Hills, Calif.: Sage, 1979.

Knight, B., Wollert, R., Levy, L.H., Frame, C.L., & Padgett, V.D. Self-help groups: The members' perspectives. *American Journal of Community Psychology,*

1980, 8: 53-65.

Kropatkin, P. *Mutual Aid: A Factor in Evolution*. New York: New York University Press, 1972.

Kureshi, & Dutt, Dimensions of alienation—A factor-analytic study. *Psychologia*, 1980.

Kushner, R. *Breast Cancer: A Personal and Investigative Report*. New York: Harcourt, Brace Jovanovich, Inc., 1975.

Lamb, D.H., & Clack, R.J. Professional versus paraprofessional approaches to orientation and subsequent counseling contacts. *Journal of Community Psychology*, 1974, 21: 61-65.

Lang, A. *Synanon Foundation: The People Business*. Cottonwood, Arizona: Wayside Press, 1978.

Latz, J. The psychiatric inmates' liberation movement. *Currents: A Review of Innovative Mental Health Programs*, 3: 18-22. Philadelphia: Pennsylvania Office of Mental Health, Spring 1979.

Lavoie, F. Elaboration d'un mode d' analyse descriptive des processes interactifs dans les groupes d'entraide. Unpublished Ph.D. dissertation, Universite du Quebec a Montreal, 1982.

Lazarus, A. *Multi-Model Behavior Therapy*. New York, Springer, 1976.

Lee, D.T. Recovery, Inc.: A well-role model. *Mental Hygiene*, 1971, 55: 194-198.

_____. Therapeutic type: Recovery, Inc., in A.H. Katz and E.I. Bender (Eds.). *The Strength in Us: Self-Help Groups in the Modern World*. New York: Franklin Watts, 1976.

Levin, L.S. Self-care: An international perspective. *Social Policy*, 1976, 7: 70-75.

Levin, L.S., Katz, A.H., & Holst, E. *Self-Care, Lay Initiatives in Health*. New York: Prodist, 1979.

Levine, M., & Levine, A. *A Social History of Helping Services: Clinical, Court, School and Community*. New York: Appleton Century Crofts, 1970.

Levine, M., Tulkin, S., Intagliata, J., Perry, J., & Whitson, E., The paraprofessional: A brief social history. In S.R. Alley, R.E. Blanton, and R.E. Feldman (Eds.), *Paraprofessionals in Mental Health: Theory and Practice*. New York: Human Sciences Press, 1978.

Levy, L.H. Mental health professionals' views of self-help groups. *American Journal of Community Psychology*. In Press

_____. *Processes and activities in groups*. In M.A. Lieberman and L.D. Borman (Eds.), *Self-help Groups for Coping with Crisis: Origins, Members, Processes, and Impact*. San Francisco: Jossey-Bass, 1979.

_____. Self-help groups viewed by mental health professionals: A survey and comments. *American Journal of Community Psychology*, 1978, 6: 305-313.

_____. Self-help groups viewed by mental health professionals: A survey and comments. *American Journal of Community Psychology*, 1978, 6: 305-313.

_____. Knight, B.G., Padgett, V.P., & Wollert, R.W. Patterns of help-giving in self-help groups. Paper presented at meeting of the American Psychological Association, San Francisco, August 1977.

Lieber, L. Parents Anonymous. *Child Abuse and Neglect Reports,* 1976, 3: 1–2.

_____. & Bond, G.R. The problem of being a woman: A survey of 1700 women in consciousness raising groups. *Journal of Applied Behavioral Science,* 1976, 12: 363–380.

_____. Self-help groups: Problems of measuring outcomes. *Small Group Behavior,* 1978, 9: 221–241.

_____. Self-help and social research. *Journal of Applied Behavioral Science,* 1976, 12: 455–463.

_____. (Ed.) Special issue on self-help groups, *Journal of Applied Behavioral Science,* 1976, 12:(3).

Lieberman, M.A., & Borman, L.D. *Self-Help Groups for Coping with Crisis: Origins, Members, Processes, and Impact.* San Francisco: Jossey-Bass, 1979.

_____. & Gardner, I.A. Institutional alternatives to psychotherapy: A study of growth center users. *Archives of General Psychiatry,* 1976. 33: 157–162.

Lieberman, M.A. & Gourash, N. Evaluating the effects of change groups on the elderly: The impact of SAGE. *International Journal of Group Psychotherapy,* 1979, 29: 283–304.

Lind, E. The female-impersonators. In A.W. Herzog (Ed.), *Medico-Legal Journal,* 1922, pp. 154–157; 159–163.

Litwak, E., & Meyer, H. *School, Family and Neighborhoods: The Theory and Practice of School Community Relations.* New York: Columbia University, 1974.

Low, A.A. *Mental Health through Will Training: A System of Self-Help in Psychotherapy as Practiced by Recovery, Inc.* Boston: Christopher Publishing House, 1951.

Luce, G.G. *Your Second Life: Vitality and Growth in Middle and Late Years.* New York: Delacorte Press/Seymour Lawrence, 1979.

Mahoney, M.J., & Kazdin, A.E. Cognitive behavior modification: Misconceptions and premature evaluation. *Psychological Bulletin,* 1979, 86: 1044–1049.

Marieskind, H.I. Gynecological services: Their historical relationships to the women's movement with recent experience of self-help clinics and other delivery modes. Doctoral dissertation, University of Michigan, Ann Arbor, 1976, (University Microfilms: No. 762-5222-01500).

_____. Helping oneself to health. *Social Policy,* September/October 1976, 7 (2): 63–66.

_____. *Women in the Health System: Patients, Providers, and Programs.* St. Louis, Missouri: C.V. Mosby Co., 1980.

Mattachine Society, Missions and purposes. In J. Katz, *Gay American History.* New York: Thomas Y. Crowell Co., 1951.

Mayer, M.J. Kin and neighbors: Differential role in differing cultures. Paper given at the 29th Annual Meeting, Gerontological Society, New York, October 1976.

McNett, I. Made for each other—Mental health pros and self-help groups could be a perfect match. *APA Monitor,* December 1979.

Mechanic, D. *Medical Sociology.* New York: The Free Press, 1978.

Medalil, J.H., & Goldbourt, U. Angina pectoris among 10,000 men. *American Journal of Medicine,* 1976, 60: 910–921.

Melville, C. Social networks interventions in mental health. 1978. (Mimeographed).

Miller, J.G. Toward a general theory for the behavior sciences. *American Psychologist,* 1955, 10: 51–58.

Moeller, M.L. *Selbsthilfe Gruppen.* Hamburg: Rowhalt, 1978.

Moos, R.H. Conceptualizations of human environments. *American Psychologist,* 1973, 28: 652–665.

Mowrer, O.H. Changing conceptions of 'neurosis' and the small groups movement. *Education,* 1976, 97: 24–62.

————. *The Crisis in Psychiatry and Religion.* Princeton, New Jersey: D. Van Nostrand Co., 1961.

————. Is much psychotherapy still misdirected and misapplied? *Canadian Counsellor,* 1979, 13: 120–135.

————. *The New Group Therapy.* Princeton, New Jersey: D. Van Nostrand Co., 1964.

————. Peer groups and medication, the best therapy for professionals and laymen alike. *Psychotherapy: Theory, Research and Practice,* 1971, 8: 44–54.

————. Possibilities for constructive interaction between professionals and mutual-help groups. Paper delivered as part of a symposium, "Toward an Understanding of Natural Helping Systems," at the annual convention of the American Psychological Association in San Francisco, 1977. (Mimeographed).

————. and Vattano, A.J. Integrity groups: A context for growth in honesty, responsibility, and involvement. *Journal of Applied Behavioral Science,* 1976, 12: 419–431.

————. Baxley, G.B., and Mowerer, M.C. *Integrity Groups-The Loss and Recovery of Community.* Urbana, Illinois: Integrity Groups, 1975.

Noll, G.A., & Watkins, J.T. Differences between persons seeking encounter group experiences and others on the Personal Orientation Inventory. *Journal of Counseling Psychology,* 1974, 21: 206–209.

Nuckalls, K.B., Cassel, J., & Kaplan, B.H. Psychosocial assets, life crisis and the prognosis of pregancy. *American Journal of Epidemiology,* 1972, 95: 431–441.

O'Briant, R., & Lennard, H. *Recovery from Alcoholism: A Social Treatment Model.* Springfield, Ill.: Charles C. Thomas, 1973.

O'Brien, W.B. A View from Daytop—The city and a sixteen-year drug watch. Testimony before the U.S. House of Representatives, November 30, 1979.

Ottonberg, D.J. Addiction as a metaphor. *Alcohol Health and Research World,* Fall 1974, pp. 18–20.

————. Brief description of Lincoln-Eagleville master's program. Eagleville Hospital and Rehabilitation Center, Eagleville, PA. 1977. (Mimeographed).

————. The process of recovery in the therapeutic community. In P. Vamos and J.J. Devlin (Eds.), *First World Conference on Therapeutic Communities.* Montreal: Portage Press, 1976, pp. 146–163.

_____. Responsible concern. Eagleville Hospital and Rehabilitation Center. Eagleville, Pennsylvania, 1978, (Mimeographed).

_____. The TC in conflict—Internal and external. Third World Conference of Therapeutic Communities, Rome, 1978.

Therapeutic community—Bastard child of public health. Second World Conference of Therapeutic Communities, Montreal, 1977.

_____. Traditional and non-traditional credentials in addiction problems—A dispatch from the battlefield. *The Addiction Therapist*, 1977, 5 : 56–63.

Ozanoff, V.V., & Ozonoff, D. On helping those who help themselves. *Hastings Center Reports*, February 1977, pp. 7–11.

Patterson, E. Mansell. Clinical social systems interventions. *Psychiatry Digest*, 1977, 38: 25–33.

_____. Social system psychotherapy. *Journal of Psychotherapy*, 1973, 17: 396–409.

Patterson, S.L. Natural helping approaches: Implications for humanizing professional practice. Presented at the 86th Annual Convention of the American Psychological Association, 1978.

Pearlin, L., & Schooler, C. The structure of coping. *Journal of Health and Social Behavior*, March 1978, 19:21.

Phillips, J. *Alcoholics Anonymous: An Annotated Bibliography*, 1935–1972. Cincinnati: Central Ohio Publishing, 1973.

President's Commission on Mental Health. Report of the task panel on community support systems. Volume II. Washington, D.C.: U.S. Government Printing Office, 1978.

Raiff, N. Recovery, Inc.: A study of self-help organization in mental health. University of Pittsburgh, Unpublished Ph.D. dissertation, 1978.

Recovery, Inc. *National Policy Booklet*. Chicago: Recovery, Inc., 1969.

Reichenback, H. *Experience and Prediction*. Chicago: University of Chicago Press, 1938.

Report of the President's Commission on Mental Health. Washington, D.C.: The Commission, 1977.

Richow, W.C. Training of lay helpers. In J.C. Albrams (Ed.), *Supervision, Consultation, and Staff Training in the Helping Professions*. New York: Jossey-Bass, 1977.

Riessman, F. The 'Helper-Therapy' principle. *Social Work*, 1965, 10: 27–32.

Riessman, F. The President's Commission on Mental Health: The self-help prospect. *Social Policy*, May/June 1978, 28–31.

Rioch, E., Elhea, D., & Flint, A. *A Pilot Project in Training Mental Health Counselors*. Washington, D.C.: U.S. Government Printing Office, 1965.

Robinson, D. & Henry, S. *Self-Help and Health: Mutual Aid for Modern Problems*. London: Martin Robertson, 1977.

Roepel, C.E. A Study of California Public Attitudes and Beliefs Regarding Mental and Physical Health, 1979.

Rogers, C. *On Personal Power*. New York: Delacorte Press, 1977.

Roncali, M. A therapeutic strategy with obsessional patients. *Perspectives in Psychia-*

tric Care, October-December 1974.

Rosenberg, M. *Society and Adolescent Self-Image*. Princeton N.J.: Princeton University Press, 1965.

Rossi, P.H., Freeman, H.E. & Wright, S.R. *Evaluation: A Systematic Approach*. Beverly Hills: Sage, 1979.

Russell, R.K., & Wise, F. Treatment of speech anxiety by cue-controlled relaxation and densitization with professional and paraprofessional counselors. *Journal of Counseling Psychology*, 1976, 23: 583-586.

Ruzek, S. *The Women's Health Movement: Feminist Alternatives to Medical Control*. New York: Praeger, 1979.

Sagarin, E. *Odd Man In*. Chicago: Quadrangle Books, 1969.

Sanders, D.H. The Lodge program in community rehabilitation. In A. Katz and E. Bender. *The Strength in Us*. New York: Franklin Watts, 1976.

Schactel, S. *The Psychology of Affiliation*. Stanford: Stanford University Press, 1959.

Scheffe, H.A. *The Analysis of Variance*. New York: Wiley, 1959.

Scriven, M. The methodology of evaluation. *Perspectives of Curriculum Evaluation*. American Educational Research Association Monograph Series on Curriculum Evaluation, No. 1. Chicago: Rand McNally, 1967.

Seeley, J. Self-help and mutual aid: Some reflections on principles and policies. Presented as part of the International Conference on the Role of Self-Help and Mutual Aid in Contemporary Society in Dubrovnik, Yugoslavia, September 1979.

Shanas, E. The family as a social support system in old age. Presented at the Symposium on Natural Support Systems for the Elderly, 30th Annual Meeting of the Gerontological Society, San Francisco, 1977.

Silverman, P.R. Anticipatory grief from the perspective of widowhood. In B. Schoberg et al. (Eds.), *Anticipatory Grief*. New York: Columbia University Press, 1974.

_____. Factors involved in accepting an offer of help. *Journal of Thanatology*, 1971, 3: 161-177.

_____. *Mutual Help Groups: A Guide for Mental Health Workers*. Washington, D.C.: NIMH Monograph, DHEW Publication No. (ADM) 78-646, 1978.

_____. *Technical Assistance to Mutual Help Groups: A Report to Professionals*. Washington, D.C.: U.S. Government Printing Office, DHEW, ADAMHA. In Press.

_____. & Murrow, H.G. Mutual help during critical role transitions. *Journal of Applied Behavioral Science*, 1976, 12(3): 410-418.

_____. MacKenzie, D., Pettipas, M., & Wilson, E. (Eds.) *Helping Each Other in Widowhood*. New York: Health Sciences Publishing, 1975.

Skovhold, T.M. The client as helper: A means to promote psychological growth. *Counseling Psychologist*, 1974, 4: 58-64.

Smith, D.H., & Reddy, R.D. The impact of voluntary action upon the volunteer participant. In D.H. Smith (Ed.), *Voluntary Action Research*. Lexington, Mass.: D.C. Heath and Co., 1973.

Sobey, F. *The Nonprofessional Revolution in Mental Health*. New York: Columbia University Press, 1970.

Society for Human Rights. Chicago Charter. In J. Katz, *Gay American History*. New York, Thomas Y. Crowell Co., 1976.

Sokolovsky, J., Cohen, C., Berger, D., & Geiger, J. Personal networks of ex-mental patients in a Manhattan SRO hotel. *Human Organization*, 1978, 37: 5-15.

Speck, R., & Attneane, C. *Family Networks*. New York: Pantheon, 1973.

Sprague, C. (Ed.). *GROW Comes of Age—A Celebration and a Vision*. Marrickville, Australia: Grow Publications, 1979.

Steinglass, P. Family therapy in alcoholism. In B. Kissen and H. Begluter (Eds.), *The Biology of Alcoholism*. New York: Plenum, 1978.

Stewart, D.A. The dynamics of fellowship as illustrated in Alcoholics Anonymous. *Quarterly Journal of Studies on Alcoholism*, 1955, 16: 251-262.

Strupp, H.H., & Hadley, S.W. A tripartite deviance: The self-help challenge to the human services. *Journal of Applied Behavioral Science*, 1974, 12: 347-362.

Sugarman, B. *Daytop Village—A Therapeutic Community*. New York: Holt, Rinehart and Winston, 1974.

Tax, S. Self-help groups: Thoughts on public policy. *The Journal of Applied Behavioral Science*, July-September 1976.

Tiebout, H.M. Therapeutic mechanisms of AA. *American Journal of Psychiatry*, 1944, 100: 468-473.

de Toqueville, A. *Democracy in America*. New York: Vantage, 1959.

Tolsdorf, C.C. Social networks and coping: An exploratory study. *Family Process*, 1976, 15: 407-418.

Tomeh, A.K. Formal voluntary organizations: Participation, correlates, and interrelationship. *Sociological Inquiry*, 1973, 43: 89-122.

Tracy, G.S., & Gussow, Z. Self-help groups: A grass-roots response to a need for services. *Journal of Applied Behavioral Science*, Summer 1976, 12.

Trice, H., & Roman, P.M. Delabeling, relabeling and Alcoholics Anonymous. *Social Problems*, Spring 1970, 17 (4): 538-546.

Tyhurst, J.S. The role of transition states—including disasters—in mental illness. In *Symposium on Preventive and Social Psychiatry*. Washington, D.C.: U.S. Government Printing Office, 1958.

van Bertalavffy, L. *General Systems Theory*. New York: Braziller, 1968.

van Harberden, P., & Lafaille, R. *Zelfhulp*. Graevenhage: Vuga, 1978.

Vattano, A.J. Power to the people. *Social Work*, 1972, 17: 7-15.

Videka, L.M. Psychological adaptation in a medical self-help group. In M. Lieberman and L.D. Borman (Eds.), *Self-Help Groups for Coping with Crisis*. San Francisco: Jossey-Bass, 1979.

Walker, K., MacBudi, A. & Vachon, M. Social support networks and the crisis of bereavement. *Social Science and Medicine*, January 1977, 11: 35-41.

Webb, E.J., Campbell, D.T., Schwartz, R.D. & Sechrest, L. *Unobstrusive Measures: Nonreactive Research in the Social Sciences*. Chicago: Rand-McNally, 1966.

Wechsler, H. The self-help organization in the mental health field: Recovery, Inc.,

A case study. *Journal of Nervous and Mental Disorders*, 1960, 130: 297–314.

Weinman, B., Sanders, R., Kleiner, R. & Wilson, S. Community-based treatment of the chronic psychotic. *Community Mental Health Journal*, 1970, 6: 13–21.

Weiss, C.H. Evaluation research in the political context. In E.L. Struening and M. Guttentag (Eds.), *Handbook of Evaluation Research, Vol. 1*, 1975.

Weisman,, A. *On Dying and Denying*. New York: Behavioral Publications, 1973.

Welziznsmaandblad. Haarlem, April 1979.

Wheat, P., with Lieber, L. *Hope for the Children—A Personal History of Parents Anonymous*. Minneapolis, Minn.: Winston Press, 1979.

Winth, L. Urbanism as a way of life. *American Journal of Sociology*, 1938, 44: 1–24.

Wollert, R.W., Knight, B., & Levy, L. Make Today Count: A collaborative model for professionals and self-help groups. *Professional Psychology*. In Press.

Yalon, I.D. *The Theory and Practice of Group Psychotherapy*. New York: Basic Books, 1975.

Zunker, V.G., & Brown, W.F. Comparative effectiveness of student and professional counselors. *Personnel and Guidance Journal*, 1966, 44: 738–743.

INDEX